ROLAND BARTHES' CINEMA

D1562844

ROLAND BARTHES' CINEMA

Philip Watts
MANUSCRIPT EDITED FROM THE AUTHOR'S
UNFINISHED CHAPTERS

Dudley Andrew

Yves Citton

Vincent Debaene

Sam Di Iorio

OXFORD
UNIVERSITY PRESS

OXFORD
UNIVERSITY PRESS

Oxford University Press is a department of the University of Oxford. It furthers
the University's objective of excellence in research, scholarship, and education
by publishing worldwide. Oxford is a registered trade mark of Oxford University
Press in the UK and certain other countries.

Published in the United States of America by Oxford University Press
198 Madison Avenue, New York, NY 10016, United States of America.

First Edition published in 2016

Library of Congress Cataloging-in-Publication Data
Names: Watts, Philip, 1961–2013. | Andrew, Dudley, 1945– editor. | Barthes,
Roland. Essays. Selections. English.
Title: Roland barthes' cinema / Philip Watts ; manuscript edited
from the author's unfinished chapters by Dudley Andrew, Yves Citton,
Vincent Debaene, Sam Di Iorio.
Description: New York, NY : Oxford University Press, 2016. | Includes
bibliographical references and index.
Identifiers: LCCN 2015037603| ISBN 9780190277543 (cloth) | ISBN 9780190277550
(pbk.) | ISBN 9780190277567 (updf)
Subjects: LCSH: Barthes, Roland—Criticism and interpretation. | Motion
pictures—Philosophy.
Classification: LCC PN1998.3.B3748 W38 2016 | DDC 791.43092—dc23
LC record available at http://lccn.loc.gov/2015037603

1 3 5 7 9 8 6 4 2
Printed by Webcom, Canada

CONTENTS

CONTENTS

CONTENTS

CONTENTS

EDITORS' PREFACE

For Sophie, Madeleine, and Louise

The life of Roland Barthes, last century's cleverest cultural critic and one of its most nimble and influential literary theorists, coincided with that century's most powerful artistic medium. Born the year of *Birth of a Nation*, he achieved adolescence at the coming of sound, and died in 1980 before videotape and digital technology decisively altered the viewing and making of films. This was the year Global Hollywood showed it could exercise its power, as *The Empire Strikes Back* blanketed the world in a new mystique, if not a new mythology. But it was also the year something as cerebral and poetic as Tarkovsky's *Stalker* managed to claim the higher ground that art cinema had struggled to gain for three decades, the decades corresponding in fact to Barthes' illustrious career, the 1950s, 1960s, and 1970s. There simply must have been a connection between Roland Barthes and cinema; and indeed there was one—more than one, as we shall see—but it is not simple to identify or track. For cinema troubled Barthes; his relations with it were intermittent, ambivalent, and variable.

Just as his criticism can be parsed into phases (mythologies, structuralist semiotics, poststructuralism, and autobiography), so the cinema meant different things to Barthes at different times. Not to mention the fact that cinema was simultaneously going through its own evolution. Hence, the myriad potential connections linking this mercurial critic to this multilayered medium. No wonder Barthes shows up so regularly in the bibliographies of film theorists. No wonder so many audacious works of film criticism take him as a model. No wonder he is taught in film curricula, even though he never addressed the medium at length, and even exhibited a certain allergy to it.

THE FIRST SYNTHETIC ESSAY ON BARTHES AND CINEMA

Since several articles have been devoted to this topic,[1] we all assumed that someone would dare to write a book probing Barthes' cool affair with the moving image. This did not happen, however . . . not until a few years ago, when some of us began to hear about Philip Watts' research and realized he was the perfect scholar for the task. As a PhD student at Columbia in the 1980s, he studied with Antoine Compagnon, who studied with Roland Barthes. As a professor of twentieth-century French Literature and soon chair of the department of French and Italian at the University of Pittsburgh (from 1992 until 2006), and then as a chair of the French Department back at Columbia, he taught inspiring classes on Céline, Francophone literature, and—more and more—on cinema. Throughout his career he was appreciated by his students and colleagues for his devotion, generosity, collegiality, and inexhaustible kindness.

Phil Watts' first book, *Allegories of the Purge: How Literature Responded to the Postwar Trials of Writers and Intellectuals in France*, analyzed the caustic debates over the political and ethical responsibility of writers in the aftermath of the Second World War, paying particular attention to the work of Sartre, Eluard, Blanchot, and Céline. In the wake of its publication, Watts began work on a manuscript that dealt with the resuscitation of aesthetic classicism among French writers and intellectuals of the mid-twentieth century. Aspects of this project were sketched in a series of articles on figures like Genet, Camus, Bazin, and Straub and Huillet. Another part was published in a special issue of *Yale French Studies*, which he coedited with Richard J. Golsan and was titled

Literature and History: Around Suite Française *and* Les Bienveillantes. As the son of a French mother and an American father, and equally at ease in both languages and cultures, Phil Watts also devoted much of his time to translating and introducing French and Maghrebian writers to US audiences. He was instrumental to the American discovery of the work of Jacques Rancière, organizing a series of invitations and conferences which culminated in 2009 with *Jacques Rancière: History, Politics, Aesthetics*, the collection of essays he coedited with Gabriel Rockhill for Duke University Press.

As his humorous introduction to this book recounts, Phil Watts' familiarity with Roland Barthes' writing began during his student days in New York, when the author of *Mythologies* offered an ideal example of how a literary sensibility can be translated into sociopolitical critique. This interest continued through his years in Pittsburgh, when his work on the self-styling of French intellectuals found in Barthes' elusive political positioning rich material for reflection. Watts' increasing focus on film studies during his last years at Columbia led him to address the vexing issue of Barthes' mixed feelings and mixed signals toward cinema. He spent three years accumulating material, stealing time from his administrative duties as chairperson to write several talks on the topic. A brief sabbatical enabled him to organize and complete his research and to prepare the first draft of a book manuscript by the beginning of 2013.

Tragically, however, Phil Watts would not be given quite enough time to finish the task. Diagnosed with cancer in Spring 2013, he passed away that summer while organizing drafts of chapters that he felt sure he could complete as his crowning book. At the request of his wife, Sophie Queuniet, we four, who cared for him and knew his work quite well, read those drafts, consulted each other at length, and determined that the book could and must be published. We revised and polished his manuscript, limiting our interventions to the minimum—completing footnotes, occasionally rearranging the order of an argument or adding a sentence to ensure a better flow. We had to come to terms with the fact that this collectively edited text would never match the book Phil Watts would have published.[2] In the most ambitious version of his prospective table of contents, for example, he had planned an introductory chapter titled "Prehistory" that would have covered Camus, Sartre, and Merleau-Ponty's writing on cinema. Unfortunately, this promising beginning was too unfinished to include here.[3] He also intended to write a final section to explore the filiation between Barthes' reflections on cinema and later writing by Gilles Deleuze and Jacques Rancière. We have compiled his notes for this section in what is now the book's conclusion, but it would be more accurate to cast these pages as an invitation to *poursuivre la réflexion*. Nevertheless, while these frustrating absences prevent this text from being exactly the one that Phil Watts envisioned, we can safely say that the reader is holding his exceptional book in its entirety, as it was actually written.

This book, *Roland Barthes' Cinema*, has four centers of gravity. First it explores Barthes' relation to certain postwar intellectual currents adjacent to film (such as philosophy and sociology) especially as these help fund his breakout *Mythologies*. Second, it takes on Barthes' more direct relations to classical film theory through his responses to André Bazin and Sergei Eisenstein. Third, it examines the particularly complex period, his semiotic and then poststructural phase from 1965 to 1975, during which he responded to two distinct ideological concerns: on one side, the potentially insidious effects of any apparatus of representation, particularly so potent a one as cinema; and on the other side, the attraction of popular forms of representation that flow into apparatuses of all sorts. As a prime carrier of the melodramatic imagination of our age, cinema both thrilled and troubled Barthes. Fourth, in his final years, Barthes reflected increasingly on broad topics that could clearly include cinema, such as forms of solitude and social life; he also composed *Camera Lucida*, his brilliant meditation on photography, published the year he died. One can only imagine what might have become of Barthes' relation to cinema had he accompanied it as the century moved toward its close.

There is no shortage of discussions about Barthes' relation to the ideas of his times, but what has been the consequence of his thought on those aspects of aesthetics and philosophy that edge close to cinema? While Watts pursued this question intermittently in this study, we have nothing like his full response. Rather than attempting to surmise what he would have written had he lived—doing so with the fragmentary notes and quotations he collected for this concluding chapter—we decided instead to complete his book with an interview with Jacques Rancière, who knew Phil Watts and his agenda. Rancière fills out the picture from today's perspective, wryly addressing his own long-lasting and complex relation to Barthes' writings.

A generation younger than Barthes, Rancière has had a similarly illustrious career; he has contributed substantially to many domains (philosophical, sociological, and aesthetic) and hence has always appealed to an international readership the way Barthes did. Moreover, cinema has accompanied Rancière from his days as a philosophy student in the 1960s. His public engagement with film dates back to a 1976 interview in *Cahiers du Cinéma*'s prescient special issue on Brand Image ("Images de Marque"), and since 1995 he has been a prominent figure in the vibrant interdisciplinary conversation that goes under the rubric "film and philosophy." He benefits, like Barthes, from a reputation for being able to drive aesthetic insights into the heart of the most profound discussions of our age, whether in philosophy or politics. His remarks provide a fitting and exciting end point for *Roland Barthes' Cinema*.

A SELECTION OF BARTHES' WRITINGS ON CINEMA

The final words in this volume, however, have been given to Barthes himself. The articles on film that are cited by Phil Watts and Jacques Rancière form an elusive part of the Barthes corpus: some are only available in Les Éditions du Seuil's multivolume *Oeuvres complètes*, which is organized chronologically. Others are reprinted in smaller collections of Barthes' writing, but here as well they are rarely, if ever, set side by side. The situation is similar outside of France: though Richard Seaver and Stephen Heath have translated key pieces like "Garbo's Face," "Leaving the Movie Theater," and "The Third Meaning" for Anglophone readers, other significant texts have remained frustratingly inaccessible. To remedy this situation, we conclude this volume with nine new translations meant to complement the material that is already in circulation. In addition to the essays that feature prominently in Watts' manuscript, we have included a handful of other pieces from different stages in Barthes' career: a 1943 review of Robert Bresson's *Les Anges du Péché* written for a student journal at the sanatorium where he was treated for tuberculosis; an answer to a 1960 questionnaire from *Positif* contributor Michèle Firk regarding left-wing criticism; a text for *Le Monde* about Pasolini's "irrecuperable" final film *Salò*, whose French release took place six months after the director's murder. We also append an article that remains absent from many Barthes bibliographies as well as the *Oeuvres complètes*, a two-paragraph note written to accompany the 1961 release of Mario Ruspoli's rural portrait *Les Inconnus de la terre*. Originally published in Raymond Bellour's journal *Artsept*, this forgotten piece reinforces the underacknowledged proximity between Barthes and cinéma-vérité at the outset of the 1960s. A concluding bibliography lists additional references in English and French so that interested readers can locate all of this book's primary source material. Unable to publish Barthes' complete writings on film here, we want the texts we have included, as well as the bibliography, to open paths for future research.

Phil Watts indicates many of those paths in his work, some of which Jacques Rancière starts exploring in the interview. For instance, Watts convincingly explains how André Bazin and *Cahiers du Cinéma* intersect Barthes' career, but we hope others will reverse the dynamic and explore how Barthes' writing might have affected Bazin during the 1950s, or investigate the more definite relationship he maintained with the 1970s *Cahiers*, where articles by Sylvie Pierre, Pascal Bonitzer, and Jean-Pierre Oudart testify to the tonic impact of his essays. On a practical level, chapter 2's discussion of Barthes and the New Wave invites further study of the films Barthes was personally involved in during this period: his punctual impact on *Wrestling*, the collective film Michel Brault, Claude Jutra, and friends made for Canada's National Film Board in 1961;[4] his direct involvement with Hubert Aquin's *Of Sport and Men* the same year;[5] his invisible "appearance" in Jean-Luc Godard's *Alphaville* in 1965.[6] Finally, we hope the future sees more developed accounts of the connections traced in the final chapters between André Téchiné and melodrama, or how Barthes' understanding of cinema relates to the conceptions of the medium that are associated with Foucault and Deleuze.

It was only once we had started editing the manuscript that we began to appreciate the full scope of the material Phil Watts had left us.

WHY ROLAND BARTHES' CINEMA MATTERS

Finding such a wealth of possibilities was all the more surprising given Barthes' well-established antipathy toward movies. In the most remarkably synthetic and well-informed article to date, Charlotte Garson states that "cinema was the object of no particular interest" for Barthes and that he used it mostly as a "methodological foil" in haphazard articles written with "nonchalance."[7] She finds two main reasons for what Barthes himself characterized as his "resistance to cinema," explaining why, in his own words, "he did not go to the movies very often."[8] First, "he expressed his repugnance towards a mode of representation in which 'everything is given.'"[9] The written text, because it relies on the symbolic, lets the reader imagine what is to be seen and heard in a narrative, whereas movies tend to provide images and sounds already made for us, forcing themselves upon us with an overbearing impression of naturalness. Second, the cinematic experience frustrates Barthes because of the relentless rhythm it imposes on the viewer: "The moving pictures leave no choice to the spectator, he can neither slow down what he sees, nor (since he is carried by the flow) can he imagine other potential developments of the action."[10]

In the interview included in this volume, Jacques Rancière fundamentally agrees with Charlotte Garson (and with the general perception of Barthes' resistance to film). He stresses that Barthes never really writes about moving pictures at all, even when he discusses his cinematic experiences. In *Mythologies* Barthes effectively freezes Greta Garbo's face as if it were a mask, or fixates on the rigid hairstyle of actors playing Roman soldiers. Later, his analysis reduces Eisenstein's cinematic art to a few instants, and these are discussed not as scenes but simply as individual stills.[11] In his 1975 essay, tellingly titled "Leaving the Movie Theater," Barthes takes into account only what happens to the bodies of the spectators, not even mentioning what is actually projected on the screen! The point seems irrefutable: Barthes did not like the movies, did not see many of them, and even when he happened to find himself in a theater, he paid attention to his fellow-spectators and couldn't wait to exit and at most transform the moving picture into isolated images that could be handled more comfortably.[12]

Phil Watts never denies Barthes' resistance to the experience of motion pictures: he made it the starting point of this book. But he invites us to inquire more deeply into this resistance, and to register how a discreet but insistent "cinephilic" voice accompanies Barthes' ostentatiously "cinephobic" postures. Charlotte Garson herself tantalizingly suggested, toward the end of her article, that Barthes may have (reluctantly) returned so often to an art toward which he felt so suspicious precisely because it provided him with a corrective to theory, which otherwise ran rampant and unbridled across every domain:

> The resistance that cinema opposed to the analytic instruments Barthes found in his [structuralist] toolbox played a privileged role in the upsetting of literary theory: because cinema could not be analyzed in purely linguistic terms, it pushed Barthes to take more distance from semiology and narratology.[13]

Phil Watts patiently and meticulously accumulates evidence to demonstrate the pivotal role played by Barthes' apparently minor articles on movies during his dramatic "turn away" from the structural analysis of narratives and images. Watts brings out more than the (well-known) resistance that Barthes felt toward the cinematic experience, by documenting the irresistible urge Barthes felt toward a form of art that resisted in turn what he himself very keenly identified as the shortcomings of "scientific discourse" and its belief in a "superior code."[14] In other words: Roland Barthes' cinema matters because it functioned as a crucial site of self-questioning, until it helped unravel, and eventually demote, Theory for this major theorist of the twentieth century.

At the outset of the 1970s, quite unexpectedly, film even provided Barthes with a model for thinking through what the remembrance of a past life could be. He imagines silent cinema as an idealized form of remembering, one that could offer more than a mere collection of fragments, photographs, or still images, but one which could also retain its independence from the forward motion of narrative. For Barthes, it becomes an ideal medium that would destabilize narrative coherence through a plurality of codes, and preserve movement without reducing it to progression:

> Were I a writer, and dead, how I would love it if my life, through the pains of some friendly and detached biographer, were to reduce itself to a few details, a few preferences, a few inflections, let us say: to "biographemes" whose distinction and mobility might go beyond any fate and come to touch, like Epicurean atoms, some future body, destined to the same dispersion; a marked life, in sum, as Proust succeeded in writing in his work, or even a film, in the old style, in which there is no dialogue and the flow of images (that *flumen orationis* which perhaps is what makes up the "obscenities" of writing) is intercut, like the relief of hiccoughs, by the barely written darkness of the intertitles, the casual eruption of *another signifier*.[15]

But there are other, more important reasons why Roland Barthes' cinema matters to us today. In the first place, when he was not eyeing his neighbors or walking out on the movie, the literary critic did at least occasionally take a look at what was being projected on the screen. Quite often, especially during the *Mythologies* era and under the rather judgmental spell of his Brechtianism, Barthes condemned what he saw—mostly in mainstream Hollywood (Kazan, Mankiewicz) or in French movies (Guitry)—in the name of a demystifying attitude prone to denounce the culture industry for luring the masses via its stultifying apparatus of representation. But the most important merit of Phil Watts' study is to trace a much more subdued and humble voice with which Barthes uttered his appreciation for the work of a few directors, to whom he clearly paid abiding attention. The first article he devoted to cinema lauded Robert Bresson's *Les Anges du Péché* (*Angels of Sin*, 1943) for its ascetic simplicity, and his last—the very rich and vibrant essay "Dear Antonioni" (1980)—elevated its subject to the status of model artist. In between (i.e., in the 1970s), one finds him discovering the "sens obtus" in Eisenstein and admiring the work of filmmakers like André Téchiné.

Indeed, his frequent affecting encounters with moving pictures were opportunities to develop multifarious fragments of a "lover's discourse."

His piece on Antonioni, in particular, deserves a closer look, since it patently reverses the second indictment Barthes levels against cinema. This second point of resistance starts from the idea that film saturates the imagination by imposing ready-made images and sounds which resist structural analysis and numb symbolic interpretation. Even more importantly, perhaps, it uses calculated montage to bind and glue our attention to the alienating cadence of a generally unrelenting pace. A late statement about radio broadcasts expresses quite accurately this rhythmic resistance that generated a great deal of Barthes' discomfort with mainstream movies: "the announcers spoke at dizzying speed: faster, faster, always faster ... The media are so desperate to 'bring messages to life,' that we'd be justified in thinking that they consider the messages themselves dead—even deadly."[16] However, the directors praised by Barthes find ways to circumvent this stultifying effect. While certain "cinematographers" like Robert Bresson use techniques of "fragmentation" in order to create images that invite the spectator to imagine what she or he is not given to hear or see,[17] other directors, like Antonioni, use "filmic techniques" which generate a "syncopation of meaning" capable of emancipating the viewers from those alienating rhythms of attention.[18] If Barthes watches his neighbor in the theater, it is because he feels that many films put little to see on the screen. Sketching an argument that would soon be reconfigured by Gilles Deleuze, he suggests that most mainstream movies prevent us from *seeing* anything, because they merely relay "clichés" (which Barthes would have analyzed as "myths" a few decades earlier). Bresson, Godard, and Antonioni "break" such clichés by means of a particular deployment of time (Deleuze's *image-temps*) or of rhythm (Barthes' *idiorrythmie*).[19] In "Dear Antonioni," emancipation begins as soon as one is led to "look at something one minute too many," to "look longer than needed," thus interrupting the informational flows constitutive of "power":

> Power of any kind, because it is violence, never looks; if it looked
> one minute longer (one minute too much) it would lose its essence
> as power. The artist, for his part, stops and looks lengthily, and

I would imagine you became a film-maker because the camera is an eye, constrained by its technical properties to look. What you, like all film-makers, add to these properties is to look at things radically, until you have exhausted them. On the one side you look lengthily at what you were not expected to look at either by political convention (the Chinese peasants) or by narrative convention (the dead times of an adventure). On the other your preferred hero is someone who looks (a photographer, a reporter). This is dangerous, because to look longer than expected (I insist on this added intensity) disturbs established orders of every kind, to the extent that normally the time of the look is controlled by society; hence the scandalous nature of certain photographs and certain films, not the most indecent or the most combative, but just the most "posed."[20]

Like Vilém Flusser, who began calling for "contemplative images" at around the same time,[21] Barthes identifies artistic work with a certain freezing of the stream of images—hence his constant tendency to extract photographic stills from the flow of moving pictures. But, as his love letter to Antonioni demonstrates, he also appreciated the possibility offered by cinematic montage to intensify our gaze, through its artistic instrumentation to allow our look to "pause" and remain longer than warranted on certain portions of reality. Hence a second reason why Roland Barthes' cinema matters: three decades after his death, his resistance to film remains more relevant than ever, since it calls for cinematographic creations to be sites of emergence for much needed counterrhythmic gestures. This amounts to a deeply political claim, very much in sync with today's "slow" movements (slow food, slow travel, and of course slow cinema).[22]

Beyond issues of rhythm, Phil Watts' essay recovers throughout Barthes' career a constant attraction for cinema as *a site of sensory excess*, serving as a reserve of meaning always ready to undermine the shortcomings of the cinematic mode of representation.[23] In the 1950s, this sensory excess pushed him to measure and sometimes overcome his Brechtian positions, as in the case of the much neglected *Mythologie* article dedicated to Claude Chabrol's *Le Beau Serge* (1958), a film condemned for its right-wing politics but vindicated for its attention to the sensual world. In the 1970s, sensory excess is the engine that makes the theorist diffident toward the arrogant poverty of Theory, when confronted with the mute wealth of our sense perceptions. In the few months Barthes enjoyed of the 1980s, we can detect the insistence of this sensual attention underneath his praise for Antonioni's *vigilance* and his claim that "the meaning of a thing is not its truth."[24] Of course, first and foremost one should understand this phrase to mean that "the *meaning* of a thing is not its truth." But after reading Watts' essay, it is hard not to hear that the *sensory* dimension of any "thing" receives its independence from the theoretical truth one can project upon it. And it is hard not to envisage the cinematographic art as one important site for this declaration of independence.

As early as chapter 1, Phil Watts announces what will become a guiding principle in his study:

> Barthes approaches film in two ways. On the one hand as an "inter-preter," who applies a hermeneutic model to films (one closely resembling what Paul Ricoeur called the "hermeneutics of suspi-cion"). On the other hand as a sensualist, who looks to describe the surface of films, the effects they produce on spectators and his own emotional response to the sounds and images of movies. This is one of the key tensions in the field of film studies—summarized as the "hermeneutic" versus the "poetic" approach—and while Barthes has most often been placed in the hermeneuts' camp, it is the tension at the heart of his writing that makes *Mythologies* a book for our modern times.

By unfolding the consequences of this tension generated by a con-stant sensory excess in Barthes' writings on cinema, Phil Watts has been led to compose an exemplary book situated at the crossroads of three disciplinary currents which have played a major role in fertil-izing film studies. In the first place, *Roland Barthes' Cinema* is closely allied with queer studies: without ever deserting the respectable her-meneuts' camp of mainstream French academia, Barthes laced his writings with subtle allusions and cryptic references to his sexual orientation, which Watts' essay unfolds with delicate care and loving humor. The background of "camp poetics" certainly sheds a new light on what Barthes wrote about film in the 1950s, anticipating a concern with queerness which would find a fuller definition for the generation after Barthes' death, yet which already underpins his readings of films like Mankiewicz's *Julius Caesar* (1953) and Mamoulian's *Queen Christina* (1933).

Secondly, *Roland Barthes' Cinema* also sets out a template for literary reading. Without ever misinterpreting Barthes' writing, Phil Watts tirelessly exploits the sensual excess of the textual grain in order to elaborate the wealth of its multifarious meanings. He may have been one of our finest, most subtle, and most Barthesian literary critics, maintaining a fine balance between an awareness of historical context and a fascination with the rejuvenating power of meaning in the present. For him too, literary studies are driven by a somewhat paradoxical urge to work as "a science of nuances"—which Barthes labeled *diaphoralogy* at the time of his courses at the Collège de France. As sharp and playful in its use of *punctum* as it is well-researched in terms of *studium*, Phil Watts' method of reading relies on pointing our attention to apparently minor details in the texts, making their recurrence surprisingly significant under the light of his clever interpretations. Look again at the insistent focus on hairstyles in chapter 1.[25] Like Barthes, he also revels in suspending the flow of discourse, isolating motifs as if they were film stills and "fetishizing" their endlessly polysemic potential. The clear-eyed focus of Watts' prose exemplifies a critical tenet Barthes had sketched as early as his 1944 essay "*Plaisir aux classiques*": it is disciplined attention to detail that best reveals a text's propensity to take on diverse meanings in light of constantly renewed contexts of reception. Watts mines this insight: more than a philosopher, more than a film theorist, more than a cultural critic, he is first and foremost a *literary* scholar, insofar as he fetishizes *the letter* of the texts, trusting it to carry more important meanings (more *sens*) than any truth that can be read into them.

Finally, and more surprisingly, *Roland Barthes' Cinema* matters as an oblique lesson in media archaeology. Barthes' fetishism—which Phil Watts allows us to trace all the way back to the period of the *Mythologies*—leads him to invest the images, moving or not, with a quasi-magical, spiritual, and sacred power. If chapter 3 shows the close interaction that took place between Barthes and André Bazin in the 1950s, chapter 6 discloses how *Camera Lucida* developed a *hauntology* of photography that is indeed very different from the ontology of photography brilliantly articulated by Bazin three decades earlier. More than ten years before Derrida's *Specters of Marx*, Barthes was already practicing hauntology when he reflected on his own persistent visions of his mother. His constant urge to transform moving pictures into still photographs should be interpreted less as a denial of movement in cinematic images than as the obscure assertion that still pictures move by their own power: as soon as a viewer is pierced by their *punctum*, they appear deeply "animated"—endowed with the inner movement of a "soul" [*anima*]. The echoes compellingly constructed in chapter 6 between *La Chambre claire* (the French title for *Camera Lucida*) and François Truffaut's film *La Chambre verte* (*The Green Room*, 1978) invite us to consider Barthes as a true *fetishist*, not only because of a potentially "perverse" pleasure taken in partial objects, but also, and much more interestingly, because of a more-than-rational belief that (apparently) inanimate things (a wooden statue, a lock of hair, a book, a film frame, a photograph) may contain a form of life that can still reach us from beyond the borders of matter, history, and death.

Jacques Rancière makes a very enlightening point when he notes, in the interview that complements the essay, that it was not simply the sensual nature of images that interested Roland Barthes most keenly, it was also their *tactile* dimension: "Leaving the Movie Theater" describes an apparatus in which the spectator is "touched" and "caressed" by the light of the projector. The writing of *Camera Lucida* originates precisely in a somatic experience which belongs both to the son looking at pictures of his dead mother and to the old man staring at a photograph of a handsome boy sentenced to die; neither can help but be "touched" by what they see. Of course Rancière is right to note that nothing in the picture itself shows that the boy is about to die, or that the mother just passed away. It is indeed a crazy idea "to see death in photos where there is no death," but for Barthes as for the media archaeologists who followed him along these tracks,[26] pictures, in motion or not, are more than inanimate objects: they are *media*—inextricably *médiatiques* and *médiumniques,* inescapably putting the living in communication with the dead. Something of the mediated reality is carried by its mediation, and emanates from it as yet another form of sensual excess—which, to return to Barthes' idea, inevitably touches us outside of reason and beyond our control. It is this unsettling experience that Roland Barthes confronted and attempted to account for during his very last years, an experience for which the techniques of the novel seemed more appropriate than those of the essay.

Though still images are deprived of movement, they may still contain the traces of vivid forms of life. Insofar as these forms have retained the capacity to move us deeply, *Roland Barthes' Cinema* is an important contribution to media studies, a study of film and photography's overlapping power to mediate our relation with our fellow humans, our selves, our ideas, our imaginations, our hopes, our future, our memories, our past, and our dead.

DEAR BARTHES

Roland Barthes' Cinema can simply be read as an assessment by a literary critic of the contribution to film studies made by another literary critic, over a forty-year span. But it also deserves to be read as a kind of love letter in its own right, as an exercise in benevolent empathy and as a testimony.

In both cases, Phil Watts attends to an author who went through a series of "turns" in his career and in his relation to cinema. In his assessment of Barthes' overall trajectory, Jacques Rancière summarizes very well the most vexing question it raises: how are we to understand "how he went from *Mythologies* to *Camera Lucida,* from trying to demystify images, asking what they were saying and what they were hiding, and transforming them into messages, to making them sacred, as if the images were like the very emanation of a body coming towards us?" Barthes indeed seems to have spent his life turning away from what he came to be identified with; in our interview with him, Jacques Rancière situates this will to emancipation in "the way that he freed himself from what he had created, whether that involved critically burdensome hyper-Brechtian positions or the pseudo-scientific ponderousness of semiology." One of the most knowledgeable and closest interpreters of his work recently published an admirable book cunningly titled *Bêtise de Barthes*, in order to show how intimately his constant struggle against the *doxa* and its myths was linked to a no less constant struggle against his own blind spots and intellectual shortcomings—geared by the stated goal of "exploring his own *bêtise*."[27]

There are at least three possible ways for Barthes scholars to position themselves in their interpretation of such reversals. Most studies published about him tend to view his trajectory as a (series of) generally *positive* turns, contrasting a later and wiser Barthes, more prudent and self-critical, against a younger, more arrogant, and somewhat foolish theorist, eager to deride popular culture in the name of dogmatic Marxism or scientific analysis. The literary critic corrected the rigid formalism of *Elements of Semiology* by musing on *The Pleasure of the Text*. The theorist of visual culture compensated for the scientific pretense of his projected "semiology of images" by reintegrating the subjective dimension of our relation to pictures in *Camera Lucida*. Such interpretations assume that the thinker went through a radical reversal, which turned him around from being wrong to being right.

Both Jacques Rancière and Phil Watts reject this dominant interpretive scheme, but they do it from very different perspectives and with very different results. According to Rancière, Barthes did indeed make a slow U-turn, which reversed the direction of his analyses and judgments—but he was as "modernistically" wrong after the turn as before: his reading of Barthes, in *The Emancipated Spectator* but even more evident in his very recent *Le fil perdu*, rests on the assumption that Barthes is "someone who embodies the 'modernist' misunderstanding about modernity—but in such a rigorous way that I find him to be an absolutely ideal partner."[28] According to this view, Barthes' evolution represents a perfectly exemplary synthesis of a certain historical transformation that characterized a whole generation of intellectuals in the second half of the twentieth century. Barthes' brilliance consisted in pushing to its furthest limits what could be felt and thought within this deeply unsatisfactory transformation—and our philosophical task is to read him as a "methodological foil" indeed, in order to understand and, if possible, overcome the obstacles and contradictions against which his modernist intelligence came to hit a modernist wall.

This paradoxical praise of Barthes as a brilliantly mistaken thinker does not amount to a mere condemnation. One feels a good deal of admiration, gratitude, and respect—and a fair amount of dry wit—in the way Rancière describes his evolving relation to Barthes over the years. And this "symptomatic" reading of his work, analyzed as a trace of a certain modernist mistake about modernism, corresponds to an attitude Barthes himself sketched in a 1977 interview where he described the intellectual as a *déchet* (waste, refuse):

> For my part, I'd say that [intellectuals] are more like the refuse of society. Waste in the strict sense, i.e., what serves no purpose, unless it's recuperated. There are regimes that do try in fact to recuperate the refuse we represent . . . Organic waste proves the *passage* of the matter it contains. Human waste, for example, attests to the digestive process. Well, intellectuals attest to a passage of history of which they are in a way the waste product. The intellectual crystallizes, in the form of refuse, impulses, desires, complications, blockages that probably belong to society as a whole. Optimists say that an intellectual is a "witness." I'd say that he's only a "trace."[29]

Phil Watts' general attitude toward Roland Barthes is quite different. He too questions the dominant interpretation of an intellectual trajectory turning away from a sinful dogmatic and theoretical youth toward a late sensual conversion to poststructuralist enlightenment. But instead of reading him as always modernistically mistaken, he invites us to observe how always-already-sensual Barthes always had been. Well before Tiphaine Samoyault published her beautiful biography, which largely confirms his intuitions,[30] Phil Watts saw Roland Barthes practicing poststructuralism as early as the *Mythologies*. His fetishist attention to hairstyle in peplum films of the 1950s, his description of certain moments of grace in Chabrol's *Le Beau Serge*, his camp poetics, his constant awareness of a fundamental excess of meaning over truth, his search for the positivity of sensation beneath the negativity of demystification—all of this prepared the way for his supposedly dramatic turn in the 1970s. Rather than a reversal or a conversion, Phil Watts describes the persistence and metamorphoses of a *tension* between "the interpreter" and "the sensualist"—something that Gilbert Simondon would have called a "metastability": a dynamic state of imbalance in which incompatible impulses struggle to find a superior form of composition and reorganization. In other words, Barthes was always right from the beginning; his writings always already contained the sensual corrective to their theoretical drive; he never turned away from himself, but progressively unfolded a sensitivity that was there from the start.

And this is where the writings on cinema play a crucial role in Barthes studies, in spite of (or rather, thanks to) their apparently scattered, haphazard, and "nonchalant" status: these "minor" articles were best positioned to allow for a different voice to emerge from very early on. Because he tended to consider cinema as a "methodological foil," it served as an open and fertile field of exploration of the tensions at work within this metastable state. Since film studies were just emerging at the time, Barthes did not have to storm the Sorbonne in order to assert his sensitivity to moving pictures. A brief notation on an early Chabrol film, a commentary on a few photograms in Eisenstein, some memories of being on a film set with Téchiné, the letter to Antonioni: it is indeed in the waste basket of his complete works that Phil Watts went to dig in order to reveal the other "sensualist" face, always present behind the official mask of the master interpreter. All he had to do was to *give literary credit* to neglected writings and to the excess of intelligence provided by the details of the texts over the self-aware claims of their author—a highly Barthesian attitude if there is one.

It is no coincidence that such a fundamentally generous attention to Barthes' writings comes from a literary critic. Phil Watts remained a philologer much more than a philosopher: he loved sensuous texts and images far more than ideas or meanings. Rather than deliver an assessment of Barthes' work, his book aspires to empathic understanding and engaged gratitude. Watts became the literary critic he was because of something he had received from his reading of Barthes, and this book gives back to Barthes some of the inspiration he had received, in the form of their shared faith that the letter of the text could transcend the interminable battles waged over their meaning. Rather than start from a position of skepticism, Watts' analyses display a disciplined but contagious approach and are written in terms of endearment. It is therefore no surprise if his *Roland Barthes' Cinema*, sadly posthumous, sounds very much like a (duly reserved) love letter to its subject, in tragically deep resonance with the nearly posthumous love letter Barthes himself wrote to Antonioni.

In a passage which can easily be read as the very last rewriting of *Roland Barthes par Roland Barthes*, the essayist-about-to-turn-novelist—another turn that would never take place—praises the Italian director as the epitome of the artist, someone who "is capable of astonishment and admiration," whose "look may be critical but is not accusatory," whose work is "neither dogmatic nor empty of signification." It is not hard to read this letter to Antonioni as a striking self-portrait of Barthes as an artist:

> Each of your films has been, at your personal level, a historical experience, that is to say, the abandonment of an old problem and the formulation of a new question; this means that you have lived through and treated the history of the last thirty years *with subtlety*, not as the matter of an artistic reflection, or an ideological mission, but as a substance whose magnetism it was your task to capture from work to work . . . The social, the narrative, the neurotic are just levels—pertinences, as they say in linguistics—of *the world as a whole*, which is the object of every artist's work; there is a succession of interests, not a hierarchy. Strictly speaking, the artist, unlike the thinker, does not evolve; he scans, like a very sensitive instrument, the successive novelty which his own history presents him with; your work is not a fixed reflection, but an iridescent surface over which there pass, depending on what catches your eye or what the times demand of you, figures of the Social or the Passions and those of formal innovations, from modes of narration to the use of color. Your concern for the times you live in is not that of a historian, a politician or a moralist, but rather that of a utopian whose perception is seeking to pinpoint the new world because he is eager for this world and already wants to be part of

it. The vigilance of the artist, which is yours, is a lover's vigilance, the vigilance of desire.[31]

This *vigilance amoureuse* is a unique mix of intelligence, generosity, subtlety, experimentation, magnetism, sensitivity, nuance, desire, and, yes, utopia—insofar as neither Michelangelo Antonioni nor Roland Barthes nor Phil Watts gave up on the hope to contribute with their work to a less dogmatic and more significant future. Barthes addressed his letter as a contribution to a celebratory event which offered a "this peaceful, harmonious moment of agreement when a whole collectivity joins together to recognize, admire and love your work. For tomorrow the labor begins again."[32] *Roland Barthes' Cinema* should also be received as Phil Watts' effort to open a peaceful and conciliatory space designed to acknowledge, admire, and love Barthes' writings. We hope this posthumous edition of the book will by the same token provide a welcoming space to acknowledge, admire, and love Phil Watts' intelligence and generosity. Not only did Phil Watts and Roland Barthes share the fate of a cruelly premature death, they can also be reunited under Antonioni's response upon learning of the French critic's passing:

> The first thing that came to mind was this: "So, there's a little less sweetness and intelligence in the world now. A bit less love. All the love which *through living and writing*, he put into his life and his work." I believe that the longer we proceed in this world (a world which regresses brutally), the more we shall miss the virtues which were his.[33]

The editors wish to thank the following people for their contribution to the publication of this volume: François Albera, Laure Astourian, Antoine de Baecque, Raymond Bellour, Dana Benelli, Yve-Alain Bois, Steven Bradley, Nicole Brenez, Claude Coste, Madeleine Dobie, Nataša Durovicová, Danny Fairfax, Gregory Flaxman, Marie Gil, Lynn Higgins, Alice Kaplan, John MacKay, Éric Marty, Brendan O'Neill, Sophie Queuniet, Violette Queuniet, Michel Salzedo, Steven Ungar, Raji Vallury, Richard Watts, Madeleine Whittle, and Dork Zabunyan.

ROLAND BARTHES' CINEMA

Introduction

The paradoxical power of understanding things as they are and of imagining them with a freshness never before seen.

Michel Foucault on Roland Barthes[1]

It is often said that Barthes was allergic to film, that he didn't like the movies. Marie Gil, one of Barthes' biographers, speaks of his inability to "understand" cinema.[2] But the term Barthes used was "resistance."[3] Resistance is a sort of compromise between fascination and repulsion, or rather the alternation of critique and fascination, of turning away from while turning toward the sensual delectation of the image. Barthes wrote about movies his whole life, as a kind of working-through of this resistance. Along with demystification comes a delight in the trivial, the ordinary, the sensual existence of common things. This is all the more evident in his writings on cinema where we see both the heavy-handed apparatus of demystification and the enthrallment with cinema's ability to reveal the ordinary, to present the everyday for our pleasure.[4]

Much of these writings register a fascination with the medium's newness and improbability. They display enthusiasm for technological advances (CinemaScope, for instance), amazement at cinema's capacity for analogical representation, curiosity about its places of exhibition (the movie house as the site of erotic encounters), vehement resistance to the transformation of movies into a byproduct of consumer capitalism and then, near the end of his life, anxiety about the possible disappearance of this fragile and magic art.

Is there a specificity—beyond resistance—to Barthes' writings about film? To separate Barthes' essays about film from the rest of his work is, in a sense, to betray the interdisciplinarity—to use this old-fashioned word to which I will return—of his project. Still, if one could locate a kind of specificity in these writings, it might be this: of all the forms of art that Barthes writes about, film is the most *political*, and this for two reasons. First, it is the art form most closely tied to ideology, to producing mass conformity, to "naturalizing" or, alternately, defamiliarizing our ways of being and perceiving. Barthes' reaction to this is evident in the *Mythologies*. Second, it is the most *social* of all arts—social in the sense that cinema is never consumed alone. It is always public, always tied to mass reactions. Cinema thus crystallizes Barthes' ambivalences toward the collective; it is at once an arm in the ideological struggle and the canonical example that helps dismiss the opposition between mass culture and art.

> As a child, he was not so fond of Chaplin's films; it was later that, without losing sight of the muddled and solacing ideology of the character, he found a kind of delight in this art at once so popular (in both senses) and so intricate; it was a *composite* art, looping together several tastes, several languages. Such artists provoke a complete kind of joy, for they afford the image of a culture that is at once differential and collective: plural. This image then functions as the third term, the subversive term of the opposition in which we are imprisoned: mass culture *or* high culture.[5]

Cinema, for Barthes, belongs to (and exemplifies) the *sensus communis*, the common sense. It is deeply linked to the common, to plurality, since cinema, more than any other art, poses the question of equality. It is an "emblem of democracy," and as such poses problems for teachers and scholars who address their topics as experts. One can hear an early echo of Jacques Rancière's *The Ignorant Schoolmaster* in the way Barthes describes his relation to teaching—an attitude that may apply particularly well to his writings on cinema. Quoting Michelet, he writes: "I have always been careful to teach only what I do not know . . . I have transmitted these things as they were then, in my passion—new, lively, blazing (and delightful for me), under love's first spell."[6] Such a remark, and there are others like it,[7] is important for two reasons. First, because it shows that the question for Barthes remains how to think about equality and particularity. Second, because it helps us understand why cinema remains the art that Barthes always approached as an enthusiast and as an amateur. As we will see, this double resistance to mass culture on the one hand, and to the elitist denigration of mass culture on the other, was at the core of Barthes' writings on film.

Why is it important to reflect on Barthes and the movies today? His writings on film are hardly systematic, yet they inevitably return to issues that are central to the history of film studies: mechanical reproduction, the apparatus, film and desire, the perception of the sensible. So far, Barthes' contribution to film studies has mainly been seen as part of what D. N. Rodowick has called "political modernism."[8] As film studies redefined itself in the 1960s and 1970s, many leading theorists turned to a left-wing critique of mass media. Barthes' *Mythologies* as well as essays like "The Third Meaning" seemed to perfectly calibrate with (and justify) film theory's general distrust of images, as well as of visual storytelling, of cinematic pleasure, of mass entertainment. While Barthes' writing certainly constituted an important contribution to this "political modernism," and while his literary studies such as *S/Z* and translations of his essays on film in journals such as *Screen* allowed American film scholars to "shift the ground of the whole realm of the humanities,"[9] my contention is that this work, and his writing on film in particular, poses other, larger problems when reread today.

From a contemporary perspective, Barthes' essays on film—and the multitude of brief references to films, actors, scenes, and so on—seem structured around recurring concerns: How does cinema configure the relation between the individual and the masses? How does it change our relation to the sensuous world? How does one think about this intermediary object located somewhere between mass communication and art? How does cinema configure desire? How does it engage skepticism? Such questions come back with surprising regularity in Barthes' work, from his early review of Bresson's *Les Anges du péché* to his last essay on Antonioni. This does not mean, of course, that his position on cinema doesn't change over his thirty-year career. What it does mean is that Barthes' essays on this topic are still relevant, and might once again be able to make an important contribution to our understanding of film as a complex network of aesthetics and politics.

If Barthes' opinions evolved over those three decades, his method of reading did not. His writings on cinema are almost always grounded in a hermeneutics that takes a part (hairstyles, for instance, as we will see in chapter 1) for the whole and that interprets the film based on that part. But this metonymic process inevitably involves a sensual attention to detail; it is always grounded in an awareness of beauty. At the end of *The Pleasure of the Text*, it is cinema that embodies what Barthes calls "an aesthetics of textual pleasure": "In fact, it suffices that the cinema capture the sound of speech *close up* (this is, in fact, the generalized definition of the 'grain' of writing) and make us hear in their materiality, their sensuality, the breath, the gutturals, the fleshiness of the lips, a whole presence of the human muzzle (that the voice, that writing, be as fresh, supple, lubricated, delicately granular and vibrant as an animal's muzzle), to succeed in shifting the signified a great distance and in throwing, so to speak, the anonymous body of the actor into my ear: it granulates, it crackles, it caresses, it grates, it cuts, it comes: that is bliss."[10] Barthes was a writer of displacements, and this surprisingly carnal description of the moviegoing experience confirms that his writings on film have to be understood in this light.

What is, then, the legacy of these writings? Not the pseudo-scientific language he adopted and (sometimes quickly) abandoned. Not the defense of specific films or a film corpus. Instead, Roland Barthes' writings on film remain significant because they attempt to restore an imaginative power (fictional, creative) to art. Just like painting and literature, cinema has become a way through which we enter into and rearrange our world. From equality to sensuality, from politics to aesthetics, from technology to hermeneutics, his abundant references to cinema did indeed help to "shift the ground of the whole realm of the humanities."

An important part of this book belongs to what might be called a *historical poetics*, and this takes two forms. The first is a history, or prehistory, of film studies. Barthes occupies a somewhat paradoxical place within the discipline. On the one hand, his work became one of the major references of U.S. academic film theory: it is so present that even David Bordwell, a self-proclaimed "post-theorist," begins his book on film criticism with a quote from Barthes.[11] It is also true, however, that in this context Barthes' writing on film matters less than the essay on the "reality effect," or books like *S/Z* and *The Pleasure of the Text*. In other words, it was Barthes' literary essays, his properly semiotic analyses, that helped to redefine film studies in the United States and in France.

What gets found, what gets lost, when a theorist is imported from literature to film, from France to the United States, from French to English? What are the conditions of their work's reception? The present study is, in part, a reconsideration of problems that arose in the transatlantic reception and translation of a primary representative of what became known as "French theory." At the same time, I also hope to open up some of Barthes' lesser known writings on films, essays that were not part of his semiotic enterprise and that were either overlooked, not included in the *Oeuvres complètes*, or never translated into English. These essays, as well as more practical connections like his relationship with André Téchiné and his small role in Téchiné's film *Les Soeurs Brontë* (*The Brontë Sisters*, 1979), challenge our received ideas about Barthes and cinema. They testify to the productive dialogue he maintained with the medium, a dialogue which, in my opinion, has something to tell us today about Barthes' understanding of aesthetics and his attempt to think through the relation between aesthetics and our experience of the world.

The second aspect of this historical poetics is what I might call *the conditions of production of thought about film* in France. Barthes came to occupy the particular position of the literary intellectual, a position he inherited from Sartre and Camus and shared with a number of contemporaries—Foucault, Deleuze, Althusser, Lacan—during one of the most intellectually creative moments in the history of European thought. One of the demands placed on this acutely public figure was that he or she be polyvalent; in the case of Barthes, this meant that he write not just about his specialty—literature—but also about a wide range of subjects, including popular ones such as cinema. Taking a position on specific movies and on cinema in general became almost a necessity for intellectuals working in France in the postwar years.[12]

How does one describe the reaction of literary intellectuals to film in France? For Martin Jay, these reactions, including Barthes' own, are overwhelmingly characterized by an "anti-visual discourse," by "antiocularcentrism."[13] More precisely, however, I would say that there is a distrust of the common among these writers, even among those who argued for equality: many share the conviction that the movies serve as an opiate of the people, that they are a popular spectacle which exercises deleterious effects on the masses. The problem they faced was not defining cinema as an art, it was extracting the art of cinema from the illusions, the mystification of capitalist spectacle and from its social and economic dependencies. For Camus such an extraction was impossible;[14] for Merleau-Ponty, it was desirable and possible.

This "extraction" of cinema from a purely commercial and banal use participates in what for me is the major contribution of Barthes' turn to the cinema. This has to do with what I will call, following Stanley Cavell, *an attempt to overcome skepticism*.[15] If one were to trace a rough trajectory of Barthes' copious writings on film, it would look something like a voyage from deep distrust (as evidenced in *Mythologies*) to a "celebration" (even if the word may sound too strong) of the poetics of film as a tool that allows one to enter into a renewed relation with the world of the body and of emotions. This overcoming of skepticism is visible in some of Barthes' essays on cinema, as well as in the work of one of France's most important post-New Wave directors, André Téchiné, whose poetics, and in particular his attempt to construct films around marginal spaces and social positions in Europe today, owes an acknowledged debt to Barthes.

If there is a coherent intellectual itinerary in Barthes, we might describe it as a journey from—and with—skepticism toward epicureanism.[16] The former term implies restraint, left-wing Puritanism, suspicion of the spectacle, demystification, distrust of the surface, distrust of images, irreconcilable distance from society and forms of sociability, "alienation." Barthes suffers from what Stanley Cavell describes as "ordinary skepticism," a feeling of not belonging to the world, a quotidian solitude, an inability to relate to one's experiences with others. This feeling, of course, never quite leaves him.

Epicureanism, on the other hand, suggests sensuality, happiness, and corporeal pleasure. In Barthes, it takes the form of a desire to understand the ways in which aesthetics structures our living in the world.

What Roland Barthes is looking for in the work of art is what Michael Fried called "absorption,"[17] an ability to be fully in the work of art, to lose the contingency of the self in the work of art and, most important, to erase the effects of skepticism. Nowhere is this journey played out more clearly, more poignantly, than in his relation to cinema.

These mixed feelings are characteristic of larger tensions: Barthes served as a link between two generations of philosophers, literary intellectuals, and social scientists, all of whom found themselves writing on film, and writing as amateurs. The first is the generation of Camus, Sartre, Merleau-Ponty, Duhamel, and Leiris, who expressed tentative, and often disparaging, opinions on the subject. The second generation is that of Deleuze, Rancière, Jean-Luc Nancy, Alain Badiou, for whom film has become an integral part of their philosophical reflection. Barthes is located between these two modes of writing: he paves the way for the writings of Deleuze and Rancière, but at the same time he is haunted by the hesitations and, dare one say, the "antipopulist" prejudices of an earlier generation.

This intermediary position gave Barthes a pivotal role in the shaping of film studies in France.[18] His writings stand in a dynamic relation with much of postwar film theory: Gilbert Cohen-Séat's "filmologie," André Bazin, auteur theory, Christian Metz (and then, posthumously, Gilles Deleuze and Jacques Rancière). He often gave articles or interviews to film journals, and these were always in full sympathy with film studies. Those exchanges as well as his early commitment to interdisciplinarity (what was semiotics if not the spearhead of a new, modern, interdisciplinarity?) contributed to cinema's growing legitimacy as a theoretical object.[19] There is also a professional dimension in this contribution. University teaching jobs for film specialists were nearly inexistent in France in the 1950s and 1960s. Serious film writing was almost entirely limited to journalism or, in the case of someone like Edgar Morin, a sociology of contemporary culture in which cinema is just one object among others. In Barthes' case, literature had been a path out of journalism and toward an academic career; cinema would play a similar role for a generation of younger film scholars he trained: Raymond Bellour, Patrizia Lombardo, Thierry Kuntzel, Stephen Heath, and Marc Vernet were all students of Barthes, either at the École pratique des hautes études or in his seminar at the Collège de France. As a matter of fact, in 1968, nearly half the students in Barthes' seminar, devoted that year to the structural analysis of Balzac's "Sarrasine," listed cinema as their primary field.

On a more personal note, I can say without hyperbole that Barthes' writings have always been with me, as they have been with so many of us. I remember once in a diner in New York where I often had breakfast in the 1980s, I chatted with one of the older waiters who called me "Dr. Linguist" in a way that displayed both affection and amusement. One day, over scrambled eggs, he asked me what I wanted to do in life and I answered that I wanted to become a critic. Did I really say that? At twenty-two, had I really wanted to be a critic, an intellectual? Shouldn't one dream of greater stuff when one begins graduate school in New York? Why hadn't I simply answered, "I don't know yet"? Or, "I guess I'll be a teacher"? As I look back at that answer, it seems to me now to have been the height of an intellectual snobbery that I prided myself on distrusting. In any case, the waiter was nonplussed, not hostile but puzzled that someone would, of choice, become a critic. As for me, I'm still embarrassed when I think of my answer that was so spontaneous as to have revealed a truth of some sort. My only explanation today is that when I made this somewhat incomprehensible declaration—"I want to be a critic!"—I was thinking of Barthes and that for me at the time there was something heroic about his role as I imagined it: a thinker, solitary (of course), discreet, melancholy, somewhat withdrawn from the world but always generous in his writings, spot-on in his analyses, refusing to be duped by society, able to move from writing about books to writing about love and life. I remember my excitement when I discovered Susan Sontag's essay on Barthes; when Jack Murray, my professor in Santa Barbara, told me he had sat next to Barthes in a café in Paris; when my friend Dave D. announced that he too had read Barthes, but that he didn't believe "all that semiotics crap." I remember reading Barthes' Critical Essays in college in an edition with a strangely granular picture of Barthes on the cover. I understood little of the essays at the time, but something drew me to Barthes—perhaps the self-assured tone of the essays, the rigor of his demonstrations, but perhaps also the celebrity status of a literary intellectual, a mystification from which I have not entirely freed myself.

Chapter 1

A Degraded Spectacle

Alongside the celebrated essays on wrestling, steak frites, the Tour de France and laundry detergent—"l'euphorie d'*Omo*"—that make up Roland Barthes' *Mythologies*, we find a surprising number of essays devoted to movies, actors, and film technology. Barthes writes about Joseph Mankiewicz's *Julius Caesar* (1953), Elia Kazan's *On the Waterfront* (1954), Chaplin's *Modern Times* (1936), Fred Zinnemann's *From Here to Eternity* (1953), the Italian anthropological documentary *Continente perduto* (1955), Greta Garbo in *Queen Christina* (1933), Sacha Guitry's costume farce *Si Versailles m'était conté* (1954), Visconti's *La Terra Trema* (1948), the Biblical epic *The Robe* (1953), a French espionage film set during World War I (*Deuxième Bureau contre Kommandantur*, 1939), a biopic of l'abbé Pierre, Jacques Becker's *Touchez pas au grisbi* (1954), Claude Chabrol's *Le Beau Serge* (1958), the advent of CinemaScope, the airy gestures of *film noir* gangsters, studio portraits of actors, Audrey Hepburn's modernism, Marlon Brando's wedding, and Michèle Morgan's divorce.

Suffice it to read the 1954 article "On CinemaScope" to understand that Barthes was, if not quite a *cinéphile*, at least a "film lover" (*amateur du cinéma*).[1] Nine years later, in 1963, he explained to Jacques Rivette and Michel Delahaye that he went to the movies around once a week and tried to maintain a relation of gratuity to them.[2] His taste in films and the wide range of his references are clear indications of a real engagement with the medium, an engagement suggesting that, for Barthes in the 1950s, cinema was both an instance of the popular culture he was investigating in *Mythologies* and an aesthetic form that posed specific problems. This engagement with film has often been overlooked by readers, in part due to the vicissitudes of the publications and translations of the volume. The original 1957 French edition did not include the essays on CinemaScope, Sacha Guitry, or *Le Beau Serge*, and English readers have not been well-served with translations.

THE INTERPRETER AND THE SENSUALIST

Barthes approaches film in two distinct ways. On the one hand, *Mythologies* famously proposes to demystify the petit bourgeois capture of everyday life in 1950s France. For Barthes, contemporary society had made "natural" and obvious various objects and actions that had nothing obvious or natural about them. Writing the *Mythologies*, Barthes became a prominent exponent of a hermeneutics of suspicion, seeking to "account *in detail* for the mystification which transforms petit bourgeois culture into a universal nature."[3] In this schema, movies, because they are the culmination of capitalism's "ideology of consumption," because they are produced in order to be watched only once, because they are highly coded mass spectacles that attempt to get audiences to suspend their awareness of the artifice of the cinematic experience, were easy prey for critical analysis.[4] Several of Barthes' essays attempt to demystify the elements—such as the "roman haircut" in *Julius Caesar*—that participate in a film's verisimilitude, its ability to make us believe, or at least suspend disbelief. What Miriam Hansen says about Siegfried Kracauer's approach to cinema in the 1920s describes well Barthes' project in the 1950s: he approached movies as an aesthetic form "relating to the organization of human sense perception and its transformation in industrial-capitalist modernity."[5] "Transformation" here is a key word, and the subject of the essays in *Mythologies* are often new forms of mediation: newspaper articles, magazines, advertisements, political speeches, photographs, and movies; by the time Barthes was writing movies had become the emblematic leisure activity in postwar France. What is more, they played a specific role in postwar European culture as the spearhead of American capitalism directed at large-scale consumption in Europe.[6] In this sense, Barthes approached cinema as a site of Cold War confrontation, as a consumer good that is also a potentially dangerous force of mass mobilization. As such, it becomes the prime object of an ideological critique, and *Mythologies* remains today one of the strongest, most convincing, and wittiest ideological critiques of mass culture in postwar Europe.[7]

At the same time, however, Barthes saw film as a way of "refreshing the perception of the world," of seeing things differently.[8] Barthes demystifies: he makes movies seem strange, different, unnatural. But he is an ambivalent demystifier, and *Mythologies* should also be read as repeated attempts to describe marvelous encounters with a world of undetermined sensations, with the sensible tissue of aesthetics.[9] One often hears today that for Barthes, the only reality was writing and that nothing he did fell into what Éric Marty calls the "ordinary triviality of life," the "grey sphere of daily life."[10] My contention, however, is that it's the other way around. Barthes' writing can be understood as an encounter that transforms the ordinary triviality of life into an object of fascination. And cinema plays a particularly important role for Barthes in offering him moments of a kind of pure sensation, not yet determined by what he will later call the "shelter" of interpretation and commentary with which we protect ourselves. Barthes says as much in the last footnote in his book, when he writes that in contradiction to his ideological critique of myths, he began to write about the pleasures of the real, "to make it excessively dense, and to discover surprising compactness in it, *which I have savored*" (274). A brick wall, a flooded street, a child's wooden toy, a soap bubble can all become ways of reconfiguring the world, of seeing the world afresh. When Barthes writes in "Saponids and Detergents" that the soap ad he sees in movie theaters seems to give the suds "a mode of contact at once light and vertical, pursued like a sort of bliss in the gustative order . . . as well as in the vestimentary" (33), one feels that he is not just giving us a tongue in cheek psychoanalysis of detergent ads, but that the pleasure is also his. It is this pleasure, and not demystification, that is at work in what he calls at the beginning of the essay the "euphoria of *Omo*."

What strikes me most today reading *Mythologies* is how Barthes' aggressive ideological critique is accompanied by this sense of enchantment, of "savor" of sensations—or what he will later label as a "polyphony of pleasures" in his essay on the Eiffel Tower. Part of Barthes' critique of the petit-bourgeoisie has to do with what he calls their "impotence to imagine *the other*" ("Bichon Among the Blacks," 68), that is, with the importance of seeing differently, of transforming the optics of the everyday. Film, of course, is not the only means of refreshing the perception of the world. Barthes calls the medium a "degraded spectacle" (21), in the sense that there is no innovation, that it traffics in the repetition of stereotypes, but it holds the potential to see the world anew, transforming the commonplace, initiating an aesthetic revolution, and reimagining our relation to others. It is this tension that I think is worth saving, worth rereading today, in an age when ideological critique seems to have run its course.

Barthes thus approaches film in two ways. On the one hand as an "interpreter," whose method of analysis closely resembles what Paul Ricoeur called the "hermeneutics of suspicion." On the other hand as a sensualist, who looks to describe the surface of films, the effects they produce on spectators and his own emotional response to the sounds and images of movies. This is one of the key tensions in the field of film studies—summarized as the "hermeneutic" versus the "poetic" approach—and while Barthes has most often been placed in the hermeneuts' camp, it is the tension at the heart of his writing that makes *Mythologies* a book for our modern times.

ROMAN HAIR

Barthes published the majority of his "mythologies" in Maurice Nadeau's monthly *Les Lettres Nouvelles*, which was launched in 1953 and quickly became one of the leading publications of postwar modernism. Regularly featuring writers like Henri Michaux, Samuel Beckett, Richard Wright, Heinrich Böll, Kateb Yacine, Michel Leiris, and Édouard Glissant, the journal positioned itself as more literary than *Les Temps Modernes* and more worldly and modern than Jean Paulhan's *La Nouvelle Nouvelle Revue Française*.[11] Barthes published an article on theater in its first issue, and in February 1954, with an essay on CinemaScope, he began regularly publishing the short essays that would make up the *Mythologies* volume, usually at a rate of four a month, all under the rubric "Petite mythologie du mois."

Barthes' *Mythologies* are made up of the author's reactions to what he encountered in his everyday life as a *flâneur*, as a *reader*, and of course, as a *spectator*, always curious and at times aghast at what he was being forced to watch. A case in point is "Romans in the Movies"—originally published in *Les Lettres Nouvelles* as "Jules César au cinéma" in January 1954. It is one of the wittiest essays of the collection in its lighthearted attempts to make strange to French audiences Hollywood's adaptation of Shakespeare's tragedy. The essay begins: "In Mankiewicz's *Julius Caesar*, all the male characters have bangs. Some (bangs, not characters) are curly, some straight, others tufted, still others pomaded, all are neatly combed, and bald men are not allowed, though Roman History has a good number to its credit" (19). It goes without saying that Barthes showed little interest in storyline or any of the technical elements of movies (with the exception of acting, as we will see in a minute), nor was he really concerned with the film itself: as Louis-Jean Calvet has written, contrary to Barthes' assertions, there are plenty of bald Romans in the film and we never see anyone sweat.[12] Under Barthes' lingering gaze, Mankiewicz's film suddenly becomes a movie about hair, more precisely about "bangs."[13] Barthes goes on to add that the "film's principal artisan" (19) is neither the scriptwriter nor the director but the hairdresser. The hair in *Julius Caesar* tells us all we need to know about the rules of verisimilitude governing Hollywood movies. It is both that which makes a Hollywood movie seem real, and the moment when the verisimilitude breaks down and "betrays a degraded spectacle, one which fears the naïve truth as much as the total artifice" (21). Barthes seems close here to relying upon a hierarchy of genres in which tragedy, Shakespeare's *Julius Caesar*, for example, would be the most prestigious spectacle, while a Hollywood rendition of that tragedy would be nothing more than "bourgeois folklore,"[14] folklore that turns out to be the antithesis of two aesthetic models that Barthes cites as ideals: the abstract "algebra" of Chinese theater and the "simple reality" of the theater of Stanislavsky.[15] In this respect, the opposition he establishes may have been a way of choosing theater over cinema. But one is hard pressed not to see that this opposition is also structured by an opposition between national and political forms of popular spectacle—the theater of the two communist powers on the one hand, and, on the other, the cinema of Hollywood.

Marlon Brando as Marc Antony in *Julius Caeser* (Joseph L. Mankiewicz, 1953)

A COLD WAR CINEMA

In the March 1955 issue of *Les Lettres Nouvelles*, Barthes published an essay on Elia Kazan's *On the Waterfront*, a film that in France as much as in the United States embodied the conflicts of the Cold War. Barthes' original title was "Comment démystifier," as if the essay on Kazan were a programmatic text for the *Mythologies*. Barthes, who throughout the original essay misspells Kazan as "Cazan," is extremely critical of *On the Waterfront*, a film he labels a "mystification," in reference to his sense that the film duped some French movie critics into believing it to be a "leftist" (70) and progressive piece of filmmaking.[16] *On the Waterfront* would have us believe that the real danger in modern society, the real threat to workers, is corrupt union bosses, a mystification that distracts us from what Barthes calls "the real evil"—the capitalist exploitation of labor. This is what Barthes labels the "vaccination of truth," in which the spectators are shown a small part of the problem and then asked to make wider conclusions that, in the end, reinforce the dominant order. Barthes accuses Kazan of having portrayed workers in his film as "a group of weaklings [*veules*], submitting to a servitude they clearly recognize but lack the courage to shake off" (70). Barthes claims that the film forces us to identify with the one "sympathetic worker" in the lot, longshoreman Terry Malloy, the character played by Marlon Brando, and that in the final scene, when Terry recovers from the beating and returns to work, the spectators have only one option: "the restoration of order" (71). When Terry walks back into the warehouse, we spectators, along with "Brando, with the longshoremen, with all the workers of America, we put ourselves, with a sense of victory and relief, back in the boss' hands" (71). *On the Waterfront* has led us to our oppression. And in the end, what Barthes improbably prescribes is a "Brechtian demystification"—though one can hardly imagine Brando engaging in this exercise—that would give the spectator enough distance from Terry Malloy to identify not just with this worker but with all the workers, and to condemn not just one union boss but the system of exploitation on which capitalism relies.

Nowhere in *Mythologies* or any other of his writings for that matter will Barthes come so close to calling a film a work of capitalist propaganda. "*A Sympathetic Worker*" is a rhetorically perfect piece of Marxist and Brechtian demystification. It identifies an illusion, reveals the duplicity of the filmmaker, and shows the reader concrete reality, in this case, the workers' struggle in Western democracies. And one senses Barthes' agitated engagement not just with the polarizations of the Cold War but with the crisis of the McCarthy hearings, even though by the time the film was released in France in January 1955 the hearings in . Washington and in Hollywood had cooled down somewhat. Elia Kazan, a former member of the communist party, had testified and "named names" before the House Committee on Un-American Activities in April 1952, and there is no doubt that these hearings are in the background of Barthes' essay. Kazan himself has offered a reading of the film that goes in this direction.[17] For the American left, as Victor Navasky has written, "Kazan emerged . . . as the quintessential informer" and "ultimate betrayer."[18] Kazan was no favorite of French Marxists either, and one has the sense that Barthes' decision to write about *On the Waterfront* may have been motivated by a desire to respond to Kazan's denunciation of communists in Hollywood.[19]

What is more, in July 1955 Barthes wrote a brief "petite mythologie" titled "Suis-je marxiste?" in which he answers a question posed in the *Nouvelle Nouvelle Revue Française* by one Jean Guérin. After reading several installments of Barthes' column, Guérin demanded that he state clearly, once and for all, his allegiance to Marxism. Barthes' response: What does it matter? "This kind of question usually only interests the McCarthyites."[20] If Guérin wants an answer, the essay continues, he should look through Marx and decide for himself. This was how Barthes had made up his mind about the *Nouvelle NRF*: simply reading it was enough to tell it was "perfectly reactionary." As Philippe Roger has shown, this little moment of Cold War theater was indeed straight out of the McCarthy hearings, with Guérin as prosecutor and Barthes duplicating "the speech strategy adopted by presumed communists in the United States during the McCarthy era,"[21] responding to hostile pressure to confess a political allegiance with digressions, asides, and feints. The scale of the hearings was different, of course, since Barthes was not facing anything like the United States Congress; nevertheless, his adversary was more powerful than he appeared. Jean Guérin, as it turns out, was none other than Jean Paulhan, the director of the *Nouvelle NRF* and an influential figure in French letters whose visceral anticommunism dated back to the postwar literary purges.[22]

This clash between Barthes and Paulhan is symptomatic of a moment in which the literary world in France, or a portion of it, seemed interested in revisiting the McCarthy hearings the year after they ended. If Barthes' essay on Kazan is so strident, the choice of tone has to do with these French re-enactments of Cold War skirmishes. Barthes was prickly about McCarthyism—he called Billy Graham's 1955 sermons delivered at Paris' Vélodrome d'hiver "un épisode maccarthyste"—and the French release of *On the Waterfront* provided a further outlet for this growing vexation.[23] His essay on Kazan participates in his general project of demystifying bourgeois culture, but something else is at stake here, as is often the case with his texts on cinema. "A sympathetic worker" is by far the most pointedly political of the mythologies, but the choice of precisely this film suggests that for Barthes cinema is also caught in a struggle between the rival political, economic, and cultural systems of the Cold War, a struggle in which Kazan became an all too willing actor.

DEMYSTIFICATION, 1957

In *Mythologies* we can see just how far Barthes is from the aesthetics and the politics of the New Wave, but his demystifications fit squarely within a current of leftist cultural criticism.[24] Demystification of Hollywood films, after all, was part of the cultural work performed by film critics on the left during the 1940s and 1950s. The model for this type of writing might very well have been André Bazin's 1946 essay "Entomology of the Pin-Up Girl," in which he shows the cultural lie that underpinned images of the Hollywood starlet.[25] A product of "military sociology" (158), writes Bazin, the pin-up girl is "artificial, ambiguous, and shallow," and provides "nothing more than chewing gum for the imagination" (161). The pin-up girl belongs to a society where "Protestantism" still dominates, just as Barthes' Romans reveal the "Anglo-Saxon lawyer" under their togas.[26]

Bazin was not alone in this type of exercise, however. Again and again, in the pages of *L'Écran Français*, *Les Lettres Françaises*, *Positif*, and *L'Humanité*, we read that Hollywood is the spearhead of capitalist culture intent upon mass-producing mythic representations in order to indoctrinate European spectators. In May 1948, Henri-François Rey published an article titled "Hollywood Makes Myths the Way Ford Makes Cars" in which he denounced Hollywood's "artificial" vision of the world. This cinema, according to Rey, was interested primarily in "defending [American] economic, political and moral views" and in imposing its culture on the world.[27] In 1951, *L'Écran Français* ran a series on the "storehouse of myths" in Hollywood films. For Hollywood, wrote journalist Jean Thévenot, doctors and patients fit into three or four well-determined categories. There is "the good old doctor" with "snowy white hair ... [a man] of unlimited devotion" who cures his patients with "a smile . . . a pat on the cheek . . . or, when the patient is a young girl, by listening attentively to her story of heartache." The other types include the surgeon "who always has beautiful eyes . . . and often an agitated love life" and the psychoanalyst who is the "subject of amorous passion" and who "tortures his patients." Finally, there is the patient who only suffers from "noble diseases," and never, ever "from digestive problems . . . infections . . . dermatosis, boils [or] venereal diseases."[28]

This low level hermeneutics of suspicion sets out to tear away the artifice of Hollywood cinema, to make strange, foreign, "Anglo-Saxon," a cultural form to which the French public is too quickly becoming acclimated. A higher-level essay on the myth of the movies is Edgar Morin's *Les Stars* published in the same year (1957) and by the same publisher (Le Seuil) as *Mythologies*. In his book, Morin sets out to study the mythical "demi-Gods" that populate the movie screens of the 1950s, and though in his 1972 preface he denied he was engaging in "demystification," he casts a self-avowed anthropological gaze on the standardized production of Hollywood stars, whom he sees fabricated and sold in the same way as chewing gum or Frigidaires.[29] It is thanks to their almost limitless eroticism that their fans engage in a "stellar liturgy," forming fetishistic cults that involve mimetic behavior and quasi-mystical worship. Most of these idolaters, Morin asserts, are adolescents and women from the "*intermediary social levels.*"[30]

However, like Barthes, Morin is cautious about his own position as sociologist. He provides taxonomies and analyses in the language of the social sciences, even going so far as to compare fans to "archaic people" (85) and "primitives" (96), in the heart of a rational society and a rationalized economy, engaged in a version of magical thinking that invests the star with a kind of omnipotence. But Morin is also critical of the position of ironic superiority that he occupies, and claims, near the end of his book, that movie fans know very well that they are playing a game, and that they only half-believe the stories they read and write about movie stars. "The star is at the border of aesthetics and magic. She overcomes the skepticism of the spectator's consciousness, who, nonetheless knows that she is participating in an illusion" (95). This position of the scientific observer who is weary of his own scientific superiority is very much at the heart of Barthes' own project of demystification, and separates both Morin and Barthes from the vulgar demystification of the journalists at *L'Écran Français.*

In all cases, demystification posits a critique of artifice that relies upon identifying the foreignness of the cinematic illusion. But the counterpoint to this artifice is different in each case—for Thévenot and the writers at *L'Écran Français,* it is their perception of the economic reality of American empire behind Hollywood films, for Bazin it is the ontological realism of cinema, for Barthes it is both economic reality and what he calls poetry's search for the "inalienable meaning of things."[31]

Demystification of the type practiced in the 1950s, with its constant denunciation of Hollywood's artifice and excess, also has a more strictly aesthetic dimension; it participates in what we might call leftwing asceticism. In the *Mythologies* it is precisely the moments of excess that trigger Barthes' demystifying reflex. Wrestling, for instance, is "a spectacle of excess" (3), the Roman locks "flood us with evidence" (19), Pierre Poujade's rhetoric is "tautological" (93), everything Poujade says, he says twice. What Barthes calls "ideological abuse" (xi) in the *Mythologies*—and which he will label *doxa* or power a few years later—is also a rhetorical abuse, a violation of aesthetic rules of balance, subtlety, sobriety.[32] It is in one of his earliest essays that Barthes lauded Robert Bresson's *Les Anges du péché* precisely on the grounds that it avoided excess: "The convent is modest, subtle, and, clean . . . no organ, a bell rings once or twice . . . the dialogue [is] simple, steady, virile. Bresson's nuns . . . are fresh without being touched up, gracious without being provocative . . . Not a single sentimental sentence or pedantic remark; no catechism, no emotional outbursts."[33] While never espousing the cause of cinematic realism, Barthes' early essays on film depend upon an ideal of asceticism, of stylistic paring-down, of an almost classical or rather Atticist aesthetic purity. If, in certain essays in *Mythologies,* Barthes denounces classical rhetoric, it is precisely the flourishes, the "flights," the abuses of this rhetoric that he condemns.[34]

Therefore, cinema participates in the "ideological abuse" of bourgeois culture not only in and of itself, but inasmuch as it participates in rhetorical excesses (breaches of verisimilitude, obviousness, overproduction). By the time of his essays on *Julius Caesar* and *On the Waterfront,* Barthes had identified what he thought of as the antidote to the compulsory power of Hollywood cinema and located it in a perhaps equally mythical ideal of Chinese and Russian theater.[35]

Barthes' trajectory has often been described as a shift from a dogmatic advocacy of structuralism to a dismantling of the scientific approach to culture; it could also be described as the advocacy and then the dismantling of demystification. But by 1956, as his desire for a "synthesis between ideology and poetry" at the end of *Mythologies* makes clear, Barthes was already a reluctant demystifier.[36] For he took too much pleasure in the popular.

"THE FACE OF GARBO"

Do Barthes' little essays collected in *Mythologies* participate in what has been called a "camp poetics?"[37] His Marxism, the seriousness of his demystifying project, the occasional revulsion he felt at the vulgarity and the obviousness of Hollywood movies, would all seem to distance him from this sensibility that began to identify itself as camp in the 1950s. But his emphasis on style, on the sensuous surface of things, and on the outrageous detail (the Roman haircut, for instance), his fascination with the excesses of rhetorical pronouncements, gangsters' gestures or an actor's makeup, his delight in the artifice of popular culture, his attraction to knickknacks (Barthes calls plastic a "magical" substance), his performance of a kind of democratic aesthetics in which anything at all can become an object of delectation, his ability to signal homosexual desire without declaring it (*"Omo euphoria"*), all these point to Barthes' proximity to a camp sensibility of which Hollywood was one of the main purveyors in the 1950s and 1960s. Barthes' attitude toward something that we might today identify as camp is complicated but might best be characterized as both fascination and suspicion. It is an attitude of "resistance" not so different from the resistance that Barthes displays toward movies as a whole, a desire to simultaneously take pleasure from and demystify an aesthetic system that, while it fascinates him, he also deems conformist, oppressive, and reactionary. Nowhere is this ambivalence to the camp aesthetic more visible than in "The Face of Garbo," a short essay on the actor whom Susan Sontag called "the great serious idol of Camp taste."[38]

Barthes published this essay in April 1955, a few months after *Queen Christina* (1933) had been rereleased in Paris, and his reading seems to gesture towards an exploration of Garbo's sexuality in that film. Christina kisses her girlfriend Ebba on the lips, spends half the film dressed as a man and, still dressed as a young nobleman, ends up sharing her bed with the Spanish ambassador. "Alternately a woman and a young cavalier," Barthes' Queen Christina seems to be an early figuration of Sarrasine (74). He reads Garbo as "sexless" [*désexué*] without being "dubious" [*douteux*]. She is neutral, a star who demystifies the categories of normative gender roles. Yet Barthes' emphasis here turns out to be less on Garbo's sexuality than on her role as an archetype, a "Platonic idea" (74). The close-ups in *Queen Christina* expose cinema as a machine that produces affect by transforming Garbo's face into a mask of antique theater, a kind of idealized form that sends moviegoers into a trance—"the greatest perturbation" (73). Cinema, once again, is cast in the role of a mystification machine whose qualities resemble the wizardry of ancient rituals and inspire what Barthes calls "mystical

Greta Garbo in the title role of *Queen Christina* (Rouben Mamoulian, 1933)

sentiments of perdition" (73) in the audience. The myth of Garbo, as Barthes sees it, is a pacifying, mystifying spectacle that Garbo herself played to by never allowing herself to be photographed.

As always with Barthes' essays on film, however, mystification (and the process of demystification) is a fractured, contradictory, unstable process. "The Face of Garbo" was written just as the Hollywood star system was beginning to falter, and Barthes sees Garbo as a harbinger of this change, an embodiment of what he had recently termed a "degraded spectacle" (21). This narrative of the twilight of the movie stars was common enough in the 1950s. In his anthropology of film spectatorship, *Les Stars*, already mentioned above, Edgar Morin had made a similar claim: the new stars of 1950s Hollywood, such as James Dean and Marilyn Monroe, participated, through their own self-destruction, in the demolition of the old star system. Dean and Monroe helped launch the youth movement, Morin later claimed, and embodied a new type of star, the "neurotic hero."[39] In Barthes' version of this story, Garbo's face plays a transitional role, embodying the terrestrial as well as the divine. Through "a deliberate and therefore human relation between the curve of the nostrils and the superciliary arcade" (74), she moves towards what Barthes calls an "existential beauty," marking a transition from the "terror" of the Gods to the "charm" of the human. For Barthes, Garbo's face is a moment in the history of cinema where Hollywood demystifies its own illusions. It might not be wholly irrelevant to note that Queen Christina is herself an ambivalent ruler—she is an absolute monarch who tames the mob with her speeches, but who at the same time sues for peace, wants to bring "freedom" to her people, and, in the end, abdicates the throne to be with the man she loves. What Barthes sees in Garbo is the end of the absolutism of the cinematic image.

This helps to explain why, at the end of his essay, Barthes cites Audrey Hepburn as the incarnation of a more fully human face on the screen, a new face that refuses mystifications and reveals the complexity and the uniqueness of the individual. Audrey Hepburn, Barthes tells us in a phrase oozing with hyperbolic technicity, has "a virtually unique specification of the face, which has nothing essential left in it but is constituted by an infinite complexity of morphological functions" (75). Barthes imagines Hepburn as the existential counterpart to the "essential beauty" of early stars, with Greta Garbo serving as a transitional model from one regime to the next. Was Barthes thinking of *Sabrina* (1954), also released in Paris in early 1955, the film in which Hepburn plays the daughter of a chauffeur who falls in love with the fabulously wealthy Linus Larrabee?[40] *Queen Christina* and *Sabrina* are both stories of the triumph of love, but *Queen Christina* is a pageant of aristocratic power, and *Sabrina*, the story of class barriers and upward mobility. In any case, Audrey Hepburn's face is "unique," "individualized," and of an "infinite complexity" (74–75). And in this, Barthes concludes, it is "an Event" (75), a term which, as far as I can tell, works as a synonym for "history" in the sense that Audrey Hepburn would be the emblem of the potential of cinema and of its audience to effect change, movement, and progress from one political regime to the next, from one way of watching movies to another. On the one hand the face of Garbo, which mystified crowds; on the other Hepburn's face, which reconfigures the star as an emblem of individual action. On the one hand myth, on the other history, change, and perhaps equality.

In the 1950s, among cinephiles and film critics, there were two ways of writing about Hollywood stars and about Garbo in particular. One approach was to celebrate. Writing about *Queen Christina*, in an essay that Barthes probably read, André Bazin had compared Garbo to Venus, to Racine's Bérénice, to Eve herself.[41] The alternative approach, at once clever and banal, was to demystify. Barthes' essay on Greta Garbo—and this might bring it closer to a camp sensibility—is situated somewhere between these two approaches. Under the guise of demystification, Barthes discloses a massive investment in the sensuous surface of the close-up (the eyes become "wounds," the "arch of the eyebrows" emblems of the humanization of Garbo). His cryptic phrase about the "infinite complexity of morphological functions" is characteristic of his project to make the trivial significant, to take seriously the beauty exhibited on the movie screen. "The Face of Garbo," and indeed much of the *Mythologies*, can be defined by an emphasis on artifice at the expense of what Marxists would qualify as the economic "real." The essay on Garbo reveals a hypertrophic attention to what Barthes' own Marxist colleagues would consider politically trivial, back-page material. It is the refashioning of American mass culture into a radically new

sensory experience. There is a playfulness to Barthes' essay, even to
his overblown technicality, that situates his experience in the realm of
delectation and, if not ecstasy, then at least pleasure. And this aesthetic
pleasure is also political in the sense that Barthes is interested in how the
close-ups of a movie star might serve to outline new forms of collective
existence, new forms of being in civil society.

Chapter 2

Refresh the Perception
of the World

A favorite target for the demystifier, cinema at the same time allows Barthes to have a unique encounter with the world, to see people and things in a way that no other medium would let him. One finds his clearest statement on this in an article on Stendhal written in 1957, the same year he published *Mythologies*. Reviving the shopworn cliché that Stendhal is somehow a "cinematic" author, Barthes writes:

> The real, for Stendhal, is Italy. Stendhalian Italy . . . is reality in its pure state, and thus intensified, heightened. The modern phenomenon that can give an account of this mode of reality is photogénie: the cinematic image neither distorts nor embellishes the real: it intensifies it, revealing the potential charge of its meanings, and pulls out from within it, all by itself, that which could become man's secret nutrient, everything that ties the world to human subjectivity . . . only the image can register the intensity of the real. [The imagination is] a mental power that succeeds in restoring to the real the multiplicity of its dimensions.[1]

The use of the somewhat archaic term *photogénie* is all the more telling, since Barthes here seems to follow its common acceptation which is tied to French Impressionist cinema: the camera's ability to capture the poetry of the everyday, the *cinématographe* as an intensifier of the real.[2]

"ON CINEMASCOPE"

This is not the first time Barthes makes this point. An earlier version of these ideas appears in one of the most surprising "petites mythologies du mois," a text which was never included in the *Mythologies* volume, "On CinemaScope." First published in February 1954, the month that Twentieth Century Fox released its Biblical epic *The Robe* in France, this enthusiastic essay shows Barthes overwhelmed, not by *The Robe* of course, but by the potential of CinemaScope to "transform the film lover's inner sensibility" and to create what he called "a new dialectic" between men and the world that surrounds them.[3] In an analogy that Jean-Louis Baudry will place at the heart of his apparatus theory ten years later (and which is a common comparison), Barthes likens the spectator to a prisoner in Plato's cave, enshadowed and passively taking in the images on the wall. But CinemaScope, as Barthes sees it, frees the spectator's gaze and allows it to wander through a world seen afresh. It transforms viewers from being "larval" into being "a bit Godlike," someone who is no longer in the traditional position beneath the image, and ventures "in the midst of it." The new space it creates is no longer a forum for close-ups—for "kisses, drops of sweat [and] psychology"—instead, it has become the space of History. With CinemaScope, film is finally able to attain the tragic, that is, the moment when the individual is engaged through art in History. For Barthes, it is as if the new process allowed the medium to attain the ideal that he had only previously found in Brecht's theater. Perhaps unsurprisingly, his model for this tragic engagement with History is not Twentieth Century Fox's production of *The Robe*; on the contrary, it is the possibility of watching a CinemaScope version of *Battleship Potemkin*: "Imagine yourself watching *Battleship Potemkin*, no longer positioned behind a spyglass but pressed up against the very air, the stone, the crowd: this ideal *Potemkin*, where your hand can finally reach out to the insurgents, where you can share in the light and receive the blow of the tragic Odessa steps right to your chest as it were."

This vision of *Potemkin* brings together two of the elements Barthes associated with a kind of cinematic ideal. Cinema—or at least in this case, CinemaScope—changes how we see and hear; it creates a "euphoria born of circulating equally between the spectacle and [the] body," enabling a revolutionary aesthetic experience that Barthes rarely finds in standard 35mm projections. Furthermore, in arguing that the process changes sensation, he also suggests that its radical reshaping of "inner sensibility" is necessarily tied to a political revolution and, very specifically, to a solidarity with the insurgents of *Battleship Potemkin*. Of course, Barthes' little essay is a fantasy, a utopia of sorts, and as far as I know, he never commented on—or never wrote specifically about— another movie in CinemaScope. Nevertheless, this short text speaks to a dream that he located in cinema, a dream in which a technological inno- vation could lead to a radical transformation in the perception of the world and, thereby, a radical transformation in the spectator's relation to the common people, the poor, the workers whom a feature like *On the Waterfront* attempts to lure down the wrong path.

A few months after having sketched this utopian project of cinema as a means of facilitating (or even creating) the viewer's solidarity with the worker, Barthes wrote an essay about *Modern Times* that praises Chaplin's film as the apogee of revolutionary art. This, of course, is not an unusual claim—in the mid-1930s, Walter Benjamin had already mentioned mass audiences' "progressive reaction" toward "a Chaplin movie"[4]—and in the postwar years, his shorts and features were emblems of progressive politics, especially after he was suspected of communist sympathies and denied re-entry into the United States in 1952. For Barthes, Chaplin's character in *Modern Times* is an unemancipated, pre- revolutionary worker who, even as he is working on the assembly line, embodies the characteristics of the poor rather than of the proletariat. That is, he is driven by basic needs such as hunger and not, or not yet, by class consciousness. At the same time, and because Chaplin's films have a real "representative force," they allow the spectator to visualize the gap between the poor and the worker—we see Chaplin's blindness, we see what he doesn't see, we see his humiliation: "No socialist work has yet managed to express the humiliated condition of the worker with such violence and generosity." In this sense, Chaplin's *Modern Times* is the very definition of political art, according to Barthes: an art that cre- ates the proper distance for seeing. And Barthes concludes his essay by writing: "His anarchy, while politically dubious, represents through art what is perhaps the most effective form of the revolution."[5]

BARTHES AND THE NEW WAVE

Since so many of Barthes' essays from the 1950s confirm his critical engagement with popular culture, we might wonder how his work related to France's most significant group of young directors. Barthes never wrote about the New Wave as such, but he did voice reservations about a film movement that, in its early years at least, had a reputation for being on the right and flirting with reactionary politics. Did Barthes have troublemaking critic François Truffaut in mind when he wrote about Sacha Guitry's Si Versailles m'était conté . . . (1954), a film about the *mores* of the French kings and their courts? Among the Young Turks, Truffaut was undoubtedly the most vocal of Guitry's admirers, going so far as to place him alongside Jean Renoir in a tribute written after his death in 1957.[6] Three years earlier, in April 1954, under the pseudonym R. L. (Robert Lachenay), Truffaut had defended Guitry's historical pageant, claiming that the French public misunderstood this film about "the greatness of France," because "the rabble" was, in his words, "thirsting for equality"; Truffaut adds: "A regime whose watchword is 'You are the State' understands nothing of the Sun King and would not know how to honor him."[7] Read today, Truffaut's right-wing provocations seem like nothing so much as an attempt to sound original by defending a figure decried as a political opportunist and former supporter of Marshal Pétain's Vichy regime.[8] While it is not certain that Barthes had read Truffaut's defense of Guitry, less than a month later, in May 1954, he published a quick but devastating "mythology" on Si Versailles m'était conté . . . where he chides the director for his reactionary vision of history.[9]

Barthes doesn't waste any time demystifying Guitry's feature. He calls it "a lethally boring film whose stupidity really corrupts; you come out of there feeling soiled." Barthes held boredom to be unforgivable in a movie, but he objects even more to the caricature of history in Guitry's film, its cloying libertinage, its ostentatious display of money at every turn.[10] The film seems guided by financial logic (after all, what is the palace of Versailles for, if not for the ostentatious display of State wealth?): Versailles cost a lot of money, Sacha Guitry argues, therefore it must be great. The same reasoning applies to the cast: *Si Versailles m'était conté* . . . puts on screen some of the biggest and highest paid French movie stars of 1953: Jean-Louis Barrault, Danièle Delorme, Edith Piaf, Gérard Philipe, Jean Marais, Daniel Gélin, Claudette Colbert, and, in a brief appearance, the still unknown Brigitte Bardot. Each star systematically degrades the historical record: "History in its entirety is swallowed up by a bunch of histrionics who humiliate her by trying to pass themselves off as her." Added to this is what Barthes calls "the fundamental ineptness of the imagery" with those "dull and pinched" costumes and "the platitude of those wigs!" (here we are with hair again). All this adds up to a spectacle that claims to be popular and historical, but that ultimately plays on the presumed idiocy of a popular audience expected to laugh at its jokes about cuckolds without understanding that they hide a broader attempt to reassert the power of the ruling class.

In writing about Guitry's film, Barthes sets out to demystify all popular spectacles that seem to ally themselves with their mass audience while actually serving the interests of the bourgeoisie. Indeed, Guitry's film embodies a very precise type of political reaction: in claiming that *all* political regimes are corrupt and therefore that no regime is more legitimate than any other, it articulates one of the main arguments of Vichy apologists who used this type of analogy to claim that democracy and the French Republic were no better than fascism and Vichy. At the same time, however, Barthes is still arguing, as he does in the essay on CinemaScope, that cinema can participate in an emancipatory history, in progress. And indeed, his hope for a dialectical understanding of history is most evident in the essays on film: the sailors of *Potemkin*, the face of Audrey Hepburn, Chaplin's worker stand out as images culled from the movie screen that, for Barthes in the 1950s, embody a promise of progress.

Barthes' essay on Sacha Guitry might very well be a response to and correction of the adulation heaped on him by Truffaut, and thus a rebuke to the attitude he could sense developing at *Cahiers du Cinéma*. Five years later, another encounter with the New Wave is far more direct. In

February 1959, Barthes published a piece on Claude Chabrol's *Le Beau Serge*, the film which, as Michel Marie reminds us, helped give birth to the New Wave.[11] Barthes' essay addresses two significant questions associated with the movement—the aesthetic effects of location shooting and the accusation among some French Marxist critics that the New Wave was, in its early years, a reactionary trend. The title of his *"petite mythologie"* on Chabrol's film, "Cinéma droite et gauche" (Cinema right and left), is proof enough that Barthes' relation to cinema echoes the political debates of its time.[12] This short text opens with the assertion that in France talent is on the right and truth on the left. Upon reading further, however, one senses that Barthes would have liked to have liked *Le Beau Serge*. Was he drawn to Chabrol's story about a student in literature (François, played by Jean-Claude Brialy), who returns to his native rural village to recover from a bout of tuberculosis? Whatever the case, Barthes admires what he calls the film's "Flaubertian asceticism," and in particular the way Chabrol presents "the fields, the village, the hotel, the town square, the clothes, objects, faces, and gestures, everything that bears up under the gaze, everything that is literal, that only signifies an insignificant existence."[13] Chabrol had made a point of shooting on location in the Creuse region with natural light, and under cinematographer Henri Decae's control the camera does indeed linger on insignificant objects and scenes: a dog crossing the village square, a closing door, stone walls. Though such shots rarely last more than five seconds, they constitute Chabrol's attempts to break with the French *tradition de qualité* and with classical Hollywood, both of which had long been for the most part studio-bound, dependent upon shot/countershot editing, and tied to narrative.

Barthes' brief essay on Chabrol's film seems perfectly attuned to the New Wave tenet that the camera on location could reveal the wonders of the world, even in its most incidental details. Like his earlier article on Stendhal, this text suggests Barthes' proximity to theories of *photogénie*, especially its tendency to value material weight over narrative function. Indeed, after introducing the film, Barthes goes on to denounce its plot, and instead he (briefly) defends Chabrol's intermittent gestures toward what he describes in positive terms as "the wasteland of a realism without signification." Surely this is also a way of pointing to the

Chapter 3

Barthes and Bazin

The connections and relations between Roland Barthes and André Bazin continue to be a source of intrigue in our understanding of modern cinema aesthetics. A generation ago, critics and theorists turned to Barthes' writing, and S/Z in particular, in an attempt to discredit what one critic called, in the parlance of the day, André Bazin's "misrecognition of the organizing function of verbal language in filmic systems."[1] Ten years after having inspired a critique of Bazin as a naïve realist, Barthes himself put a damper on this movement when in Camera Lucida (1980) he argued, in terms that are close to Bazin's, that photography brings the "loaded evidence" of the existence of a world or a person now gone.[2] These claims have led critics to begin re-evaluating what Dudley Andrew called the "genealogy" from Bazin to Barthes, a re-evaluation that has focused almost exclusively on the proximity of Barthes' final work to Bazin's celebrated essay "The Ontology of the Photographic Image."[3] A generation ago everything seemed to separate Bazin from Barthes; today, everything seems to bring them together. The focus on Barthes' debt to Bazin in Camera Lucida remains too restrictive, however, and the relations between the two writers are more sustained and much more complex than Barthes' last book would seem to indicate. They go back, in fact, to the early 1950s, when Barthes was cutting his teeth as an essayist and publishing some of his very first articles on cinema. Bazin and Barthes may never have met, but the two writers often published in the same periodicals, sometimes appeared on the same page of a journal, and on more than one occasion wrote about the same films. Both wrote major articles for the journal Esprit, and their names appear next to one another on the cover the of the March 1952 issue, Bazin with a crucial article on Jean Renoir, Barthes on the novelist Jean Cayrol. Both appeared in *Combat* in the late 1940s, where Bazin published a piece on his conception of the cinematic avant-garde,[4] while Barthes composed the essays that became *Writing Degree Zero*. In the 1950s, both wrote frequently for the weekly *France Observateur*, at the time a left-leaning journal allied with Pierre Mendès-France, where Bazin wrote over 300 times about film and Barthes contributed theater reviews. Reading through their essays from this period, one gets the clear sense that Barthes, while never citing Bazin, read and responded to his writings on cinema. In November 1953, Bazin wrote a long article in *Esprit* on the advent of CinemaScope. Three months later, in February 1954, Barthes wrote a short and enthusiastic essay on CinemaScope for *Les Lettres Nouvelles* that seems to directly answer Bazin. "What will happen to the sacro-sanct close-up?" Bazin had asked in his essay. "It's possible that the close-up will not survive," Barthes answered.[5] In January 1955, Bazin spoke of his "irritation" at Kazan's *On the Waterfront*, writing that the unions in the film seemed suspiciously *"peu sympathique."*[6] Two months later, Barthes published his excoriation of *On the Waterfront*, denouncing Kazan's McCarthyism and later giving this essay the ironic title "A Sympathetic Worker."[7] In February 1955, Bazin reviewed *Queen Christina* comparing, as I mentioned earlier, Greta Garbo to Venus, Bérénice, or Eve.[8] Two months later Barthes published his famous "mythology" on Greta Garbo's face.

LOST CONTINENT

While some of these coincidences may have to do with the vicissitudes of cultural journalism and the small scale controversies that occupy weekly publications, the relation between Bazin and Barthes begins early, runs deep, and remains one of the most fruitful tensions for thinking about what is at stake in the understanding of film after WWII.

A case in point can be found in their responses to a now-forgotten documentary about Indonesia, *Lost Continent* (1955), directed by the Italian team of Leonard Bonzi, Enrico Gras, and Giorgio Moser. Though this film had been awarded a Special Jury Prize at Cannes, the

January 1956 issue of *France Observateur* saw Bazin give it one of the harshest reviews he would write that year. This scathing piece accuses the directors of "intellectual dishonesty," describing, in particular, the film's voiceover as "a commentary of incredible intellectual vacuity." *Lost Continent*, he writes, is a false documentary and breaks two of the genre's fundamental rules. First, it stages events and passes them off as real—the scene, for instance, where a python menaces the explorers' mascot, a domesticated bear cub, who is saved at the last minute. Second, it denies, or attempts to hide, its own methods. *Lost Continent* is not so much a documentary as it is a "perpetual fraud" that Bazin sets out to demystify.[9] Though in a surprising twist that reveals either Bazin's critical charity or his susceptibility to the lure of exoticism, he concludes by recommending that the viewer go see it if for nothing other than to marvel at the "stupefying beauty" of its landscapes.

The following month, February 1956, Barthes published his own commentary on the film in *Les Lettres Nouvelles*. He too submits it to a rigorous demystification, though his essay seems to begin where Bazin's left off.[10] Whereas Bazin concluded his review by pointing to its "beauty," Barthes equates this beauty to what he calls "the current myth of exoticism." From this point on, Barthes relentlessly denounces the Italian feature as an exercise in Orientalism, a film whose exoticism is meant to bolster European political and economic dominance of "the East," a film whose directors turn ethnography into entertainment, who remain stubbornly impervious to historical and sociological forces and who turn the East, "which has today become the political center of the world," into a picture postcard and a playground for "child-like" ethnologists. The saturated colors of this documentary are precisely the servants of mystification, as if for Barthes color film, at least in this instance, were a form of the rhetorical excess that he denounces throughout the *Mythologies*. This is one of Barthes' only commentaries on color in film, but he is relentless in his criticism: "To color the world," writes Barthes, "is always a way of denying it" (184). In this film, Barthes writes, "the East is ready for the disappearing act [*l'opération d'escamotage*] our film has in readiness for it" (184), and this "operation" consists in transforming the "Orient" into a series of "beautiful images." Now paradoxically, it is precisely beautiful images that have the pernicious effect of hiding the continent the film claims to reveal. The images of *Lost Continent* are, in Barthes' phrasing, a conscious attempt to erase colonial history and the newly independent nations of Asia. The beautiful images of *Lost Continent*, he concludes, "cannot be innocent: it cannot be innocent to *lose* the continent which has been found again at Bandung" (186).

Part of the difference between the two articles might be attributed to a difference in genres. Bazin's article is a capsule review that leaves him little space for development. Barthes' article is only slightly longer but it is an essay, a more wide-ranging piece of writing, appearing in a journal, *Les Lettres Nouvelles*, which adopted a strong anti-colonialist position in the early 1950s. Still, the differences between these texts point to greater tensions in relations between Bazin and Barthes and in their approaches to film. Both articles take as their starting point the process of demystification, a rhetorical stance that, as we have seen, had become one of the most common intellectual operations among left-leaning film critics in Western Europe by the early 1950s. We have already speculated in chapter 1 that Barthes could have learned how to demystify movies from reading Bazin, especially "Entomology of the Pin-Up Girl," which might be added to the usual list of sources (Lefebvre, Brecht, Sartre) for the *Mythologies* project. It is equally clear that both critics were at times enthusiastic and at times weary practitioners of demystification as an intellectual process. In analyzing *Lost Continent*, each navigates that process differently: Bazin compartmentalizes his analysis within a set of aesthetic and formal rules, while Barthes looks to expand the horizon of what can be said about a film, exploring the encounter when a film's aesthetics meets anti-colonialism and an emerging anthropological discourse.[11] Barthes' reference to the Bandung conference of April 1955 makes evident his attempt to think film through the forces of decolonization and workers' rights. In this respect, it is worth noting that Bazin and Barthes both use the word "situation" (by 1956 Sartre had made the term his own), but in distinct ways. Bazin states that a documentary filmmaker must remain in his "situation as a witness" when making the film, a phrase that implies that the filmmaker must not attempt to manipulate events (such as feeding the crew's mascot to a python). Barthes, for his part, criticizes *Lost Continent* for giving a small dose of historical "situation" (Barthes uses the term in quotes) as an inoculation of sorts, in order to avoid the larger historical context of European colonialism. Bazin and Barthes were both devoted readers of Sartre, who for his part wrote infrequently and sometimes disparagingly about the movies, and both returned again and again to Sartre's 1940 work *The Imaginary* (*L'Imaginaire*), but their articles on *Lost Continent* reveal a dispute about the legacy of his writing, about what his concept of "situation" means when applied to cinema.

Most significantly, Barthes' essay suggests a turn to anthropology and to the work of Claude Lévi-Strauss as a new, scientific way to engage film—and culture more generally—in a manner distinct from Bazin. As Vincent Debaene has shown, Lévi-Strauss' anthropology in the 1950s was in part motivated by a critique of "mediatized stories of 'explorers'" whose work tended to deny history and who substituted adventure and exoticism for rigorous study and an ethical engagement with the other.[12] Debaene cites Barthes' essay on *Lost Continent* as a particularly telling example of the way highly mediatized tales of adventure tend to mask historical reality (298). While Barthes' demystification of *Lost Continent* draws less upon Lévi-Strauss' structural anthropology than upon his critique of celebrity explorers, it nonetheless remains an early but significant moment in this transition of the French intellectual field, and of its engagement with film. In Barthes' text we see the formal model of close reading that Bazin had perfected give way to another model that allies itself with a new form of anthropology, weary of exoticizing non-European civilizations and soon on its way toward full-blown structuralism. Despite what has so often been suggested, the opposition between Bazin and Barthes isn't between Bazin's ontological realism and Barthes' linguistic model. At least not in the 1950s, when, as I will show, Bazin and Barthes shared a common understanding of the image as analogon. Rather, the salient opposition between the two in the 1950s is political and institutional, with Barthes constantly on the offensive. The opposition is between Bazin as an advocate of an immanent critique, and Barthes for whom film was necessarily understood as part of a larger ethnography of everyday life and tied to ever-widening geopolitical and economic forces.

What is more, to draw on Bourdieu, we could say that behind this tension lurks a struggle for dominance within the restrained and highly competitive field of cultural commentary. This explains, at least in part, why Barthes' essay on *Lost Continent* can be read as a corrective to Bazin. Barthes is one of the first literary intellectuals in France to attempt to write seriously, even scientifically, about the movies, to make cinema a new object of academic discourse, and to introduce film studies into academic institutions such as the CNRS and the École Pratique des Hautes Etudes. This move coincided with Barthes' increased rate of publication in journals such as Gilbert Cohen-Séat's *Revue Internationale de Filmologie* and *Communications*.[13] Bazin's association with the cinephiles at *Cahiers du Cinéma*, and with cultural journalism more generally, meant that Barthes likely read him through a veil of institutional and professional rivalry in the competitive field of cultural criticism, with the result that perhaps more than any other critic of his time, Barthes contributed to what Hervé Joubert-Laurencin has called the "erasure" of Bazin from the French intellectual scene and from the significant theoretical and hermeneutic film debates of the 1960s right into the 1980s.[14] And this erasure relies, as is so often the case, upon an unacknowledged debt, a debt that plays out not just in Barthes' refusal to cite Bazin, but in Barthes' repeated revision of Bazin's writings. Bazin is Barthes' lost continent.

FROM ONTOLOGY TO RHETORIC AND BACK

A few years after their essays on the documentary, we find a second point of contact. When Barthes takes his "scientific turn" in the early 1960s, precisely at the moment when he wants to leave cultural journalism behind so as to further dismantle theories of realism and referentiality, his writings on the photographic image reveal a strong debt to Bazin. Barthes' 1964 article "Rhetoric of the Image," a landmark of his semiotic analysis, once again enters into a complex but productive relation with the author of "The Ontology of the Photographic Image." First published in *Communications*, a CNRS journal devoted to the transdisciplinary study of mass media, "Rhetoric of the Image" is Barthes' attempt to systematize how we read photography, and, specifically in this essay, how we might understand an advertisement for Panzani pasta.[15] Barthes famously identifies three levels of interpretation, three "messages," delivered by the advertisement. First, we have the "linguistic" message, which tells us what we are looking at and which, Barthes says, limits the possible (and dangerous) proliferation of meaning dormant in all photographs. Second, there is the "connoted message," which brings a supplement of meaning to the image: in the advertisement for Panzani, for instance, the composition of pasta, tomatoes, and a green pepper (the red, white, and green of the Italian flag) connote Italy, or what Barthes calls "Italianicity." Finally, there is the "denoted" message, the object photographed—a shopping bag, a packet of pasta, a tomato, an onion.

Shortly after having made this distinction between three levels of meaning, Barthes distinguishes photography from drawing. If the latter practice is invariably associated with style and the artist's intentions, photography is fundamentally seen as a "recording." It is at this point that Barthes comes very close to citing Bazin:

> In the photograph—at least at the level of the literal message—the relationship of signifieds to signifiers is not one of "transformation" but of "recording," and the absence of a code clearly reinforces the myth of photographic "naturalness": the scene *is there*, captured mechanically, not humanly (the mechanical is here a guarantee of objectivity). Man's intervention in the photograph (framing, distance, lighting, focus, speed) all effectively belong to the plane of connotation; it is as though in the beginning (even if utopian) there were a brute photograph (frontal and clear) on which man would then lay out, with the aid of various techniques, the signs drawn from a cultural code. Only the opposition of the cultural code and the natural non-code can, it seems, account for the specific character of the photograph and allow the assessment of the anthropological revolution it represents in man's history. The type of consciousness the photograph involves is indeed truly unprecedented, since it establishes not a consciousness of the *being-there* of the thing (which any copy could provoke) but an awareness of its *having-been-there* . . . It is thus at the level of this denoted message or message without code that the *real unreality* of the photograph can be fully understood . . . its reality that of the *having-been-there*, for in every photograph there is the always

stupefying evidence of *this is how it was*, giving us, by precious miracle, a reality from which we are sheltered.[16]

There is a puzzling shift in this passage. At the beginning Barthes uses the phrase "myth of photographic 'naturalness,'" with "naturalness" in scare quotes, but by the end of the passage it is quite clear that for Barthes this "myth" is no myth at all but the very ontology of photography, with the scare quotes around "naturalness" having been replaced by the assertive italics of *having-been-there*. Barthes ends with this conclusion: at its core, a photograph provides "stupefying evidence" of a world that once existed, of "a reality from which we are sheltered," a claim that will return many years later as the central hypothesis of *Camera Lucida*. Alongside the rhetoric of the image, its linguistic message and the meaning constructed by advertisers, photography records a brute reality that escapes or at least precedes imposed meanings. Photography is, for Barthes, a mixed medium, both rhetorical in the sense that it is put to specific uses by market forces, and fundamentally, inescapably, realistic. Barthes' 1964 essay is thus not just an argument for a rhetorical approach to the image, as is commonly claimed. It is an attempt to come to terms with what Barthes calls, in a language that sounds surprisingly Bazinian and unscientific, the "precious miracle" of photography.

Did Barthes have Bazin in mind when he wrote this piece? The very title, "Rhetoric of the Image," echoes and revises Bazin's famous 1945 "Ontology of the Photographic Image."[17] Furthermore, when Barthes writes about a photograph that "the scene *is there*, captured mechanically, not humanly (the mechanical is here a guarantee of objectivity)," he reprises the very terms Bazin used in "The Ontology of the Photographic Image" when he spoke of the "essentially objective character of photography," and of the camera lens.[18] And when Barthes speaks of the "stupefying evidence" brought forth by the photographic image, it is hard to hear this as anything other than an echo of what Bazin had called the "quality of credibility" of the photograph that forces us to "accept as real the existence of the object reproduced." A final link between the two essays occurs when Barthes uses the phrase "man's intervention in the photograph," which directly echoes Bazin's famous phrase "For the first time an image of the world is formed automatically, without the creative intervention of man." Both writers use the French term "*intervention*," with the one difference that Barthes turns this phrase around. For Bazin, photography's exceptionalism was located in the fact that the image happened *without* the creative intervention of man, whereas Barthes uses "man's intervention" to identify everything—framing, focal distance, lighting, and so on—that the photographer brings to an image and that belongs to the realm of connotation. Still, this does not detract from Barthes' conclusion that the photographic image is a brute recording of reality.

One might push this analogy between the two essays even further. When he rewrote his article for inclusion in the 1958 volume *Qu'est ce que le cinéma?*, Bazin added this final phrase: "On the other hand, of course, cinema is also a language." One might suggest that Barthes' project of accounting for "the opposition of the cultural code and the natural non-code" rests precisely on Bazin's identification of the tension in the photographic image as both a brute recording of the world and a language. Barthes' "Rhetoric of the Image" subscribes, at least in part, to claims made in Bazin's "The Ontology of the Photographic Image," to the point of using much of the same language, for it is clear that Barthes doesn't seek to deny photography's realism but rather to add to it. At the very moment when Barthes is developing the approach that in the 1970s, for a short time at least, would allow critics at *Cahiers du Cinéma* and *Screen* to produce an elaborate critique of Bazin's ontological realism, we find Barthes making claims about the "analogical" nature of the photographic image. The image may be a code, Barthes tells us, and it may produce readings of itself as a code, but it is also, fundamentally, a recording of "brute reality." And the proximity of Barthes' language to Bazin's own essay on "The Ontology of the Photographic Image" seems to confirm that if Barthes didn't have that essay at hand when he was writing, he certainly had it in his mind.

Another sign of this proximity can be found in the 1963 *Cahiers du Cinéma* interview. The photograph accompanying the interview shows a young Barthes, smoking, wearing a tie, his desk neatly arranged. In the background, on the shelf behind Barthes, we see a copy of Claude Lévi-Strauss' *The Savage Mind*, clearly identified by a *viola tricolor* on its cover.[19] In due fashion, Barthes insists upon the possibilities of applying structural analysis to cinema, but his conclusion is not what we might think. As we saw in the previous chapter, Barthes admits he has difficulty analyzing cinema because it is, to use his expression, an "analogical expression of reality."[20] If cinema has a future as an art, he continues, this future lies precisely in its ability to exploit this first-level quality and to suspend meaning. "Suspended meaning" argues for aesthetic sensation as opposed to the production of meaning, and this may be at the heart of Barthes' understanding of literature, but he also uses this phrase to define a fundamental component of the cinematic experience.[21] Already in his 1959 critique of Claude Chabrol's *Le Beau Serge*, Barthes had claimed he would be happy watching an endless stream of such images, which he described as the film's "light touch" [*frôlage*] with "sensuous" existence.[22] Here again, Barthes' argument for the photographic and cinematographic image as a recording of "brute reality" seems to consciously escape the scientism he is so intent upon promoting in the mid-1960s. In an extremely smart essay on Bazin's presence in Barthes' *Camera Lucida*, Adam Lowenstein traces how Bazin's writings helped Barthes negotiate the relation between photography and cinema. He convincingly traces a common "investment in surrealism" in both authors, in particular in their mutual understanding of the photograph as combining "rational fact with irrational belief."[23] Lowenstein shows how both critics turn to a vocabulary of "magic" and "emanation" to describe the photographic image. One might also point to a common link to the *photogénie* movement that both knew well, and which Barthes describes precisely as the understanding of cinema as the modern phenomenon that can reveal "the intensity of the real."[24] The vocabulary of "miracle" and "grace" that Barthes uses to describe the aesthetic experience of the cinema lays the groundwork for the more explicit rejection of scientific and cultural approaches to photography in *Camera Lucida*, and certainly belies the idea that his work is irremediably distinct from Bazin's realism.

Comparing these critics born less than three years apart, I want to insist upon two similarities. The first is what I would call their shared idiosyncratic classicism. Both Barthes and Bazin voice a suspicion of rhetorical excess and of what they designate as fraudulent and mystifying images. Second, and more important, their calls for rhetorical restraint were a way to clear the ground for aesthetic sensations related to the ordinary world. What counts for both is cinema's ability to intensify the real and evoke through the image an emotion. Bazin calls this emotion "attention" and "love."[25] Barthes calls it "pleasure." In each case the primary effect of cinema, and indeed the fundamental cinematic experience, can be located in the intensity generated by images of the commonplace. Both critics associate this with wonder. I would add that, as we have seen, both are in step with intellectual currents (Surrealism, *photogénie*) that understand sensation as something associated with the most common, the most trivial. In sharing this understanding, both advocate a kind of democratization of aesthetic sensibility.

CAMERA LUCIDA

By the time Barthes finally directly quotes André Bazin in *Camera Lucida* he had already engaged in a sustained, if unacknowledged, reflection on Bazin's work, including both a hostile move away from Bazin's humanism and a shared attempt to account for the emotional shock, the aesthetic intensity, generated by a cinematic image unshackled from plot, character, and editing. True, *Camera Lucida*, one of the great modern elegies, is often taken as proof of Barthes fascination with the still image and what he himself calls his "resistance" to cinema: "I decided I liked Photography *in opposition* to the Cinema, from which I nonetheless failed to separate it" (3). However, we need to take Barthes seriously when he speaks of the inability to separate photography from cinema, in part because of what Barthes says within the covers of this book, in part also because, as Barthes was correcting the proofs of *Camera Lucida* in January 1980, he wrote one of his last and most moving essays, a letter to Michelangelo Antonioni, a director whose films Barthes had watched his whole life and whose work he now sees as the embodiment of melancholic reflection and political resistance.[26] And once again, at this crucial moment in his meditation on the image, Barthes turns to Bazin.

    Camera Lucida is dedicated to Sartre's *The Imaginary*, and while Barthes has moved away from the early Sartre's phenomenology of the image, his conclusion that the image brings irrefutable proof that a person or object once existed—the famous *that has been*—might very well be Barthes' translation of what Sartre identified as the image's *given-absent*.[27]

It is, of course, the Bazin of "The Ontology of the Photographic Image" who seems most present in this essay. For when Barthes claims that a "photograph . . . is never distinguished from its referent" (5), he reveals, as he himself admits, his "'ontological' desire" (3), that is, a desire to get to the ontology of photography. Later, Barthes claims that photography "certifies" (78) that the object visible in the image once existed, referring to the Shroud of Turin as a kind of proof that photography was not made "by the hand of man" (82). Finally, Barthes' desire to link photography to a reflection on love and death, as well as his use of the terms "magic" and "hallucination" to qualify the image, are references which point directly to the first edition of *Qu'est-ce que le cinéma?* where a photograph of the Shroud of Turin is in fact reproduced.

When Barthes actually quotes Bazin, however, it has nothing to do with the "ontological realism" of the image. About half way through his book, Barthes sets out to describe the effects of the *punctum*, that element of the photographic image that evokes an overwhelming emotional intensity in the viewer, and distinguishes viewing a photograph from watching a moving picture. Whereas the moving picture launches us into the incessant voracity of images, the photograph allows for what Barthes calls *pensivité*, thoughtfulness, the ability to add one's thought to the image. Bazin appears at a moment that qualifies this idea, as Barthes begins to reflect on the possibility of thinking not just while contemplating photographs but while watching movies. Here is the passage where Barthes cites Bazin:

> Yet the cinema has a power which at first glance the Photograph does not have: the screen (as Bazin has remarked) is not a frame but a hideout [*cache*]; the man or woman who emerges from it continues living: a "blind field" constantly doubles our partial vision . . . Yet once there is a *punctum*, a blind field is created (is divined). (55–57)

Barthes is referring here to a passage from Bazin's 1951 article "Théâtre et cinéma" where Bazin had written, "The screen is not a frame like the frame of a painting, but a *mask* [*cache*] that reveals only part of an event. When a character walks out of the camera's field of vision, we know that he has left the visual field, but he continues to exist in an identical state somewhere else in a hidden part of the setting."[28] Though he gets the passage partially right, he misquotes Bazin, who never used the words "blind field" [*champ aveugle*] in his essay, nor, to my knowledge, anywhere else. Barthes' source for this term "champ aveugle" may well have been Pascal Bonitzer, a critic (and later a filmmaker) who had been a student in Barthes' seminars and who had begun writing essays on the "blind field" in the 1970s precisely as a way of breaking out of the discourse that all cinema is pure ideology.[29] More important is the fact that by speaking of a photograph's "blind field" Barthes is coming very close to turning the photograph into a film frame. As Adam Lowenstein contends, it is with the blind field that "the *punctum* animates the photograph with cinematic power."[30] If elsewhere Barthes focused on individual frames, photograms from the films where they appear, here he is suggesting that the imagination adds off-screen action to the still. Thus, at the very moment he seems to be claiming that cinema spectatorship is necessarily unthinking, he also arrives at the opposite conclusion: in giving a "cinematic" quality to the still photograph, he continues to reflect upon the imaginary potential of the cinematographic image.

A final, perhaps more evident, moment of contact occurs in Barthes' short encomium to Antonioni, where he insists on three aspects of the Italian filmmaker's art. One of his three theses is that Antonioni is aware of art's fragility. As an artist, and not simply a producer of culture, he is conscious that art remains vulnerable precisely because it does not necessarily produce meanings sanctioned by society. The State can ban it at any time (as the Chinese authorities had censored Antonioni's film on China), and liberal capitalist society can censor it in a more passive way, simply by ignoring it: "The artist is threatened . . . by a collective feeling, ever latent, that society can do perfectly well without art."[31]

Art is a luxury and, according to Barthes, even a society in the stages of late capitalism, such as that of contemporary Europe, does not know what to do with this excess of meaning. We might pause here at this paradox: the late Barthes is construing cinema—albeit art house cinema—as the aesthetic form that can resist an ever more powerful capitalism, a capitalism that by 1980 in any case has overcome the challenges of May 1968. But he also asserts that if Antonioni's films provide a form of resistance to late capitalism, it is because they never attempt to impose a truth on the spectator. Antonioni's film embodies the suspension of meaning for which Barthes had advocated at least since his 1963 interview in *Cahiers du Cinéma*. What is more, and this is the third thesis, Barthes locates this suspension of meaning in a very precise cinematographic technique, what Barthes calls "the insistence of the gaze" [*l'insistance du regard*]. In an argument that brings to mind the penultimate, seven-minute shot of *The Passenger*, where the tracking camera hovers in and around the hotel where the film's protagonist lies dead, Barthes maintains that Antonioni's films are constructed around a sustained gaze on the world which undoes fixed meaning precisely because the shot or sequence lasts too long. This "insistence of the gaze" according to Barthes "leaves the path of meaning open." That is, according to Barthes, Antonioni's films do not impose a meaning, they allow for the production of thought, of hypotheses, of the simultaneous working of perception and imagination, of what Barthes calls *pensivité*.

Might we not, in this final instance, think one more time of Bazin? What Barthes calls "the insistence of the gaze" and "the ambivalence of meaning" seem close to what Bazin identified as the "ambiguity" of the image. An article such as "The Evolution of the Language of Cinema" was precisely elaborated around this notion that extended depth of field and long takes demand an "active mental attitude" on the part of the spectator and what Bazin calls "an ambiguity in the structure of the image." He concludes, "the uncertainty in which we find ourselves as to the spiritual key or the interpretation we should put on the film is built into the very design of the image."[32]

At stake for both Bazin and Barthes is an attempt to define cinema as an aesthetic form that generates thinking, and both authors were writing against a long and particularly engrained literary tradition in France that equated cinema with passivity and thoughtlessness. For both Barthes and Bazin, cinema must be depicted as an instrument of thought as well as an aesthetic form of intense emotional power. Barthes, of course, takes longer to get to this point, and to overcome his skepticism, than Bazin. But he does get there. And at the end of a long and tortured relation with the movies, his letter to Antonioni seems to find him looking toward his younger colleague once again, turning to ideas Bazin developed to think through his reaction to film.

Chapter 4

Another Revolution

The first filmmaker for whom Barthes expressed a sustained enthusiasm, the first director whose films he did not feel the need to demystify,
the first figure in film history with whom Barthes, at least for a few years,
was in sympathetic dialogue, was the Russian director Sergei Eisenstein.
Two articles from the early 1970s, "The Third Meaning" and "Diderot,
Brecht, Eisenstein," confirm this enthusiasm, and attest to Barthes'
attempt, in the years after May 1968, to define a new relation to film,
one in which demystification, an intellectual operation associated with
Mythologies but largely discredited after 1970, played no part and no longer served even as a pretext for writing about film. Both these essays are
dedicated to friends—critic and cinephile Noureddine Saïl for the first
and the director André Téchiné for the second.[1] Dedications of essays
were a rare occurrence in Barthes' writing, and they give Barthes' essays
on Eisenstein a slightly different tenor, one distinct from the scientific
rationality of semiological analysis, in that they gesture to friendship,
affect, and "an emotion which simply *designates* what one loves."[2]

Between *Mythologies* and the articles on Eisenstein, there is a shift
precipitated by May 1968 and a reconfiguration of what politics might
portend. In the 1950s Barthes primarily understood film as the product
of Hollywood, itself the spearhead of U.S.-dominated consumer capitalism that was transforming the French postwar landscape. In his articles
on Eisenstein, he sees the medium opening up the possibility of reconfiguring new ways of being and seeing, ways that he calls the "politics" of
tomorrow (62–63). After 1968 he began to develop a tendency that had
been present in his writings all along but given a minor role: an effort to
think about film as a configuration of the sensible, an art form that could

lead the viewer to think through the political and social consequences of minute aesthetic events, and about the revolutionary potential of affect, of sensation, of love. This was not a post-'68 retreat from politics, as some have said, it was an attempt to articulate a micropolitics in which film would play a substantial role, precisely the role of opening up new possibilities of desire and designating what one loves differently. The shift from demystifying Elia Kazan to reconfiguring Eisenstein was not accidental. Nor, as it turns out, was it a way of simply declaring Barthes' clear sympathy with the revolutionary politics of the post-'68 leftists who were now running *Cahiers du Cinéma*. On the contrary, the turn to Eisenstein was a way for Barthes to stage another, more subtle revolution that would take place inside the reels of revolutionary cinema.

This other revolution raises two sets of questions. First: why is Barthes so interested in Eisenstein at this historical juncture? Is it because Eisenstein is a gay filmmaker in a profession that in the early 1970s is still aggressively heteronormative? Is it because Barthes is also responding to a trend—the rediscovery and translation of Eisenstein's work by the left in France?[3] Eisenstein is of the left, of course, but his films had posed problems for the French Communist Party during the late 1940s and early 1950s. Barthes' writings on Eisenstein undo the stakes of Cold War polemics and polarization; they use the director to counter U.S. capitalist cinema (if one can still use such an expression) as well as Soviet-style Marxism in France.[4]

Second: what larger consequences for Barthes' evolution are lodged in his writing about Eisenstein? A change in politics, from grand narratives to "micropolitics"? The promotion and discovery of new ways of feeling? And how might this change our understanding of Eisenstein's career? These are the questions this chapter will address.

THE FETISHIST

The focus of "The Third Meaning" is not film at all, as it turns out, but a series of still shots—"photograms" in the parlance of the times—from Eisenstein's films *Battleship Potemkin* and *Ivan the Terrible*, in particular. Still images had always been part of the culture of *Cahiers du Cinéma*, which houses an extensive collection of stills in its offices, and as Adam

Lowenstein has said, Barthes' essay can be understood as his "meditation on reading film journals like *Cahiers du Cinéma* after seeing the films discussed within their pages."[5]

Barthes begins with a still from *Ivan the Terrible* showing courtiers pouring gold over the young emperor's head. This image, Barthes tells us, has three possible, and simultaneous, meanings. The first meaning has to do with the information we can gather from the image—who is doing what to whom in the scene? The second meaning is located in symbolic interpretations contained within the scene about imperial Russia and, by extension, about the Russian Revolution, the Soviet Union, and the film industry that was in place when Eisenstein made his film. The third meaning, the "obtuse" meaning, however, is for Barthes the most important one, though it appears incidental. For what strikes Barthes in this image is not so much its place in the narrative, the information it transmits, or the interpretations it produces. What strikes Barthes is affect, the emotion produced by the insignificant detail, the trivial object, the commonplace element that somehow seems slightly out of place.

Ivan the Terrible, Part I (Sergei Eisenstein, 1945)

Here is what Barthes sees looking at the stills of Eisenstein's films: the "compactness of the courtiers' make-up, thick and insistent for the one, smooth and distinguished for the other; the former's 'stupid' nose, the latter's finely traced eyebrows, his lank blondness, his faded, pale complexion, the affected flatness of his hairstyle suggestive of a wig" (53). Or later, in commenting on stills from the funeral scene in *Battleship Potemkin*, Barthes insists upon the "obtuse meaning" of a mourning woman's "coif, the headscarf holding in the hair . . . , the closed eyes and the convex mouth" (57). Or he sees obtuse meaning in "Ivan's beard" (58), the "bun" of a woman mourner at Vakulintchuk's funeral, or the "disguised, blond silliness of the young quiver-bearer" in a still from Mikhail Romm's 1965 film *Ordinary Fascism* (60).

It's hard to read "The Third Meaning" without thinking of *Mythologies*. What Barthes sees in these images—the courtiers' pancake make-up, Ivan the Terrible's beard—seems to be a direct echo of his comments on Greta Garbo's eyebrows and the Roman hairline in *Julius Caesar*. This is the writing of a fetishist, for whom the starting point of a commentary on cinema is always the trivial detail, the mundane feature which carries "a de-naturing or at least a distancing effect" (61). And yet, these similarities aside, "The Third Meaning" also rewrites *Mythologies* by turning it inside out. For whereas the earlier essays focus on American films, "The Third Meaning" foregrounds a Soviet director. Whereas in the 1950s Barthes situated rhetorical excess on the side of "ideological abuse" and the trickery of Hollywood, in 1970 he identifies obtuse meaning as a supplement, an "accent," and, most importantly, a fold—*un pli* (62). And whereas *Mythologies* places the detail in the service of demystification, "The Third Meaning" invests it with affect: the courtiers' make-up, the old woman's *chignon*, all reveal "something *touching* . . . or *sensitive* [sensible]," words Barthes labels "antiquated" [*désuets*], out of date, untimely "with little that is revolutionary or political about them" (59). Barthes' affect is not the revolutionary pathos that usually accompanies such scenes, it is what Victor Burgin astutely identified as "a loss of reality, a porosity to the strangeness of the world, a hallucinatory vivacity of sensations" associated with meditation, melancholy, and *pensivité*.[6]

It is here that Barthes makes claims—so widely imitated for a few years and then so widely disdained—about how the obtuse meaning, the detail, "outplays meaning—subverts not the content but the whole practice of meaning" (62). The obtuse meaning proposes "a new—rare— practice affirmed against the majority practice." It is, Barthes concludes, a "luxury," and his essay proposes to account for this luxury, this sensation beyond meaning. This, Barthes tells us, is the politics of art, and he quotes Eisenstein: "Art begins the moment the creaking of a boot on the sound-track occurs against a different visual shot and thus gives rise to correspond-ing associations" (61–62). It is a question of tension internal to the signifier itself, removed from, or in any case "indifferent" to, story and to character.

Barthes' other essay on Eisenstein uses similar concepts to open larger aesthetic questions. "Diderot, Brecht, Eisenstein," first published in a spe-cial issue of *Revue d'esthétique* devoted to film and theory, is the only essay written by Barthes that, to my knowledge, ties together an analysis of the-ater and cinema. It is also an essay in which Barthes continues his explo-ration of a new aesthetic, now baptized "*découpage*."[7] Art, Barthes claims, happens when the spectator is able to cut out a segment of the visible, to iso-late and fetishize—this is Barthes' term—an object, a gesture, or a scene. Now, this revival of the fragment, and of découpage as the basis of art, is not new in itself. Modernist aesthetics, at least since Marcel Duchamp, have defined the gesture of the artist as the isolation, recontextualization, and defamiliarization of objects, and these processes are at the very heart of Barthes' writing. By emphasizing *découpage* as the most significant gesture of art, and indeed as the fundamental basis of representation, Barthes is also echoing (and expressing solidarity with) the rediscovery of montage and cut outs in the avant-gardes of the 1960s and 1970s.

In "Diderot, Brecht, Eisenstein," however, Barthes draws a slightly different genealogy, heading not through twentieth-century modern-ism but back to Diderot, whose theater, Barthes tells us, was based on the principle of the isolated scene, the "tableau," "a pure cut out seg-ment with clearly defined edges" (70). It is within such "tableaux" that Diderot located the production of meaning. Associating Diderot and Brecht is surprising, to say the least, but as Philippe Roger notes, it makes sense given "their broader concern with redefining theatre in civic terms" and their common desire to establish a truly popular theater.[8] Diderot's tableaux are based on a kind of internal montage in which objects and gestures respond to each other within the frame of the scene and do not need to go outside of it to find or produce meaning. "The epic scene in Brecht," Barthes writes, "the shot in Eisenstein are so many tableaux" (70–71), and as proof, he adds, "isn't it said that in some *cinémathèque* or other a piece of film is missing from a copy of *Battleship Potemkin*—the scene with the baby's pram, of course—it having been cut off and stolen lovingly like a lock of hair, a glove or an item of women's underwear?" (72). In Eisenstein, *"no image is boring"* (72). The interest of these films, however, is not to be found in the dialectical montage that Eisenstein promoted, but in what Barthes calls the "jubilation" communicated by the images themselves: "The film is a contiguity of episodes, each one absolutely meaningful, aesthetically perfect, and the result is a cinema by vocation anthological, itself holding out to the fetishist, with dotted lines, the piece for him to cut out and take away to enjoy . . . it is a question not of a dialectic . . . but of a continuous jubilation made up of a summation of perfect instants" (73).

Brecht and Eisenstein build their art around what Lessing, in his commentary on *Laocoön*, called the "pregnant moment." For Eisenstein, pregnant moments are those in which the gesture of an actor embodies an "idea," an abstract entity far from the naturalism or the realism of cinema. This isn't quite the same thing as Brechtian distanciation, Barthes tells us, but it can have the same effect on the spectator. Barthes ties the "pregnant moment" to the *social gest*, "a set of gestures . . . in which a whole social situation can be read." In *The General Line* (Eisenstein, 1929) for instance, they consist of "fists clenching, hands gripping tools, peasants reporting at the bureaucrat's reception-desk" (75): "The pregnant moment is just this presence of all the absences (memories, lessons, promises) to whose rhythm History becomes both intelligible and desirable" (73).

From Diderot's tableaux to Lessing's pregnant moment, Barthes constructs his Eisenstein articles as a fetishist, by emphasizing the importance of the detail. In what is still one of the most convincing books on Roland Barthes, Réda Bensmaïa draws a clear line from Barthes' enthusiasm for details in Eisenstein to Barthes' own practice of writing.[9] What Barthes sees in Eisenstein is a series of shots cut off from what Bensmaïa calls the "compositional chain." Though *découpage* is a term employed in art history and especially in cinema, it is also a word at the heart of Barthes' textual practice, since the detail, even more than the fragment or the essay, is a fundamentally discontinuous and "instantaneous" form. The detail escapes all obvious meanings or concrete referents; it is isolated from the narrative, from comprehension, from assembly. Bensmaïa folds his reading of Barthes and Eisenstein into an aesthetics of the essay, and of Barthes' essayistic writing in particular. He identifies the essay as a kind of storage room or holding cell of details, and "the 'detail' profoundly modifies the classical status of reading and its object." The detail "can . . . be considered a 'quotation': that is, an element that both 'parodies' and 'disseminates.'" It is nothing other than a "discontinuous and eccentric trait within the fragment, a parodic and disseminated trait within the Essay." In suggesting that Eisenstein is a fetishist, Barthes does not simply find in him a kindred artist. He delineates a certain political stance, related to the return to Eisenstein that took place in the early 1970s, but adding a quite distinct aesthetic dimension to that return.

EISENSTEIN, 1970

Why is Barthes so interested in promoting the isolated image in Eisenstein's films? How can Barthes claim that the "luxury" that he has identified in the detail and its "obtuse meaning" "does not *yet* belong to today's politics but nevertheless *already* belongs to tomorrow's" (62–63)? Over the course of the 1960s, *Cahiers du Cinéma* radically broke with their established critical line, turning away from their cinephilic, pro-Hollywood past to promote the European and American underground, opening their pages to Third World cinema and rediscovering questions about revolutionary aesthetics posed by the Soviet avant-garde around the Revolution of 1917—questions that, as Sylvia Harvey notes, "had been simmering within Western Marxism for sixty years."[10] According to film historian Antoine de Baecque, Eisenstein became one of the review's primary ideological reference points.[11]

And so, in writing about Eisenstein in 1970 and 1973, Barthes is very much of his moment. Before 1970 there is no extended engagement with Eisenstein in Barthes' writing.[12] When he does propose "The Third Meaning" to *Cahiers du Cinéma*, it fits into that journal's promotion of the Soviet director.[13] Barthes' text points to the import of the revolutionary narratives in Eisenstein's films, which it claims are "necessary in order *to be understood* in a society which, unable to resolve the contradictions of history without a long political transaction, draws support (provisionally?) from mythical narrative solutions" (63–64). In other words, the stories in Eisenstein's films—the story of the mutiny in *Battleship Potemkin,* for example—are necessary until society—France? the Soviet Union?—resolves the contradictions of history.

At the same time, however, Barthes seems to be writing, if not against, then at least in slight discord with the revolutionary aspirations of *Cahiers du Cinéma.* Not only does he write about still images of the filmmaker who had theorized cinema's kinetic force and the infectious movement of actors, but even as he expresses his sympathy for Eisenstein's cinema and its "obvious meaning," he displaces the political force of Eisenstein's films. Thus "The Third Meaning" becomes a kind of back and forth between narratives of revolution and the micropolitics of sensation. About the funeral scene in *Battleship Potemkin,* for instance, Barthes writes that "the obvious meaning [of the scene] must remain revolutionary" (58), and yet what he retains from the photogram is the emotion of seeing the old woman's *chignon.*

In "Diderot, Brecht, Eisenstein," he explicitly opposes the "patience" necessary for narratives to play out (or, in cinema, for a sequence of shots to unfold) to the immediately revolutionary potential of certain gestures (72). Perhaps nowhere more than in his writings on film do we see the "other" revolution that Barthes promotes and hopes to precipitate. This revolution consciously overrides the Marxist one in which society and individuals need to submit with "patience" to the operation of the dialectic. After all, didn't the French Communist Party preach "patience" to its members after May 1968?[14] Patience, Barthes seems to realize, is the end of revolution, and Barthes here enlists Eisenstein in an attempt to replace the patience of the dialectic with the "jubilation" of the shot, of a series of "perfect instants," similar to Lessing's "pregnant moments" which figure a revolution of pleasure that could begin now (73). Drawn to the immediate, his analysis revolves around the immanent power of the *gest:* "It matters little, after all, that Eisenstein took his 'subjects' from the past history of Russia and the Revolution and not—'as he should have done' (so say the censors today)—from the present of the construction of socialism; . . . what alone counts is the gest, the critical demonstration of the gesture, its inscription—no matter its period—in a text the social machination of which is clearly visible: the subject neither adds nor subtracts anything" (76).

That Barthes in 1970 should choose to locate this "loss of reality" in *Ivan the Terrible* and *Battleship Potemkin* shows both his sympathy for Eisenstein and his relative distance from the writers at *Cahiers du Cinéma*, for whom Eisenstein's films are tied to the tenacious promise of social transformation. When he writes about the emblematic figure of revolutionary cinema, Barthes is very much of his time and in the ranks of a revolutionary film journal. What he writes about the photograms, however, is strangely out of time, removed from the historical imperatives of film criticism, of avant-garde cinema, and of revolutionary vitality.

Ultimately, no matter how far his essays about Eisenstein seem from the choice of films in *Mythologies*, the two moments do have something in common: each sends us back to an ideological and aesthetic split that structured Cold War cinematic reception in France. For Barthes, ideology, or *doxa*, not only forces us to produce, to speak or write in a certain way; it forces us to take sides, and compels us to choose a camp. In writing about Hollywood in the 1950s and Eisenstein in 1970, Barthes is reproducing and putting into question a cultural split that structured European film reception: America and its cultural apparatus, the Hollywood film, on the one hand, versus the leading filmmaker and theorist of revolutionary cinema on the other. If, in some of Barthes' other writings, power and ideology remain diffuse notions, his essays on film tie power to specific political and economic regimes, and so take on tactical specificity that is absent from many of his other texts. *On the Waterfront, Julius Caesar*, and *Battleship Potemkin* were not only films produced in close proximity to state power, they also became allegories of Cold War conflicts that solicited the audience's adherence as subjects of competing empires. In this sense, Barthes' "Third Meaning" is also a "Third Way," a baroque fold that obviates the oppositions and alternatives of structuralist poetics and Cold War rivalries. This baroque fold and its historical context may help us understand the rather puzzling formula encountered above, where "this luxury [of the obtuse meaning] does not *yet* belong to today's politics but nevertheless already to tomorrow's" (62).

Barthes is indeed outlining "another" politics. This is not a politics in which the subject is inscribed in history—the importance of *Battleship Potemkin* does not reside in its representation of the 1905 naval mutiny against the Tsar's officers. Nor, for Barthes, does the importance of Eisenstein's films reside in the dialectic, even if for Eisenstein in the 1920s dialectical montage may have been cinema's most salient political tool. No, the importance of Eisenstein's films resides in the series of gestures to which they give life.

Barthes' micropolitics invest his gaze, his attention, his time, and his work in fractions and particles. This art of the miniature argues that the revolutionary potential of a film can be found neither in the story it tells nor in its style. For Barthes, what films can transmit to viewers are new conceptions of being a body, of linking one gesture to another, of moving in space, of being together. This is what Barthes means by "solidarity" (73) and "the co-ordination of gestures" (76). He certainly doesn't reject the revolutionary potential of Eisenstein's films. To suggest that he is replacing politics with sterile aesthetics would not just be a misinterpretation, it would be an underestimation. On the contrary, his reflection on Eisenstein in "Diderot, Brecht, Eisenstein" attempts to think how film participates in social solidarity and the *social gestus*. In both cases, participation starts by exhibiting the power of the smallest possible movements.

CODA: FROM LEFTOCRACY TO AFFECT AND INTIMACY

In October 1980, Wole Soyinka delivered his inaugural lecture at the University of Ife, (now the Obafemi Awolowo University), in Western Nigeria. Soyinka, a professor of comparative literature there, had been working for many years to create a popular theater and develop Nigerian proletarian culture. Just three years before, he had written *Opera Wonyosi*, a version of Brecht's *The Threepenny Opera*. Soyinka was a member of a kind of Brechtian international, and it was perhaps because of his sustained reading of Brecht that, in his 1980 lecture, Soyinka turned to another Brechtian, Roland Barthes. In his lecture titled "The Critic and Society: Barthes, Leftocracy and Other Mythologies," Soyinka engages with Barthes' *Mythologies* and the volume published in English in 1977, *Image, Music, Text*.[15]

Soyinka tells of browsing Dillon's bookshop in London and stumbling upon some new volume by Barthes—whom Soyinka's typesetter mistakenly identifies as "Ronald" Barthes throughout. Barthes' essays, Soyinka writes, were in fact "a perfect paradigm for the social reality of the radical shift in critical language in my own African community" (2) and a must-read for any leftist "if ever a genuine proletarian revolution is to overtake our universities" (11). What does this mean?

Soyinka's essay begins in earnest when he quotes from a newspaper report on violence at the University of Ibadan. He undertakes to demystify the article, showing how the journalists focus on student violence while obscuring state-sponsored violence—police slaughter of students, corruption, prohibition of unions, seizure of passports (8). They even call in an expert to "explain" the violence to the readers, a further act of intellectual mystification. Soyinka then turns to Barthes, whom he calls "a rare breed of academic worker who has tried to explore, in very concrete terms, the social situation of the critic/teacher in the practice of his profession" (10). Soyinka clearly sees the tension within Barthes' work—a bourgeois intellectual who demystifies a spectacle only to remystify it, or at least recast it, in another bourgeois language—in Barthes' case, the language of semiotic analysis. This, according to Soyinka, is the very position of the African intellectual, though he further contends that Barthes seems to see his position with more lucidity than other critics and Leftists.

Much of the second section of Soyinka's essay is aimed at critics of Soyinka's own work. Specifically, he rejects those who accuse his theater of "ambiguity," of producing art rather than committed writing, and who do not, at the same time, reflect upon their own social situation as critics and writers. In essence, Soyinka, who sees the contradictions in Barthes' position, nonetheless uses Barthes as a response to "Leftocratic" critics who would accuse him—Soyinka—of not being political enough, of not providing "social answers" (20). These "ultrarevolutionary" critics fail to see that art's role is not to lead to the direct overthrow of political aberrations. Instead, he argues that its task is more humble, more discreet: it must try to "contain and control Power" (34) through the process of naming, transforming, redistributing and breaking apart all attempts at essentializing. At this point, Soyinka provides a powerful reading of Brecht, and we can see the appeal that Barthes might have had for him in 1980.

Soyinka ends his essay—and this is where I want to end.as well—with a consideration of Barthes' "Diderot, Brecht, Eisenstein." Soyinka's question is this: how can one place Brecht in tandem with Eisenstein's "expressionist techniques" (40), how can the poet of defamiliarization and strangeness be made to work with the cineaste of revolutionary pathos? What Soyinka finds in Barthes is, if not a contradiction, then at least two different rules of art—one for Brecht, one for Eisenstein. Brecht's tableaux are there for the viewer to critique, while Eisenstein's tableaux are there to inspire the viewer's pathos. Soyinka has quite rightly identified two forms that define popular art in the twentieth century, both with revolutionary potential. One, which was Brecht's, involves distance and the intelligence. The other, Eisenstein's, is expressionistic and pathetic. One is critical, demystifying. The other emotional, full of affect, loving, open to feeling, to friendship even.

This idea invites us to return to those dedications—so rare in Barthes—at the outset of his articles on Eisenstein, since they could suggest that both belong to a politics of friendship, a reconfiguration of revolution that includes love—and of course love between men. In the 1970 piece, we see Barthes moving toward questions of affect and intimacy. As Steven Ungar has written, "'The Third Meaning' significantly revises Barthes' semiotics of the image from the social categories of *Mythologies* toward the intimate family drama of *Camera Lucida*."[16] There is, to my knowledge, no discussion about a gay or queer Eisenstein in France in the 1960s and 1970s; indeed, as Thomas Waugh has pointed out, one finds a specifically French dismissal of "queer biographical readings" of his films.[17] But it is not impossible that in speaking of Eisenstein, Barthes was also speaking in code, thinking that he might signal a certain form of queerness which would permit affect and pathos as forms of historical change to enter into scientific discourse. This at least seems to be what Eisenstein brings to Barthes' work as far back as 1954, when Barthes introduced his name in the midst of his essay on CinemaScope to promote what he came to value most: pathos as a revolutionary force, and affect as a force of historical transformation.

Chapter 5

Leaving the Movie Theater

What could be a science of cinema? Seen from today's perspective, the European *engouement* during the 1960s for science in the humanities remains perplexing. This is when the use of the term "sciences humaines" became widespread. It designated something akin to the humanities and the social sciences, as seen in the enthusiasm for structuralism and semiotics. The expansion of the École pratique des hautes études seems like nothing so much as a last-ditch effort by intellectuals trained in literary studies to stave off an inevitable turn that would deprive them of their ruling position in higher education.

Barthes' position in relation to this incursion of science is ambivalent. His adoption of an explicitly scientific approach to culture, or more precisely, his claims to scientificity, are a continuation and a refinement of the ideological critique undertaken in *Mythologies*. Compared to André Bazin, Barthes, as we have seen, doesn't hesitate to use scientific methods to correct what he perceives to be weak thought about the social implications of certain films. At the same time, as has been well documented, his enthusiasm is matched by an increasingly steady skepticism toward the validity of a systematic method applied to literature and, as we'll see, to cinema. Even in those moments when Barthes seems to think that the scientific approach affords us a break from an unreflecting consumption of cultural products, his writing suggests that a science of art or of culture cannot account for fundamental elements of signification such as the body and the self.[1]

THE SCIENCE OF FILMOLOGY

What is science, according to Barthes? Or rather, what are its manifestations?

1. A break with "ideology" and "myth." In this sense, Barthes is close to Althusser. Science is, first of all, what points to and denounces the myths and illusions of collective representations, principally the illusion that something (an object, an activity, a way of behaving) is natural rather than constructed.

2. The science of culture, or a scientific approach to culture, involves borrowing methods and most often a terminology from the social sciences—in Barthes' case anthropology, Marxism, linguistics, occasionally sociology and, to a lesser extent, psychoanalysis. Hence Barthes' frequent off-handed references to Claude Lévi-Strauss, Ferdinand de Saussure, Louis Hjelmslev, Émile Benveniste, Algirdas Julien Greimas, American sociologists, and Russian formalists (Jakobson, Propp, Tomashevskii). Science for Barthes manifests itself both in its internationalization—Barthes cites work in English but uses translations from other languages—and in interdisciplinarity. In Barthes' understanding, the traditional field of literary studies at the time, largely dominated by literary history, *explication de texte*, and the psychological interpretation of literary works, was precisely not a science. In 1967, Barthes wrote that disciplines and fields determined by universities were a way of producing specific forms of research. Convinced that "the institution directly determines the nature of human knowledge," he would give interdisciplinarity a major push after 1968.[2]

3. Science (of cinema and literature) involves producing generalizable concepts. Many of Barthes' most scientific texts are not much more than outlines of possible fields of research, but they are always written so that the claims made about a specific work can be applied to other works.

4. Science for Barthes might involve teamwork and the coauthor-
ship of texts. While rare in the Humanities at the time, Barthes
did collaborate on at least two articles on cinema: "Traumatic
Units in Cinema," written in collaboration with Gilbert Cohen-
Séat, and "La vedette: enquêtes d'audience," which he published with the assistance of sociologist Violette Morin [then
the wife of Edgar Morin] and which involved public opinion
polling.[3]

However, by 1970 Barthes would state that "[the code] of science is
known for the narrowness of its constraints: impersonality, rationality,
translucency of form with respect to content, etc." and he later called the
scientific approach to literature "reductive."[4] He comes to these conclusions if not quite as an architect, at least as a principal representative of
the tendencies he was beginning to abandon. The larger ambiguities in
his work, this complex relationship to an idea of science, are reflected in
his writing about film.

I want to take as a first example Barthes' 1960 article "Traumatic
Units in Cinema," which appeared in the *Revue internationale de filmologie*, and which was published, not coincidentally, at the very moment
that Barthes was beginning to work at the École pratique des hautes
études. Dudley Andrew reminds us that it is during this period that film
studies—as promoted by the *Institut de filmologie* directed by Gilbert
Cohen-Séat—were positioned to play a pivotal role in the scientific
study of social life:

Taking cinema to be civilization's ideal mix of qualitative experience (a sum of the arts) and quantitative impact (a global and
mass phenomenon of unprecedented proportions), he [Cohen-
Séat] called for a superdiscipline to study it, combining aesthetics
with sociology. . . . From the moment of its official license, late
in 1950, until the very end of the decade, the institute benefited
from significant support, visibly affecting the stratosphere of
French education in the process. The ancient amphitheater of the
Collège de France was, for example, equipped for projection . . . In

the late 1940s such luminaries as Maurice Merleau-Ponty, Henri Lefebvre, and Jean Hyppolite had appeared before the group. Cohen-Séat's inspired strategy was to set up cinema as a magnet to attract high-profile intellectuals from a spectrum of disciplines, principally the human sciences.[5]

Barthes was precisely this sort of intellectual, and the article he delivered was a tactical gesture operating on multiple fronts: he meant to show solidarity with Cohen-Séat's project, of course, but also to consolidate his position in the emerging field of film studies, to outline possible topics of research within this field, and, most ambitiously, to sketch the broad outlines of a positivist system that could account for the ways a film produces meaning. To demonstrate this, he tries to explain the rhetorical effects of shot duration—how, if the camera stays even a second or two longer on a character, it opens up new interpretive possibilities. As a test case, Barthes made use of what the filmologists called *tests filmiques thématiques* [thematic film tests, TFTs], filmstrips made at the Institut de filmologie which were accompanied by audience questionnaires. The latter made it easier to measure how varying the length of the shots in a sequence changed interpretation of that sequence. These strips, in other words, were Filmology's equivalent of the Kuleshov experiment.

Though his brief article may align itself with Cohen-Séat, one senses a tension in Barthes' writing between scientific positivism and an affective, indeed highly personalized, relation to any film sequence. The "thematic film test" (TFT) that Barthes chooses to discuss shows a young man and an older woman, whom Barthes identifies right away as "a mother and son with a problem"—or more precisely "a filial relation colored by ambiguity *(un rapport filial teinté d'ambiguïté)* . . . [there is] something disturbing between them and I can't or don't want to say what it is."[6] Now, it would be facile to identify this as Barthes' Oedipal scene, but what concerns me more in this case is his attempt to account for affect, for the emotional charge of film, for the production of an affective relation. For Barthes, what counts in the TFT is not the "expressivity" of the boy's gaze for the older woman; it is not this "expressivity" that signifies love. What counts is the "duration" of the shot; hence, science is deflected into a poetics that forms a relation between private response and public reception. Was this already a way for Barthes, as early as 1960, to be discreetly calling into question the scientific dogma of filmology? This minor displacement will only grow more significant in the following years, as we will see in paying close attention to one of Barthes' most widely discussed articles on cinema.

APPARATUS THEORY

The title of Roland Barthes' 1975 essay "En sortant du cinéma" has been read, more than once, as an indication that what Barthes liked best about the movies was leaving the theater.[7] As such, Barthes' essay would be a symptom of both the literary intellectual's deeply engrained suspicion of the moving picture and a manifestation of a moment in intellectual history—the mid-1970s—when film theorists were intent upon resisting the pleasure of the movies, the passivity into which films were said to throw the spectator, and what Barthes himself in the essay calls the "lure" of the moving image.[8] "Leaving the Movie Theater" does indeed participate in this moment, a kind of high-water mark of the psychoanalysis of cinema, but it does something else as well and invites reconsideration of the relationship between cinema and aesthetics, including what we might call "the political possibilities of aesthetics," the kind of phrase that Barthes increasingly lodged in his essays. It was not for nothing that Barthes published "En sortant du cinéma" in *Communications*, an academic journal that, beginning in 1960, had situated itself at the forefront of "transdisciplinary" analyses of the revolutions in communication technologies that were taking place in modern industrial societies.[9] Special issues on radio, on cable TV (what the editors called "câblodiffusion," in a kind of charming 1970s techno-speak), on advertising, and on comic strips and cartoons make up the bulk of the volumes in the 1970s. Interdisciplinary or "transdisciplinary" approaches to mass culture had been one of the innovations coming out of May 1968, an impetus responding to the desire both to open new fields of knowledge and to undo the disciplinary and social hierarchies at work in the French university system. This push was precisely what allowed Barthes, who sat on the editorial board of *Communications*, to write about cinema in this journal. As we shall see, it is this interdisciplinarity (an idea which included the very fact of its institutionalization) that would push Barthes to write an article as eccentric as "Leaving the Movie Theater."

"Cinema and Psychoanalysis," the special issue of *Communications* in which Barthes published his piece, gathered essays from authors intent upon solidifying the theoretical rigor of the psychoanalytic school of film studies. Reading it today, one is struck at how, with the exception of Raymond Bellour's meticulous "Le Blocage Symbolique," the vast majority of the essays in the volume were predicated upon a distrust of movies. The authors in *Communications* were not alone in their desire to debunk film as mass entertainment, and it is hard to read some of their texts as anything other than attempts to "break the spell" of the cinematic illusion and to do in verbal form what filmmakers like Debord or Godard were doing on-screen at the time. In this issue, Christian Metz published the first part of his essay "The Imaginary Signifier," which attempts to found a "relatively autonomous science of cinema" that would transcend cinephilia's affective relationship to the moving image.[10] Jean-Louis Baudry's contribution "Le Dispositif" famously likened the moviegoer both to the prisoner in Plato's cave, mistaking the shadows on the wall for reality, and to the sleeper voluntarily regressing to the passivity of the fetal state. And in a panicky article entitled "The Pauper's Couch" [*Le Divan du Pauvre*], Félix Guattari rejected both psychoanalysis and cinema as machines intent upon capturing the energy of desire and subordinating it to the "dominant social system." What is worse, Guattari wrote, commercial cinema is a "cheap drug" administered in massive doses to children "even before they have learned language."[11] Guattari's article makes one wonder to what extent Deleuze's work on cinema—beginning with his lectures at Vincennes in November 1981—wasn't a reaction against the suspicions his writing partner had voiced in 1975—though in all fairness, Guattari does end his article with a call for "un cinéma de combat" that will liberate the multiplicities and intensities of desire.

To be sure, the writings of Metz and Baudry were meant to counter the amorous gaze of the cinephile, which, at least since the end of World War Two, had dominated serious writing about film in France. But there is no doubt that philosophical engagement with film after 1975—the writings of Deleuze and Jacques Rancière for instance—actively refused the rather cinephobic posture of this broadly pitched call for "scientific" demystification.

In this shifting terrain, Barthes' essay stakes out a kind of middle ground. Reading it in its context in the special issue of *Communications*, one is struck at how it participates in a conversation with the other articles, and with Metz in particular. Barthes' essay relies upon the terms and premises that we find in apparatus theory circa 1975. Barthes, like Metz, speaks of the movie screen as a "mirror" and he equates this fascination with the Lacanian concept of the "imaginary." Like Metz, Barthes is attentive to the spectator's relation to the projector—Metz called the light from the projector a "beam of light" [*faisceau de lumière*] emanating from the back of our heads, Barthes calls it "that dancing cone" [*ce cône dansant*], a "laser beam" that "brushes our skull, glancing off someone's hair, someone's face."[12] Like Jean-Louis Baudry, Barthes builds his essay around an understanding of the screening room as *dispositif*.[13] And like Baudry, he speaks of the "soporific" state one enters into when watching a movie. If we wanted to be critical, we might add that Metz, Baudry, and Barthes also have this in common: none feels the need to mention specific films.

Yet Barthes' essay serves less to reinforce the tenets of apparatus theory than to undermine them. He does this quite subtly, calling them into question not through argumentation, but through the staging of his own body. "Leaving the Movie Theater" is, to my mind, one of the very first attempts to resist what is now widely recognized as the overreaching universalizing gestures of Paris School apparatus theory by opening up a space to reflect on desire and on the sensuous world of the film spectator.

Here is how the essay begins: "The subject who is speaking here must admit one thing: he likes to leave the movie theater. Finding himself on the lighted and abandoned street (he always goes to the movies at night and on a weekday) and heading softly toward a café, he walks in silence."[14] The passage reads as if Barthes were writing the first lines of a novel—he seems to be rewriting Valéry's famous line "*la marquise sortit à cinq heures,*" in terms that sound surprisingly like Sartre's

La Nausée—or even describing the opening scene of some *film noir*. A man, alone on the street, at night, walking toward a café; we could be watching the opening sequence of a Carné-Prévert collaboration, and waiting for something to happen.

In this case, it is the essay itself that happens. This first sequence sets the tone and introduces a central idea: the power of cinema resides not in its capacity to hypnotize us or render us passive, but rather in its ability to transform the sensory experience of the world around us. Contrary to the way critics have read Barthes, "Leaving the Movie Theater" is not as much about rejecting the medium as it is about delighting in the pleasure he feels when the altered state into which the film has put him lingers on beyond the end of the projection. It is a deeply melancholic essay, and the narrative fragment at the beginning quickly gives way to the description of the inner state: his melancholy and his desire. Cinema, he writes, offers a cure to his melancholia; it is a healing therapy, a *guérissement*.

Even more important is the fact that Barthes positions himself upright, walking. This posture seems to be a direct response to apparatus theory, the very starting point of which is a spectator who remains invariably fixed, seated. Two things happen in this particularization of apparatus theory. First, Barthes' essay does something that seems both obvious and rare in 1975: instead of denouncing the lure of the movies, it attempts to describe a sensibility, an aesthetics that would allow the viewer to emancipate himself from the capture of the cinema. Barthes tries to account for the sensuous quality of the moviegoing experience and the complexity of the viewer's situation in the black box of the movie theater. His turn to autobiographical writing has often been categorized as hedonist, or as an attempt to break the strictures of formalism by turning to Epicureanism. And certainly, "Leaving the Movie Theater" exemplifies Barthes' desire to reinject pleasure into moviegoing.

But Barthes' later writings, those on cinema in particular, are also an attempt to alter the way the body and desire encounter spaces, objects, and people. In order to break with what, in 1975, he still understands as the repressive potential of cinema (its ability to limit thought and render us passive), Barthes turns to aesthetics, to a reconfiguration of the sensory space of film, as if the very first foundational political gesture were

a new cinema, but a situated approach to the viewing experience that opens onto an encounter with the world.

"Leaving the Movie Theater" thus brings together a series of tensions that run through Barthes' work and, by extension, through modernism as a whole, tensions between the common and the individual, between art and non-art, between an undifferentiating theory of the apparatus and a differentiated approach to perception, between a writing that claims the status of science and one that aims to capture the affect ordinarily associated with literature. As Marielle Macé has shown, this tension between science and literature haunts Barthes as he is writing in the 1970s, when his work evolves from the science (or pseudoscience) of a semiological approach that culminates in S/Z, and toward the more open, suggestive, and personalized writing of his later years.[18] Though Barthes has been criticized for his "impressionistic" style, it was precisely the genre of the essay, because it allows for subjectivity, that permitted him to step outside the scientific and universalizing claims of apparatus theory. It is because the essay as a literary form allows for autobiographical fragments, speculative thinking, and the recording of individualized experience that Barthes was able to counter the claims of theory with an almost confessional text based on his experience at the cinema. And it is because the essay is a genre made up of the remnants of other genres, a genre that since Montaigne has included autobiographical narratives, scientific truth claims, and fiction, that Barthes was able to write about anything at all, and to include in his text heterogeneous elements—the lighted street outside the movie theater, a café, the "grain" of sound inside the screening room, "the darkness," the "obscure mass of other bodies," "the entrance, the exit"—as if the essay itself were the very form of the aesthetic regime.[19]

A LONG CONVERSATION WITH CHRISTIAN METZ

Although his reputation would dim within a decade, no star in early-1970s film theory shone as brightly as Christian Metz. Metz had attended Barthes' seminars while he was writing one of the field's foundational texts, *Le Signifiant Imaginaire*. As we saw, "Leaving the Movie Theater" was published in the same issue of *Communications* as Metz's famous study, and Barthes' five-page article is in the strange position of being supportive of Metz's theoretical claims and yet clearly, already, trying to find a way out. Like so much of Barthes' writing from these years, "Leaving the Movie Theater" is a short, speculative embodiment of his attempt to leave theory behind. As such, it is an important moment in the history of film studies and should make us wonder, nearly fifty years later, about the nature of its relationship to Metz and the tenor of their conversation about the movies.

Metz famously describes the experience of watching a movie in a movie theater as a kind of *mise en abyme* in which the spectator's gaze mimics the projector's beam of light, which mimics, in turn, the camera's field of vision. In a sense, the model for Metz's cinematic apparatus, and for the spectator, is nothing other than the Lumière Brothers' *cinématographe*, a machine made to both record and project. In Metz's essay, this recorder/projector creates a sort of feedback loop, a never-ending process of production and consumption that Metz attempts to interrupt by calling attention to the system itself, and pointing out that this process of identification is an illusion fabricated by an apparatus. Barthes attempts to break this illusion in another way, by undoing the distinction between what is on-screen and what is off-screen, between the cinematic image and the surrounding world, between art and life.

For Metz, the spectator at the movies replays a sort of Oedipal drama. He is in the position of the child who watches the parental couple at play [*s'ébattre*],[20] but is definitively excluded from the action on the screen—as opposed to the theater where the distance between spectator and actor is not so great because the actors are really there:

I shall only recall that the cinema was born in the midst of the capitalist epoch in a largely antagonistic and fragmented society, based on individualism and the restricted family . . . in an especially super-egoistic bourgeois society, especially concerned with "elevation" (or façade), especially opaque to itself. The theater is a very ancient art, one which saw the light in more authentically ceremonial societies, in more integrated human groups (even if sometimes, as in Ancient Greece, the cost of this integration was the rejection into a non-human exterior of a whole social category, that of the slaves), in cultures which were in some sense closer to their desire (i.e. paganism): the theatre retains something of this civic tendency towards ludico-liturgical "communion," even in the degraded state of a fashionable rendezvous around those plays known as *"pièces de boulevard."*[21]

This quite stunning quote, coming from France's foremost film theorist, intimates that the cinema may play the role of a degraded art, that it is degraded theater, as it were.[22] This genealogy, from theater to cinema, from Greek tragedy to commercial cinema, is phantasmal but not rare. It isn't at all odd that in the mid-1970s a French film theorist should invest considerable energy in describing a fundamental distrust of the movies because they are a product of capitalism. In a paragraph such as this Metz seems to be proving his intellectual validity, vying for a certain amount of intellectual prestige by diminishing the very object of his study. Part of Barthes' conversation with Metz has to do with the latter's replication of the prejudice that cinema is a degraded art form.

Yet while cinema might be degraded for Metz, it is far from bankrupt. In his work, the movies are never simply the extension of an existing political order:

> For the vast majority of the audience, the cinema (rather like a dream in this) represents a kind of enclosure of "reserve" which escapes the fully social aspect of life although it is accepted and prescribed by it: going to the cinema is one lawful activity among others with its place in the admissible pastimes of the day or the week, and yet that place is a "hole" in the social cloth, a *loop-hole* opening on to something slightly more crazy, slightly less approved than what one does the rest of the time.[23]

Cinema here is not an instrument of social control, and even if it does involve mystification, it also goes beyond what society approves. Metz's project, in a way, is to radicalize the film viewing experience by getting through the mystifications of plot and image. In this sense, he is close to Barthes. And it is often forgotten that, like Barthes, Metz included fragments of autobiography in his articles. In a reflexive moment of *Le Signifiant imaginaire* which could be a starting point for "Leaving the Movie Theater," he writes: "Psychoanalysis does not illuminate only the film, but also the conditions of desire of whoever makes himself its theoretician . . . I have loved the cinema, I no longer love it, I still love it. What I have wished to do in these pages is to keep at a distance, as in the scopic practice I have discussed, that which in me (= in everyone) *can* love it: to retain it as *questioned*."[24]

Metz once said that writing about films is an autoanalysis of sorts. In a passage of an essay on metonymy, he describes himself writing while, outside his window, a jackhammer pounds away at the sidewalk and triggers the author's migraines. Metz's working title for this article became "the jackhammer." Whenever he hears the jackhammer he knows he is no longer writing. Whenever he is writing he no longer hears the jackhammer.[25] Such an autobiographical fragment aims to illustrate the principle of substitution: "jackhammer" doesn't symbolize Metz's article; it stands in for it. As (relatively) popular as they might have been at one time, such analyses based on linguistic categories—the difference between metaphor and metonymy in this case—were never quite suited to the study of a medium based on images and sounds. But this personal example is revealing since it consciously avoids the scene of cinema even while it clarifies cinematic codes. Metz's writing does include analyses of specific films but, as far as I know, among the dozen or so autobiographical fragments in his work, never once does he evoke the memory of going to the movies, watching television, or seeing a photograph; the entirety of his autoanalysis takes place outside the screening room. In a sense, Metz theorized this blind spot when he claimed, in the subsection of *The Imaginary Signifier* titled "Identification, Mirror," that the experience of watching a film is akin to the Lacanian mirror stage, with only one difference, that "there is one thing never reflected" in the film: the spectator's body.[26]

In "Leaving the Movie Theater," Barthes is focusing on that blind spot. He acknowledges the importance of the *situation* in which one watches the film. It is the movie house, the seat, the other spectators, the projector, the screen, the soundtrack that draw his attention.

In some respects, the article shows Barthes' support for a French apparatus theory that was triumphant in 1975. Yet at the same time, this essay is one of the first to put into question the claims of apparatus theory, and in particular what scholars have since rightly labeled its tendency to generalize audiences.

LEAVING THEORY

We can now better understand the politics of Barthes' gesture in "Leaving the Movie Theater." This essay links the Epicureanism of personal feeling (Barthes' mood in the afternoon) to a reflection on the equality of each particular viewer. Under the guise of a universally applicable theory, Baudry and Metz elaborated positions that were implicitly grounded in a straight male gaze which excluded gender, racial, or sexual difference. Barthes' essay, on the other hand, has been read as an attempt to write about gay desire in the movie house. This desire for other bodies, other spectators, these references to "modern eroticism," this description of the body's "availability" in the movie theater, this call, in the very last words of the essay, for "a possible bliss of *discretion*," all this has led readers to understand Barthes' essay as the description of a scene in a pornographic theater.[27] We can indeed read Barthes' essay as an early attempt to question apparatus theory by postulating differentiated audiences.[28]

Writing about *Empire of Signs*, D. A. Miller situates what he calls the possibility of a "*lateral gaze*, as between equals" at the heart of Barthes' writing about Japan. For Miller, this lateral gaze is possible due to Japan's economic power, which stands up to the economic imperialism of the West. However, "laterality" and equality are also the condition of homosexuality: "The possibility of this laterality *and of its implied reciprocation* is doubled in a homosexuality that by definition neutralizes the gender hierarchy and so is well disposed to dreaming that it might suspect the operation of other hierarchies too."[29]

"Leaving the Movie Theater" is the definitive description in Barthes of the lateral (and egalitarian) gaze. Thinking equality for Barthes means first thinking the equality of the reciprocated gaze—a drastic revision of the Sartrean model. A gaze that is all the more significant at the movies because it defies film's ability to turn the audience into an undifferentiated mass. This is also why we should take seriously Barthes' choice of Eisenstein as both a gay and a communist director.

Barthes questioned the universalizing tendency of apparatus theory. He repeatedly states that the subject he is describing is himself, unique, "difficult," solipsistic even, but not generalizable, at least not in a sense that Metz and Baudry evoked. Barthes may have been famous for reintroducing the subject into the theoretical discussions of his times, but the subject of "Leaving the Cinema" serves to move the vision of film away from psychoanalytic generalization. Barthes does follow and reproduce Metz's claims that the spectator is caught in a process of identification (for Barthes, it is with the image on the screen, for Metz with the camera) and he does believe like Metz that this imaginary relation is akin to "ideology" (l'idéologique) since the on-screen world seems natural, coherent, pertinent, true. But unlike other film theorists of the 1970s, what Barthes is looking for is a way to come undone, to come unstuck from the mirror and to do so in a manner that wouldn't fall back on the methods and aims of Brechtian distanciation. Barthes is looking for a way to break the hypnotic spell of moving pictures other than through the demystification of his *Mythologies*. And he finds the way when he allows his body, what he calls his "perverse body," to look beyond the image, toward the more idiosyncratic territory of experience itself.

Chapter 6

The Melodramatic Imagination

THE BRONTË SISTERS

On March 7, 1978, Roland Barthes dressed for the role he was playing as William Makepeace Thackeray in André Téchiné's biopic *The Brontë Sisters*. As Éric Marty writes, the film "was a nightmare for Barthes. For some reason Téchiné had him hold forth at length while pacing up and down, making his presence in the film appear artificial and clumsy. The film was a failure."[1]

Roland Barthes as Thackeray in *The Brontë Sisters* (André Téchiné, 1979)

The Brontë Sisters is a melancholic film, mysterious in its object and extremely sober in its form. Filmed for the most part in the moors near Haworth, it traces the lives of the three sisters and their brother Patrick Branwell, around the time when Anne, Emily, and Charlotte were finishing their studies and writing the works that would make them famous. We see Patrick's doomed love for a married woman, his descent into depression and opium. We see Emily's death from tuberculosis and then Anne's. Though the film ends by evoking Charlotte's celebrity in the wake of *Jane Eyre*, its tone remains excessively somber. This darkness, of course, is meant to evoke the strict Methodist upbringing of the Brontës, but it can just as convincingly be put in parallel with the overwhelmingly melancholy tone of the period pieces that flourished in French cinema at the time.

Much has been written about the so-called *mode rétro* in 1970s film, about works like Luchino Visconti's *The Damned* (1969), Bernardo Bertolucci's *The Conformist* (1970), Louis Malle's *Lacombe Lucien* (1974), or Liliana Cavani's *The Night Porter* (1974). Few critics find anything positive to say about the nostalgia they express. For Michel Foucault, these films, and *Lacombe Lucien* and *The Night Porter* in particular, were political mistakes and egregious lapses in taste.

We might also recall that, as Foucault described it, the *mode rétro* movement involved films set before 1945 that replaced working-class struggles with nostalgia, and history with what Fredric Jameson called an appetite "for all the styles and fashions of a dead past."[2] Serge Daney situated French cinema's fascination with the past within an even broader frame. In 1979 he concluded that for all their formal innovation and in spite of having launched a revolution in world cinema, the films of the New Wave, and François Truffaut's in particular, were really an elaborate cult of the dead.[3] Daney, who had Truffaut's *La Chambre verte* (*The Green Room*, 1978) in mind when he made this trenchant claim, intended to challenge the widespread notion that Truffaut and the New Wave had embodied France's postwar rush to modernize.[4] For Daney, writing ten years after May 1968, nothing had a more complicated relation with France's fixation on newness after 1945 than this group of films. Was the *mode rétro* a response to May 1968? Or at the very least a response to the formal innovation and political radicalness of certain elements of the New Wave that, in works such as Jacques Rivette's *Out 1*

(1971), Godard's Dziga Vertov films, or Agnès Varda's *Black Panthers* (1968) came to the fore in its wake? In any case Daney detected in Truffaut and elsewhere a resistance to, or at least a lack of enthusiasm for, postwar society's imperative to modernize; he saw a turning away from the political and formal innovations of post-'68 cinema in Europe.

Téchiné's *The Brontë Sisters* takes its place alongside these period films, but of them all, its disconsolate mood most closely resembles the films of Téchiné's friend François Truffaut. Truffaut had, of course, been making period fictions since his third feature, *Jules et Jim* (1962), a paean to the European avant-garde around World War 1.[5] But he made the majority of them during the 1970s, including *The Wild Child* (*L'Enfant sauvage*, 1970), *Two English Girls* (*Les Deux Anglaises et le Continent*, 1971), *The Story of Adele H* (*L'Histoire d'Adèle H*, 1975), and *The Green Room* (*La Chambre verte*, 1978). These films inhabit what Sam Di Iorio has called a "non-consensual third space within the landscape of French cinema, a space which is equally removed from mainstream fare and the more radical experiments of auteur-oriented features."[6] This, it seems to me, is also the space that Téchiné's films, including *The Brontë Sisters*, have come to occupy. Both directors made films that are closely tied to literary sources, and, though shot in period costume, are markedly staid in approach, especially when contrasted with the orgy of ruffles one often finds in Hollywood's recreations of nineteenth-century dramas. Their work shares a subdued and melancholy tone that refuses to yield to the spectacle of history.

Truffaut and Téchiné share other, more practical features: the use of narrative ellipses, the importance accorded to landscape, and the assistance of some of the same personnel. Jean Gruault, who wrote the screenplay for *The Story of Adele H*, also collaborated on the script for *The Brontë Sisters*; Christian Gasc, who was the costume designer for Truffaut's *The Green Room*, served the same role in Téchiné's film, which co-stars Marie-France Pisier, who had played in Truffaut's early short *Antoine et Colette* (1962). And of course both *The Brontë Sisters* and *Adele H* feature Isabelle Adjani, who famously broke her contract with la Comédie-Française in order to make the latter feature, and who, through these successive roles, came to embody a romantic excess of passion very much out of step with both feminist aspirations of equality and societal norms emerging in the 1960s and 1970s.

In order to understand what is at stake with *The Brontë Sisters*, and with Barthes' participation in it, we need to take a step back and recontextualize the film, its project, and the tone it adopts as part of a "melodramatic turn" that had been unfolding in French cinema during the previous decade.

THE NEW WAVE'S MELODRAMATIC TURN

If the 1970s saw commercial cinema romanticize the surfaces and textures of an immediate past, they are also a period in which the star directors of the 1960s move toward a critical relationship with history. One of the more interesting and still overlooked aspects of the New Wave is their 1970s turn toward historical drama. Of course, one could also argue that by the 1970s the New Wave no longer exists. Film historians usually agree that the movement ended sometime earlier—by 1965, or by 1968 in any case.[7] Nevertheless, the following decade sees its primary representatives make a surprisingly high number of period pieces. Besides Truffaut's streak of really amazing films from *The Wild Child* on, we have Alain Resnais' *Stavisky . . .* (1974), the first genuine period drama from a director who had always focused on history and memory. Or think of Claude Chabrol's *Violette Nozière* from 1978, about a young woman who murdered her parents in 1933. Or Jacques Rivette's adaptation of *Wuthering Heights* in 1985, or even, in a slightly different register, his 1971 *Out 1*, which is not a historical drama but nonetheless claims to be a an adaptation of Balzac's *Histoire des treize* in modern-day Paris. One might even include in this list Godard's *Wind from the East* from 1970, which is, among other things, a western shot in period costume—as well as, of course, André Téchiné's *The Brontë Sisters* or Bertrand Tavernier's second and third features *Let Joy Reign Supreme* (*Que la fête commence*, 1975) and *Le Juge et l'assassin* (1976), which, even though they were made by a younger generation, still raise some of the same questions as the films of the New Wave group.[8]

The reception of these historical dramas has been mixed. Many were popular successes, but scholars and critics for the most part have either studied them in the context of the oeuvre of their respective directors, or as a return to the *cinéma de qualité* of the 1950s against which the New Wave had rebelled, or—the worst fate of all—as an embodiment of the *mode rétro* and the nostalgia films against which Foucault and Jameson inveighed as symptoms of a world that had lost all hope of change after 1968. Was French cinema an initial sign of the full-blown political restoration and reaction that François Cusset refers to as the decade-long nightmare of the 1980s?[9]

By focusing on Roland Barthes' role in Téchiné's *The Brontë Sisters* and on a number of specific and striking points of convergence between Barthes and Foucault, I would like to shift this focus, to see if we might think of all these films not simply as a nostalgic return to the *cinéma de papa*, but as films with a political stake. I would like to see them at least as mainstream films that ask questions about what stories can be told in the commercial art house context after May 1968. Rather than simply look backward, these films reach into the shadows of the past to locate and render sensible the lives of ordinary individuals that make up what Foucault called the "fine grain of history."[10] This gesture, of course, was at the heart of a certain form of Leftism, mostly after May 1968, and what I want to show is that at the heart of this Leftist project of recuperating the voices silenced by history, stands an aesthetic mode— melodrama—that, while rarely acknowledged, especially in France, nonetheless helped certain filmmakers and intellectuals to structure their thought and open up the range of their sensory faculties.

The early 1970s is a time when Anglophone scholars rediscovered melodrama with benchmark texts written by Peter Brooks, Thomas Elsaesser, Laura Mulvey, and Christine Gledhill. I believe that there is also a rediscovery of melodrama in the cultural production in France at this same moment, one that remains largely unacknowledged. Can we think about melodrama in the context of the French 1970s not necessarily as a reaction to Hollywood, but as a form that allows filmmakers and writers to deal with moments of historical violence in aesthetic or artistic terms? In order to understand what is at stake in this melodramatic turn, I want to examine two objects that, in spite of obvious differences, might have something in common: Truffaut's historical melodramas from the 1970s, in particular his most perfect historical film, *The Story of Adele H*, and Foucault's research from the same period in what he called "the technology of human abnormality."[11] By this, Foucault identified the processes intended to normalize those individuals who were deemed anomalous, marginal, transgressive, monstrous, in a word, *irregular*. In case after case he showed them to be caught up in administrative and bureaucratic machines, ranging from psychiatry to the courts, to the schools, whose goals were ever to straighten out and normalize these individuals. This is the program in *Discipline and Punish* in particular, but the same ideas also appear in *Abnormal*, his 1974 lectures at the Collège de France, and in his 1973 volume on Pierre Rivière, which René Allio turned into a film in 1976.

Both Truffaut's film and Foucault's archival research are engaged in rescuing voices and stories from what British historian E. P. Thompson called the "enormous condescension of posterity," deploying a process of rediscovery, or recreation, that involves not just telling the story but recreating a sensorium of aesthetic moments, of beauty, of emotion.[12] Melodrama is precisely the genre that allows us to engage the new sensorium in an effort of historical recovery.

No film draws more deeply on the melodramatic imagination than *The Story of Adele H*, the story of the lovesick daughter of Victor Hugo whose passion puts in play all the elements of the melodramatic genre or mode. The "young heroine," Adèle, finds herself in a hyperbolic situation, a family drama in which she is feuding with her famous father, who only grudgingly sends her money, and in love with a Lieutenant Pinson who, having seduced her and having gotten money from her, now has lost interest. It is a tale of extreme psychological violence, a violence that Adèle turns on herself, in part due to the jealousy she feels toward her dead sister, Léopoldine, who will always remain her father's favorite. After a series of increasingly abject scenes and a descent into madness, Adèle is ultimately discovered wandering destitute through the streets of Bridgetown, Barbados.

As happens in many melodramatic narratives, Adèle cannot speak her pain to anyone, except the lieutenant who, for his part, won't listen and refuses to read her letters. Her tale belongs to what Peter Brooks calls the "text of muteness."[13] This leads to her compulsive journal writing, a practice that produces the document upon which Truffaut based his film. It also triggers several sequences in which Adèle dreams that

Isabelle Adjani in the title role of *The Story of Adele H.* (François Truffaut, 1975)

she is drowning. These expressionistic scenes present Isabelle Adjani in a kind of double pantomime, gasping for air beneath superimposed images of her body submerged under water.

The film is built around a tension between verbal and nonverbal expression: neither Adèle nor Lieutenant Pinson really hear each other; Adèle confides her thoughts to a journal that no one will read (not until the end of the film at least); Adèle and her father misunderstand each other; and Adèle has to lie about getting married in order for a message to even arrive in Guernsey where Victor Hugo lives in exile. As much as *The Wild Child* (Truffaut's other great film on language), *The Story of Adele H* is about miscommunication, the inability of an individual to make herself heard, especially in confrontation with a law which alternately takes the form of her father, the bank where she draws her money, or the asylum where she spends the latter part of her life. The film concludes with a bizarre historical coda that contrasts Victor Hugo's glorious national funeral with the quiet, discrete, private, and wholly forgotten life Adèle led at the Saint Mandé asylum until her death in 1915.

Making this film drew Truffaut closer to melodrama than he had ever been before. Anne Gillain and Dudley Andrew have pointed to

Truffaut's ability to jump "from comedy to melodrama in a single pan,"[14] and earlier films, such as *La Peau Douce* (1964), contain various elements of the genre. Most commentators emphasize Truffaut's distancing techniques, his playful but irreverent references to its conventions: Vincent Canby, for instance, wrote that *Le Dernier Métro* (1980) is "a melodrama that refuses to exercise its melodramatic options."[15] The definitive example of this often ironic distance is developed in *Day for Night* (*La Nuit américaine*, 1973), where the primary narrative concerning a film crew is set off by the somewhat ridiculous melodrama they are shooting, *Je vous présente Pamela*. In part, *Day for Night* is a lesson about how to take melodrama with a grain of salt. And yet in my opinion, *The Story of Adele H*, shot just one year later, is a full-throated embrace of the melodramatic mode, without scare quotes.

There seem to be two ways to understand Truffaut's turn to melodrama in *Adele H*. The first contends that this film reflects his slide to the political center, or worse still, a return to the aesthetic choices against which he and the New Wave had revolted en bloc in the 1950s. After all, what could be more conventional in filmmaking than a nineteenth-century period piece that rehearses a tale of unrequited love—this was the bread and butter of the *cinéma de qualité*. Another, more productive reading would open up the troubling, unconventional aspects of Truffaut's films, as suggested in an article by Sam Di Iorio on "Truffaut's Radicalism" which understands the filmmaker, for all his popularity in Europe and in the United States, to be an artist whose work is traversed by "darker," "antisocial" currents that complicate its legacy.[16] From this perspective, it becomes possible to see *Adele H*'s use of melodramatic structures less as a bid for respectability than as one manifestation of a larger instability that inhabits Truffaut's work. This instability is present in the very fabric of the melodramatic storyline. Such is the role and power of melodrama: as stable as the genre might seem, it nonetheless has volatile effects on the place, the social role, of its protagonists.

Why doesn't Truffaut break the spell of melodrama? Of course, the political value of this genre has been debated at least since the 1970s, with some claiming that its emotional intensity necessarily points viewers to the contradictions of the system (capitalism) that produces it, while others, such as Geoffrey Nowell-Smith, arguing that it basically stages women as suffering, passive, and impotent heroines. Melodrama, in this reading, is a hysterical text that fails to solve the problems or contradictions that it raises. Both positions revolve around the question of whether or not a work of art provides a site for ideological critique.

But the problem that Truffaut's melodrama exposes is of a slightly different order: who, he asks, can produce emotion, what kind of individual can produce stories, and whose story are going to be told? The melodrama of *Adele H* is the story of a passion—of *passion* pure and simple—and of film's relation to affect, to emotion. This is why the ending of the film is so startling, its "unhappy, happy end" so characteristic of melodramas. Truffaut's is not just about the conflict between a father and a daughter, it is about whether or not Adèle is allowed to write, to feel, to display her work. Part of this story responds to what T. Jefferson Kline, in his fine study of the New Wave and literature, has called the "anxious affinities" that Truffaut's generation maintained toward books.[17]

MICHEL FOUCAULT'S MELODRAMATIC IMAGINATION

Truffaut's films of the 1970s deploy melodrama as a popular form that both thinks and must be thought about. This orientation is in line with a decade in which, after Thomas Elsaesser's 1972 essay, "Tales of Sound and Fury," Anglo-American criticism brought the films of Douglas Sirk and Vincente Minnelli center stage for ideological analysis.[18] In retrospect, it seems equally tied to the work Michel Foucault was producing at the time. Teasing out a relation between Foucault and melodrama might help us better understand film as not just an object of commentary for the philosopher but as a form of thought, as well as a form of sensation encountering other forms of sensation. Such an approach might also encourage us to think about theory—Foucault and Barthes' work in any case—not just as a significant moment in intellectual history, though it is that to be sure, but as a moment in aesthetic history.

Of course, the importance of Foucault's influence on film studies cannot be overstated. His work on institutions and on the apparatus as an ensemble of discourses, institutions, buildings, and sites has been central in what became known as "apparatus theory," as well as in more recent studies of the place occupied by the technology of cinema and spectacle in general. In their excellent book *Foucault va au cinéma*, two French philosophers explore the ways in which Foucault's thought was shaped in part by cinema and by film aesthetics. In the first part of the book, Dork Zabunyan shows that for Foucault cinema participates in what he calls a "requalification of knowledge."[19] Movies modify our relation to the past but they do so through an aesthetic form, through a mutation of the way we see and hear the world around us.

In the same vein, Patrice Maniglier argues that in spite of his quarrel with the *mode rétro*, Foucault had a sophisticated understanding of film as a way of making us sense forms and movements outside the confines of institutions. What counted for Foucault, according to Maniglier, was the pure movement of film, bodies in motion, gestures and words, everything that might be qualified as a microaesthetics, for this is what resists capture by technologies of normalization. Cinema helped Foucault understand the "techniques of the body" that were to become an essential part of his late work.[20] In this regard cinema is not just a storehouse of knowledge or a producer of stories, but an aesthetic form that delivers history as made up of gestures, utterances, hesitations, emotions—everything that Deleuze called "intensities."

How are such intensities organized and distributed within the genre or mode of melodrama? Within, for example, a film like *The Brontë Sisters*? And did Barthes, a theorist who thought deeply about the intensities of the body, recognize his proximity to Foucault in this regard? There is no lack of commentary on the role of theater in Foucault's work, especially the theater of punishment. In the first pages of *Discipline and Punish* Foucault describes the transition from the Ancien Régime's spectacular violence to a new "soft," hidden, masked power of the "scientifico-judiciary complex": "It was the end of a certain kind of tragedy; comedy began, with shadow play, faceless voices, impalpable entities."[21] But the model Foucault turns to is not so much comedy as melodrama—a word, however, that to my knowledge, Foucault never uses.

Melodrama provides the vocabulary, the affective charge, and the narrative potential that allows Foucault to build his research. The real melodramatic matrix in Foucault's thought has to do with the generation of emotion located in the clash between a "hero" and forces of villainy which are often characterized by their secret nature, their hidden form. A striking coincidence between Foucault's ideas and historical melodrama comes up in the genealogy of the genre. Although it emerged in the early nineteenth century as an entirely postrevolutionary phenomenon, the word "melodrama" may have first been pronounced by Rousseau, and its inception, as Peter Brooks has convincingly shown, actually took place during the Revolution. One of its chief functions was to replace tragic theater favored by the Church and the Monarchy with a more demo-cratic aesthetic form.[22] Melodrama is democratic in the sense that it appeals to a wide audience, but also in the sense that it puts ordinary, anonymous individuals living everyday lives into dreadful, extreme, hyperbolic situations. Melodrama thus came about at a time of histori-cal transformation, of "epistemological break." This was precisely the moment of the break from spectacular forms of punishment to softer, more discrete, less visible, but no less pernicious forms of discipline and punishment. Indeed, during the 1970s Foucault becomes interested almost exclusively in the first half of the nineteenth century, and in the stories of "abnormal" or "anomalous" individuals struggling to live under a completely new set of values. Surprisingly, in *Abnormal: Lectures at the Collège de France 1974–1975*, Foucault traces these anomalous individu-als back to what he describes as the fallen figure of the King, specifically Louis XVI.[23] He argues that this king was transformed into a monster by the Revolutionaries and then was reborn, in the form of extreme individuals who were incubated by institutions intent upon correcting a postrevolutionary population. "Abnormal" individuals—the physi-cal monster, the criminal recidivist, the masturbator, or more generally what Foucault calls the "sexual deviant"—are all "descendants of Louis XVI," "little monsters" who by their very existence put into question, and thereby rupture, the "naturalness" of the social pact.[24] For proof of this genealogy running from king to "ordinary monster," Foucault turns at first not to legal proceedings but to melodramatic forms, and more particularly, to gothic novels by Balzac and Ann Radcliffe.[25]

Foucault's genealogy helps to explain the origins of melodrama as a representation or staging of hyperbolic existence lived by ordinary individuals, by citizens. Perhaps we can see why, when the filmmakers of the New Wave turn to historical drama in the early 1970s, they too were attracted to the nineteenth century for material (Rohmer's *The Marquise of O*, Truffaut's *The Wild Child* and *Adele H*, Téchiné's *The Brontë Sisters*).

For who are these "monsters" Foucault uncovers in his lectures on abnormality? They include Anne Grandjean, a hermaphrodite, accused of living as a man and marrying a woman, and obliged after her trial to wear women's clothes and to cease frequenting both men and women. Or Henriette Cornier, who in 1826 killed her neighbor's baby daughter. Are these individuals not cast as though they were melodramatic characters in a theater of the age? They are and they aren't. Certainly, the heinous crime of Henriette Cornier (like that of Pierre Rivière) might not make of her the kind of "virtuous heroine" that Peter Brooks identifies as the protagonist of melodramas. And yet the confrontation of such troubled people with the techniques and powers of normalization, with what Foucault calls the "strange secret" of punishment, their entanglements with a juridical and medical system constituted in the "shadows," with "faceless voices," with "the darkest region of the political field"—all of this provides narrative material in tune with the needs of the melodramatic imagination.[26]

What melodrama enables us to see today—as scholars like Christine Gledhill have demonstrated[27]—is the texture of extreme experience, the charges of light and of sound, the microorganisms of emotion, in short, the affective dimensions of cinema. *Adele H* is a melodrama which recuperates an individual who would otherwise be lost to us in the "fine grain of history," effaced by the men in her life. It reveals the contradictions of patriarchy without necessarily being a feminist film, for it raises the figure, so crucial to the end of the nineteenth century, of the hysteric, invariably female.[28] Similarly, even though the tale is tainted by misogyny, *Moi Pierre Rivière* also recuperates an individual, this time a male, lost in the fine grain of history.

BARTHES AND FOUCAULT

The case of Pierre Rivière, of course, is of very special interest, since it was the object of a film by René Allio which came out in 1976, and which offers suggestive parallels and contrasts with Téchiné's. In featuring nonprofessional locals rather than stars, *Moi, Pierre Rivière, ayant égorgé ma mère, ma sœur, et mon frère* implicitly responds to the *mode rétro*. For Foucault, and for René Allio, *Pierre Rivière* was not a historical recreation, it was an attempt to stage the relation between the contemporary moment and what Foucault calls a "microevent" in history. Unlike the nostalgia film, which Foucault excoriated for sealing its subjects off from the modern world, Allio's feature attempts to open the past to the present, including popular memory, as exemplified in and expressed by the men and women who currently live in the part of Normandy where the crime happened and where Allio shot the movie. These men and women had roles in the film and brought their local history to life. As Foucault put it, Pierre Rivière's confession brings out the "tragic" confrontation of the peasantry with the law: "Allio's film gives ... peasants their tragedy ... The entire drama of Rivière is a drama of the law."[29]

What is more, for Foucault and Allio, Pierre Rivière represents an individual who "short-circuited" all the traps in which society attempted to capture him.[30] In his notebooks, Allio hoped the film would provide evidence of such tactics:

> We have to make a film that better articulates—that is, in artistic and poetic terms—what I'm writing here, and have often said: namely, that I want to rescue from oblivion, from death, these moments that are so violent, so dramatic or intense, or so beautiful, in all of these lives, these lives of "the poor," of those who do not have a voice, who do not even leave a trace (and so this would constitute such a trace), and who don't deploy any less know-how [*savoir-vivre*], imagination, courage, ingenuity, love, in order merely to exist, to continue existing, to change, or simply to endure.[31]

Pierre Rivière was an instance, indeed the very emblem, of those Foucault called the abnormal ("les anormaux").

Like Allio, Téchiné insisted that his film be shot on location, though *The Brontë Sisters* has little to do with popular, peasant memory. Instead, its proximity to *Pierre Rivière* lies in Téchiné's portrait of exceptional, abnormal siblings. Téchiné's film also deals with "anormaux," three sisters who keep their distance from society's taming institutions: marriage, motherhood, work.[32] Each of the sisters admires a fourth sibling, Patrick Branwell Brontë, whose initial artistic talents are squandered after an ill-fated affair leaves him addicted to laudanum and unable to leave his bed. As some remarked when the film was released, *The Brontë Sisters* is truly about the Brontë brother, his destructive love affair with Lydia Richardson, his inability to function in society, and his slow suicide.[33]

Barthes agreed to appear in Téchiné's film, almost as though he were trying to keep up with Foucault, who had been instrumental in getting the story of Pierre Rivière on-screen. These two professors at the Collège de France, both homosexual, simultaneously came to be drawn to film and to the genre of melodrama as a way to represent the anomalous individual in society. The irony, of course, is that in Téchiné's film Barthes embodies a kind of social success and *mondanité*, which, of the four Brontë siblings, only Charlotte finally attains. Barthes plays the role of the writer William Makepeace Thackeray, whose support was fundamental to Charlotte Brontë's success. It's a minor role, and Barthes is present in only two scenes. In the first, he is walking through the streets of London with Mr. Smith, Charlotte Brontë's publisher; in his slow tenor voice, he says: "Life is so unfathomable. I've never managed to learn a hundredth of its twists and turns. It would take forever. That's why youthful works are always full of errors . . . Life is too short for art. We need much more time to harden our shell. Hard and shiny . . . But here's the devilish thing: the shell is often shiny, and rarely hard."

Barthes may have been cast as a literary celebrity, but his words and his voice complement the melancholy of Téchiné's film about isolation. Barthes is also present in the film's penultimate sequence, where Charlotte, the talk of London thanks to the publication of *Jane Eyre*, goes to the opera and, in what can only be described as a strangely Proustian (and most un-Brontean) moment, sits in Thackeray's loge and scans the London crowd with her opera glasses. They are listening to the invigorating overture of Rossini's *Tancredi*, a strange counterpoint to the morose tone of the film we have just been watching.

Barthes as Thackaray and Marie-France Pisier as Charlotte Brontë in *The Brontë Sisters* (André Téchiné, 1979)

BARTHES AND TRUFFAUT: MELODRAMATIC PHOTOGRAPHY

If one were to draw a map of possible intersections between Roland Barthes and the *mode rétro*, one could include his obsession, in *Fragments of a Lover's Discourse*, with Goethe's *The Sorrows of Young Werther*. This fascination resonates with both Truffaut's and Téchiné's attempts to recover in nineteenth-century narratives what we might call "Romantic excess," a passion in the era of romanticism that is at odds with the technocratic ideals of France in the 1960s and 1970s.

Is there a rediscovery of the romantics in France after 1968? Besides Foucault's search for deviants we can look to Jacques Rancière's turn to Schiller and the Schlegels as a model for thinking political and aesthetic equality. But it seems to me that romanticism, as an emblem of passion, of excessive, extreme, asocial and ultimately destructive love, and as a kind of substitute for Marxist alienation, finds its quintessential expression in postwar France in the films of the New Wave and in the late writings of Roland Barthes. I must add that Barthes' writings, while remaining coy, open up the possibility for gay desire, while the films of the New Wave remain anchored in an unambiguous, even aggressive heterosexuality.

Nevertheless, one could almost say that Barthes had a sensibility close to that of this neo-romantic cinema, a melodramatic imagination fired by suffering, and by love before all else, even if in his case it was filtered through a restrained camp sensibility, if that phrase is not a contradiction in terms. A similar melodramatic imagination is at work in Truffaut's *The Green Room*, a film that is littered with photographs of the dead. When we first enter Julien Davenne's green room, we see him seated, a spectator in a museum of grief, contemplating the pictures of his wife that hang on the room's wall. Later, after he has built his altar to the dead, Davenne lines the walls of this chapel with pictures not just of his wife, but of Truffaut's personal friends as well as his literary and artistic idols: Jeanne Moreau; Oskar Werner; the composer Maurice Jaubert, whose music Truffaut used for *The Green Room*; the writers Jacques Audiberti, Raymond Queneau, Guillaume Apollinaire, Marcel Proust, Jean Cocteau, and, of course, Henry James, from whose stories the film's plot is drawn.

These photos are emblems of memory, aesthetic forms through which Davenne attempts to stop time, to preserve and retain the presence of his friends, his wife. It is through photographs that, as Davenne tells a grieving friend, "our dead can continue to live." And it is through photography that Truffaut's previous work "continues to live." *The Green Room* accumulates abundant references to early cinema not for nostalgia's sake, but as a way of placing itself within a historical and technological process that leads to the very film we are watching. In this sense, the still images force us to interpret the film not as distant from the present but as integral to it. The photographs of the dead in *The Green Room* are what help make the film a work of art in the present.

The self-conscious use of still images in moving pictures is an old problem that was given new life in the 1970s, as writers, theorists, and filmmakers questioned the status of the still image in relation to the movies. A year after Truffaut's *La Chambre verte*, Roland Barthes wrote *La Chambre claire*, a work that, in tone and in its relation to photography as a technology of contemplation, seems very close to Truffaut's film.[34] By the late 1970s Barthes had become Europe's foremost elegist, intimately tying his writing to reflections on love and mortality and making photography the surface on which to carry out this reflection. For both Truffaut and Barthes, the photographic image is intimately tied to death: the death of his wife and his friends for Davenne, the death of his mother for Barthes. It thus becomes the trigger of an intense affect, precisely because of what Barthes identified as its referentiality. This is what he famously, and scandalously at the time, labeled the *ça-a-été* quality that attaches itself to any photograph. For Barthes, photography provides undeniable proof that a moment has irremediably expired and exists only in memory. To look at an image in this way is to encounter an unbearable aspect of life that can lead to madness in the present. Indeed, one of the most striking ideas in *La Chambre claire* comes in the final pages, when he argues that society's relationship to the photographic image is based on a compulsion to "tame" this medium's realism. Photographic realism is cast as a "sibling of madness,"[35] and certain images, when looked at for what they really are, can only produce mental instability. In a sense, this is precisely the narrative development of Truffaut's film, which tells the story of a man driven mad by the incessant contemplation of photographs.

Was Barthes thinking of Truffaut when he wrote his book on photography?[36] Can one hear an echo of the title *La Chambre verte* in Barthes' *La Chambre claire*? And should we hear an echo of Barthes' *Le Plaisir du texte* (1973) in the title of Truffaut's collection of essays *Le Plaisir des Yeux* (1987), especially given Barthes' final paragraphs in that book on the pleasure of sound at the movies?[37] We know that Barthes had a contentious relation to film and that he wrote about photography *against* cinema, but the previous chapters of this book have also shown that he went to the movies and wrote about cinema his whole life and that connections between Barthes and Truffaut do exist. We have seen, for instance, that Barthes was thinking of André Bazin when he wrote *La Chambre claire*, and that Barthes' essay takes a position on the referentiality of photography that was similar to the position Bazin had made famous in his 1945 "Ontology of the Photographic Image." If Barthes cites Bazin dead-center in *La Chambre claire*, was he also thinking of Truffaut? For instance, when he chose Daniel Boudinet's "Polaroid," a 1979 photograph of a green room as the frontispiece of his book? Or when he cited Gorin and Godard's famous dictum "This is not a just image, it's just an image"?[38] And, turning the question around, might Truffaut have remembered Barthes' "The Third Meaning," the essay on Eisenstein and still images, when making *The Green Room*? That essay appeared in the July 1970 issue of *Cahiers du Cinéma*, alongside a long article by Serge Daney and Jean-Pierre Oudart on Truffaut's *The Wild Child*.

Francois Truffaut, starring in his own film, *The Green Room* (*La Chambre Verte*, 1978)

Though evidence of their intersection may be tenuous and circumstantial, Truffaut's film and Barthes' essay both unquestionably reinvest the image with an aesthetic aura and ask it to perform the work of grieving that for both men *is* the work of art. Both tie photographs to elegy, and in doing so they assign them a role radically different from the one that Pierre Bourdieu, for example, had given them in his 1965 essay on photography as a middlebrow form.[39] In Truffaut's film and Barthes' essay, the photographs are, in part at least, images that could figure in a family album—Davenne's wife and friends, Barthes' mother in the picture of the "Winter Garden." They are, in both cases, images that Bourdieu would have identified as belonging to the process of socialization of the individual as a member of a family.

Nothing, however, could be further from Bourdieu's analysis of family photographs as symptoms of what he called the "regularities of behavior" than the narratives of passionate love that Truffaut and Barthes are telling about their images. Nothing could be further from Bourdieu's theory of middle-class integration than the attempt by both Truffaut and Barthes to tie the image to a form of grief that spills into madness. In his introduction, Bourdieu had specifically opposed what he called the "activity of the amateur photographer" to the "image of artistic creation."[40] Truffaut's film and Barthes' essay turn this opposition on its head. Amateur photography, banal pictures of friends and family, become the site of extraordinary attention and excessive emotion. In both these works, the most trivial image becomes the object of the work of art's principal investment of affect and narrative.

Conclusion

From Barthes to Rancière?

It would certainly be an overstatement to claim that Barthes' work on cinema opened the way for Gilles Deleuze's and Jacques Rancière's own prolific writing on the topic. If anything, Deleuze's decision to teach his course and publish *L'Image-Mouvement* (1983) and *L'Image-Temps* (1985), and Rancière's reflections, which are energized by mid-1970s collaborations with *Cahiers du Cinéma*, can be tied to the encounter between French literary intellectuals, visual culture, and the media in the second half of the twentieth century.[1] Deleuze and Rancière, like Barthes, but also like Sartre, Camus, and Merleau-Ponty before them, were responding to the expansion of transdisciplinarity and image culture in Europe, an expansion which includes the assumption that intellectuals in their position would write about these topics. I don't think I am alone in claiming that *L'Image-Temps* was the first book by Deleuze that I read—I remember well buying and reading it precisely because it was a book on film by a celebrated philosopher. Deleuze's cinema books met "a horizon of expectation." But is it possible that this horizon had already been drawn by Barthes' writings on cinema? And perhaps, to a lesser extent, by Foucault's work in this area and his participation in the film *Moi Pierre Rivière*? Deleuze and Rancière certainly read Barthes, but could there be closer ties than this, especially between Rancière and Barthes' writing on film?

Kristin Ross believes that Rancière's *Chronicles of Consensual Times* constitutes an answer to Barthes' *Mythologies*, books quite comparable in their mutual attempts to critique everyday life: "Like *Mythologies*, it consists of brief journalistic essays, written by Rancière over the past ten years, in this case for a Brazilian newspaper; its themes are chosen, like Barthes', among various contemporary *fait divers*: expositions, political

events, films, crime scandals, best-sellers . . . [Rancière's book is] a critical history of the present. But the present itself has changed."[2]
Can we find more points of convergence between these two think-
ers? Rancière's writing about film is more systematic, more voluminous,
and more explicitly political than Barthes', to be sure. Still, there are at
least two similarities.

First, these writers share a distrust of demystification. Ross points
out that Rancière's project is different from *Mythologies* because of its
author's reluctance to occupy the position of "master demystifier," but
she also suggests that we should see this same reluctance in Barthes' collection, as we certainly do. Barthes' refusal, in the early 1970s, to engage
in ideological critique coincides more explicitly with Rancière's accusation of demystification as an intellectually arrogant position. In each
case, demystification is a way for the writer, the philosopher, the intellectual, to show his knowledge—he reveals the truth that others cannot
see—and to reassert his power and prestige over the other, the masses,
the public who are assumed not to be able to see. I have suggested
throughout this book that Barthes is a thinker of equality—someone
who reflects on and attempts to undo the power relations, the imbalance at work in the encounter between two individuals, particularly in
the relation between teacher and student; this is especially clear in his
denunciation of "arrogance" in his lectures on *The Neutral*, as well as in
his earlier essay on the dynamics of the seminar.[3]

The distrust of demystification as a valid intellectual operation was
one of the central tenets of late-1960s *gauchisme*. Through a feedback
loop, Barthes responded to this suspicion in a preface to a 1970 edition
of *Mythologies* that recognized that the methods that he had adopted
during the 1950s were no longer possible. By that point, demystification
had become a moribund form of thought in France, at least on the left.
Edgar Morin drew a similar conclusion in his 1972 preface to *Les Stars*
when, in a move strikingly parallel to Barthes', he repudiates the "tone
of ironic superiority" he'd allowed to creep into the first edition of his
book in 1956: "Criticism," he writes, "must first be directed at oneself in
order to have some value beyond the self."[4] For Barthes, the process had
become so common that, as he wrote in 1971, any "student can and does

denounce the petit-bourgeois character of such and such a form (of life, of thought, of consumption)."[5]

The problems this process raises have less to do with the act of denouncing than with the position it accords the demystifier. What Barthes questions is the dominant power, the scientific superiority, it confers on the intellectual. In 1956, he had already recognized that one of the limits of demystification is that the *mythologue* "cuts himself off from all the myth consumers. . . . The mythologist is condemned to live in a theoretical sociality . . . the mythologist is excluded from this history in the name of which he professes to act."[6] In essence, he fears the alienation of the intellectual from historical and cultural forces, an alienation that entails a separation from the world and from all forms of collective action—and these fears, it seems to me, are why Barthes points to Althusser at the end of that 1971 article which returns to the mythology project.[7] In pretending to enlighten individuals by showing them a reality that they couldn't see before, the demystifying intellectual sets himself over his readers, those "others," his audience.

For Jacques Rancière, demystification is a critical operation that sets up an intellectual hierarchy at the very moment that it attempts to destroy a social hierarchy. And it is perhaps for this reason that in 1979, Barthes writes: "I have long believed that an average intellectual like me could, and must, fight (even if only within himself) against the unremitting surge of collective images, the manipulation of affects. This fight could be called demystification. I still fight, here and there, but deep down I hardly believe in it any more . . . All that's left to do is to sound one's voice from the edge, from elsewhere: an unattached voice."[8]

However, even if demystification fundamentally emphasizes the wrong intellectual operation, this realization does not imply an all-out rejection of theory as an inherently arrogant posture. Barthes made the latter point clear in his disagreement with the Maoists:

> I think that Mao has been rather specific on this point. In the experiment going on right now in China, he does not want theory to be divorced from practice, and does not believe there should be specialists in theory—intellectuals, in other words—all this

being part of the socialist stand against the separation of manual from intellectual labor. In the New China, it's the people themselves who in a certain sense, and at every moment, are their own theorists. But I don't believe that Maoists in the West are right to work through this idea in order to apply it to the situation here. I believe that in a capitalist society like ours, theory is precisely the kind of progressive discourse that has been rendered at once possible and necessary by this society, in its transitory and presocialist state.[9]

While some amount of theory as well as a critical stance toward the "the unremitting surge [déferlement] of consensual images,"[10] are still needed, both Barthes and Rancière are more interested in the sensible web ["le tissu sensible"] within which humans think than in the promise of revealing to the masses some "truth" of thought.

A second significant convergence between Barthes and Rancière is that their approaches to film both emphasize the fragmentation of narrative. Barthes' dismantling of narratology in literature is evident as early as S/Z, but his visions of film have almost always been similarly fragmentary, whether he is writing about film stills in "Le Troisième sens" or Garbo's face in Mythologies. Parataxis, fragment, pregnant moment, asyndeton, anacoluthon: these are all terms and notions that Barthes situated at the center of his aesthetics, and that Rancière uses in a comparable manner, in order to emphasize interruptions and suspensions in the narrative flow.

Now, Barthes and Rancière are certainly not the only ones to think film this way—the 1970s was a time of great questioning of film narrative. One need only turn to Deleuze's cinema books to see the same kind of approach. What Deleuze calls the break with the movement-image is also a critical stance. It is not just the films that make this break; it is also critics, theorists, and film historians who, in their attempt to understand the process of film production and reception, take narrative action apart. Though they shared Deleuze's interest in this dismantling, what brings Barthes and Rancière together is their common emphasis on the tension between narrative and sensuality, their common desire to pay closer attention to the sensible tissu of film.

Interview with Jacques Rancière

Do you agree with Phil Watts that there is a continuity between certain of Barthes' film analyses and your own work?

I think that Phil Watts is grappling with something that all of Barthes' readers and interpreters deal with, that is, trying to understand how he went from *Mythologies* to *Camera Lucida*, from trying to demystify images, transforming them into messages, asking what they were saying and what they were hiding, to making them sacred, as if the images were like the very emanation of a body coming toward us.[1] So there is, on the one hand, this huge gap between the two Barthes and, on the other hand, Phil Watts' work interpreting Barthes' shift in a particular way, that led him to depict Barthes' evolution as being, in some measure, discernable from the outset. Watts saw another Barthes besides the semiologist, the structuralist, the demystifier and the Brechtian Barthes, a Barthes who had always been in love with the image and with a particular aesthetics of daily life, and that could lead to my work—in as much as being my precursor might be any sort of triumph for Barthes! Of course, I share Phil Watts' concern and appreciate his tribute, but I think we need to clarify a certain number of issues.

Of course, we can always say that there were several currents in Barthes' work, even in *Mythologies*, where Phil Watts indicates certain essays that seem to him to go beyond cinematic demystification, like the one on Greta Garbo's face. One definitely finds something in that essay that goes beyond a reading which denounces signs as being part of the naturalizing process by which bourgeois ideologies "turn History into Nature." In such moments, Phil Watts sees an interest in cinema running through the simple interest in reading and interpreting signs. When Barthes talks about Garbo's face, what interests him primarily and above all is the mask, insofar as it refers to theater, to an artifice that is external to the naturalizing process that he discerns in the images which convey the mythologies of the moment. Similarly, when Barthes talks about Chaplin, there is his dogmatically Brechtian critique on the one hand, that he makes in exactly the same terms as those in his text on *Mother Courage*—with the idea that seeing someone blind makes you lucid, which is an utterly incredible statement: only a truly instransigent Brechtian could come up with such a totally absurd remark.[2] Yet on the other hand, of course, there was this kind of reversal where Barthes showed us that Chaplin's politically retrograde art was at the same time artistically progressive. There, as Phil Watts saw quite clearly, Barthes was interested in Chaplin's gesture, his *gestus*.

Here again, it's as if there were two Brechts pitted against one another. There is Brecht the dialectician of demystification and distancing effect on the one side, and on the other, a Brecht interested in theatrical artifice. So from the outset, Barthes' Brechtian reading of images draws on two different lines of thought that can both be attributed to a particular Brechtian tradition: the one seeking the message conveyed by the image in order to understand how it tricks us and mires us in naturalism, and the other seeking the artifice itself in the image, insofar as the artificial is a critique of the natural or of naturalism.

We find this double tendency in *Mythologies* and in some film analyses. But Phil Watts doesn't seem to consider as important a text in *Mythologies* that strongly supports his argument: the essay on detective films, where everything is really oriented around the question of gesture.[3] Barthes makes the mythology of the gesture in detective films into something like an extraordinary Brechtian theater.

However, as I see it, this does not truly define Roland Barthes' interest in cinema as such. He drew on images from cinema just as he used images from advertising, from journalism, and from the press, which in no way demonstrates any specific interest in cinema, at least not when Barthes was writing *Mythologies*.

Was this still true when Barthes was writing about Eisenstein?

Phil Watts is right to look at Barthes' work on Eisenstein, but we have to put those texts back into the ambiance of the period. It's true that

Barthes never tried to demystify Eisenstein, but no Brechtians were try-ing to demystify Eisenstein in the 1960s. When Barthes wrote about Eisenstein to bring out the theory of the *punctum* based on an analy-sis of a few shots from *Battleship Potemkin*, what I find remarkable, here again, it is that Barthes wasn't interested in the *film*. He was interested in *still images*, which he called "photograms," although the idea was a bit unclear in his writing because he wasn't looking at photograms in the technical sense of a twenty-fourth of an image, but rather at stills that were made from individual shots, which was done at the time so they could be posted in cinema entrance halls—those are the images that Jean-Pierre Léaud and his pal ripped off the movie theater wall in *The 400 Blows*. The paradox is that the "obtuse meaning" that Barthes finds in the hat and pursed lips of the old woman in *Battleship Potemkin* whom we see in another shot looking furious—if I am not mistaken—this "obtuse meaning" is only meaningful for someone who sits in front of that image and looks at it for a long time. But it is unlikely that any filmgoer ever sees an image that way.

Phil Watts examines Barthes' texts on Eisenstein, and he is right to do so, because they are in fact a turning point. He interprets this turning point as Barthes' move towards an interest in the sensible that would lead to something like "another politics." It's an interesting idea, but to set this in context, we should make some mention of what was happening in the 1960s in France and of the enormous influence of the discourse on the primacy of the signifier, on its materiality. What interested Roland Barthes in these images—since he was looking at and commenting on images and not looking at a film—was "the question of the signifier," as he said quite clearly in one of his texts. He puts him-self in front of these still images, as he would do a decade later, asking, "What is it in this image that stings me?" At that time, he wasn't yet ask-ing exactly that, but rather "What conveys the features of the signifier?" There is this enormous opposition between the two sides of the sign, the meaningless material signifier and the signified with all of its deceits. In other words, there was a shift away from a form of criticism which was seeking the hidden meaning of images. The image takes the place of the signifier. Of course, at the time, the signifier represented the symbolic, which was good, whereas the signified was evil, the imaginary. So Phil

Watts is surely right in seeing that Barthes was valorizing the image in some way, yet it seems to me that in addition to the longer-term perspective in which he sees this work leading to me and to Deleuze, we need to put this idea into the context of the relationship between intellectuals and politics in France at the time, around 1968, and the role that Tel Quel's ideology played in that relationship.

Roland Barthes did indeed evolve, and I agree with Phil Watts about that. However I'm not entirely convinced that this meant that Barthes was particularly interested in cinema. Instead, I see an interest in images, an interest which focuses on images which were once the scaffolding for revolutionary faith, which were emblems of revolutionary art, but with a difference: what's interesting is no longer the expression on a face, but the face when it expresses nothing, when it becomes a pure set of abstract relationships, an "obtuse" meaning opposed to an "obvious" meaning. If something changed at that point and later moved toward valorizing the fetish and the *punctum*, it still did so in the context of an allegiance to the reign of the signifier in the late 1960s, as much as and even more than as an attraction to the sensible or to cinema as a form of sensory experience.

But isn't it true all the same that Barthes changed significantly at the end of his life?

There's no doubt whatsoever that Roland Barthes had a critical, curious mind; he was always able to discover something interesting in things that hadn't interested him previously, and to find different ways of being interested in what had interested him before. Phil Watts is right in connecting the texts on Garbo's face with the text about the courtier's mask in *Ivan The Terrible*. Barthes was always interested in certain aspects of sensible phenomena, although the modalities of that interest never stopped combining and changing according to the moment.

If I look for a general change in Barthes and consider the various phases that Phil Watts suggests from the perspective of *Camera Lucida*, I see an evolution that starts with the discovery of a message in the image, then slips toward the primacy of the signifier sought in the image as a signifying whole that was neither interpreted nor deciphered, and that finally, in the more recent article *"En sortant du cinéma"* ["Leaving the Movie Theater"], there was another turning point that Phil Watts sees as an apology for the movie theater as a form of sensible experience, eliminating the distinction between great art and popular culture, which gives a kind of vision of cinema as art in the aesthetic register of art, as I define it. I also agree with Phil Watts here, to a certain point, but I want to add a few things to fill out the picture.

Of course, Barthes is interested in the black box of the movie theater as the space where a particular cinematic experience occurs; he shares that with me, with Serge Daney, and with André Bazin, among others. But at the same time, what seems equally significant to me is that at no point in this text is Barthes interested in what is going on on-screen.

He understands the movie theater as a double experience. On the one hand, there's a form of hypnotism which, as Phil Watts makes clear, has shifted away from the hypnosis of bourgeois ideology that stupefies the miserable masses, just what Brecht condemned and critical theory endlessly denounced in its depiction of mass media. Barthes valorizes a different sort of hypnosis that Raymond Bellour, for example, sees as positive and to which he devotes considerable space in *Le Corps du cinéma*.

But at the same time, Barthes' position is also very complicated on this issue. He goes half of the way about hypnotism. On the one hand, he is trying to vindicate it. To do so, and with Brecht very much in mind, he defines something like another form of distancing effect. He says that what goes on in a cinema auditorium is a form of distancing effect that contrasts another pleasure [*jouissance*], perverse and fetishistic, with the pleasure of identification designed within the cinematographic apparatus. It's striking to me that what drives this criticism of the image, of the apparatus of cinema and of the duplicity of images, no longer draws on Brecht's distancing effect, but is rather based on fetishism. When Barthes introduces this fetishism, which is very present in his late texts, he is shifting from the primacy of the signifier to the primacy of the *"having-been-there"* and of the *punctum* in *Camera Lucida*. That's where, for my part, I see the main evolution in Barthes.

What I also see, though, is that no matter how he changes, Barthes remains unchanging on one point, which is that he is never talking about cinema when he's talking about cinema! When he talks about Eisenstein's "photograms," he is sitting in front of images, he's not in a movie theater, and when he does enter a theater, he absolutely never talks about what is going on on-screen. Compare this to Guy Debord who writes a critique of spectacle but is nonetheless fascinated by Errol Flynn running around brandishing his sword and by Johnny Guitar showing up in Joan Crawford's saloon. But there's absolutely nothing like this in Roland Barthes' work, that's what is so extraordinary. When he hails a specific fetishism, that fetishism is defined by its opposition to cinema as the art of moving images. As far as Barthes is concerned, fetishism is the possibility of always being able to cut out his little bit of film, his little fragment.

So, in a word, between *Mythologies* and *Camera Lucida*, Roland Barthes has completely reversed himself. The reversal is based on an interest in images that are occasionally identical, but it implies a reversal toward this *"having-been-there"* that he had radically critiqued in "The Reality Effect" and which became the supreme value of *Camera Lucida*.

Do you agree that we can see in "Leaving the movie theater" the beginnings of a new perspective in which the cinema spectator is no longer a victim of the effects of massification, thus opening the possibility of some kind of emancipation?

Indeed, Phil Watts shows us in this short text something like a theory of the spectator who, while not emancipated, is at least not alienated. But here again, Barthes' text is ambiguous. On the one hand, Phil Watts says, and he's absolutely right in saying this, Barthes is no longer thinking about a cinematic apparatus that catches people in its net by luring and lumping them together, turning them all into idiots who are forced into the perspective of the dominant ideology through the setup of the movie theater itself. Nor are we any longer talking about a theory that conceives of cinematographic space as a controlling enclosure of the masses, à la Foucault. But even so, has the spectator been freed? For me, the spectator is emancipated when you consider the viewer's role in relation to what is happening on the screen. But Barthes is doing something different. When he discusses "his" experience as a film viewer, he's describing the experience of someone who isn't watching the screen, as I said earlier. He is describing the experience of someone "touched" by the rays of light of the projection. For him, the viewer isn't a person looking at a screen, either to be fascinated or freed; the viewer is a person touched and caressed by a ray of light. To the overwhelming apparatus theory in vogue at the time, Barthes opposes an imaginary erotic experience which turns cinema into something tactile, with a viewer who is a character sitting in a chair caressed by a ray of light and eroticized by the site. This isn't a theory about the spectator's activity; it's a theory about the spectator's delicious, erotic passivity . . .

Barthes turned things on their head: what's important isn't what is happening in front of the viewer's eyes, it's what's coming from behind. That's why the title starts with a departure, with "Leaving" the movie theater. It's clearly a reversal; we don't walk in, we're coming out. Everything is happening backward, in a part of the auditorium where everything is coming from behind.

Precisely because of this type of inversion, do you think that we can find anything resembling a "consideration of equality" in Barthes' work?

If there is a reflection on equality in Barthes' late work, it would be linked to some kind of distance with respect to art. If photography can integrate a relationship of equality, as he described it in *Camera Lucida*, that relationship is with photographs that can all be treated like family photos. Photographs are things that you take in your hands or lift out of an album or a box, and spread out on a table. So it's not so much about denying a relationship between high art and popular culture, but about taking photography out of the realm of art—something that you look at in galleries and museums, on walls—and making it into something that belongs to everyone, at home, something we hold in our hands.

There is always this shift from the visual to the tactile that is central to Barthes' reversal. We hold the photo in our hand like we are caressed at the movies by a ray of light. The equality has to do with the fact that any idiot can be caressed by the projector's light or can hold a photo in their hands. If there is any equality at all, it depends on this individual body-to-body relationship. Everything happens as if a relationship of equality was made possible by taking the images out of their artistic presentation site which contrasts art with representation. This relation of equality deals with one body having to address another body. This is very distinctive in Barthes, even if it is tied up with other things that were being discussed at the time, like the shift from the visual to the tactile that we also see in Deleuze's work on haptic editing and in Lyotard's thinking about the shock—it was an issue at the time.

Yet at the same time, in the way that Barthes expresses it, he goes further than anyone else because for him, everything becomes a pure relationship between bodies, between an image-body and a body caressed by the image-process. When you get down to it, what Barthes considers to be a form of equality is this kind of body-to-body transportation. But it's obviously completely crazy, since he is writing this just as the digital image was being born, which is to say at the moment when the analogue photographic image subtending his reading is disappearing. The image will continue to exist just as the past does, as something "having-been-there" and now dead.

What do you consider the most important thing to be taken from Barthes and his writing on cinema?

The most interesting issue in Barthes' evolution is the way that he adopted different *positions*, in the physical sense of the term, the position of the gaze, of the body, of thought, with respect to various statuses of the image and of the message. When I talk about Barthes in my latest book, Le fil perdu, or in *The Emancipated Spectator*, I am not trying to establish the "right" theory of the image or of literature, compared to "bad" politics. I was studying the various positions and shifts in the positions of the gaze. If Barthes continues to be important for me today, it is not as the author of a method that enables me to read texts, or to interpret literary works or works of art, or to think about photography or film. What's interesting about Barthes is that he's a truly exemplary case of a thinker who travels the full route between two completely antagonistic positions regarding the fact of the image and the status of reality. We can't possibly say that Barthes is a theoretician of photographic art: *Camera Lucida* is not going to teach anyone what photography is. However, it will teach us what it was possible to think about images, and how they were problematized at a certain point in time.

From this perspective, Barthes will remain the exemplification of someone who summarizes, in the most stunning way possible, the trajectory of an entire generation of intellectuals over a period of twenty years. This generation made critiques of consumer culture, addressed the issue of daily life, Brechtian thinking, semiology, psychoanalysis, the revolutionary *revival* and then *postrevival* melancholia, and then returned to the nude image and word. Barthes embodied all of that better than anyone else. As an historical figure, he's exemplary.

At the same time, we can acknowledge that the exemplary figures who make it possible for us to reflect are not the ones who give us the *means* to reflect, that is, the methods for interpreting texts and images. They show us something like *interpreting bodies* who live for a long time like a very long film in which the same individual gets interested in seeing things, wondering what's going on, what words mean and how they have to be arranged, why images are organized in a particular way, what is hiding in them, and who ultimately sees that nothing is being hidden in the images, and that that is exactly why they are valuable. So we have someone who oscillates between denouncing hidden messages, declaring the primacy of the signifier, adopting a fetishistic devotion to the image and the melancholia of the "having-been-there." No one is better suited to that role in this great film than Roland Barthes.

This also surely has to do with the fact that he was never a professional philosopher. He was in some middle zone between the enlightened amateur, the journalist, the rigorous thinker, the dialectician, and the inventor of a new science who dropped it as soon as he'd invented it. We can see this as a *Bildungsroman*. Ultimately, intellectual history comes more from stories of *Bildungsromans* than from stories of theories.

Barthes' trajectory also included a demand to break free from the established disciplines, from what we might call "the partition of the intelligible." Phil Watts quotes and comments on a very Jacotot-like passage in "To the Seminar" (1974), where Barthes cites Michelet, and says that he had "always been careful to teach only what [he] did not know."

We can certainly pay tribute to Barthes as the person who created a space for thinking outside of any discipline or specialization, even if, at a given point in time, he wanted to see everything converge on a particular discipline, which was the great semiological dream, in the theoretical space that he constructed from the position that he pieced together between journalism and his status as a teacher at the *École des Hautes Études*.[4] If I see any affinities with Barthes, it is in the way that he located himself in an institution that is something of an intersection that allows for movement between philosophy, literature, the visual arts, and history, and which is unregulated by and unsubjected to any disciplinary standards, and where no one is asking, "what's your position on this or where do you stand on that"—as was being asked at the time.

For me, Barthes represents a model of something that we might call "a free space for thinking." Of course, at a certain point, he was also tempted to make this into a new reigning science, but his emancipation also came in the way that he freed himself from what he had created, whether that involved critically burdensome hyper-Brechtian positions or the pseudo-scientific ponderousness of semiology. Had he lived longer, he might have also thrown off some of the weight of the phantasmagoria of the image that marks *Camera Lucida*, his final work, and that we could easily imagine as being merely one stage in a path that would have taken him even further.

Barthes is interesting because, in his best moments, he was not doing any "theory of." He occupied spaces, and moved from one battlefield to another, as it were. Even if he never really called himself into question, he changed his *dispositif*, he repudiated it, he interpreted it entirely differently from the way he had done previously. Surely we can consider that to be an emancipated thinking practice.

Can we draw any particular politics from Barthes' positions or the dogmatisms that he pushed aside?

We can of course discern some connections in Barthes' evolution between the major political trends and interpretative paradigms. But can we draw any particular politics from that? I know that Phil Watts points to Barthes' mention of "another politics" to be drawn from a certain kind of cinema. But I think that Barthes made that statement for the sake of his interviewer. I don't think he really knew what "other politics" might be derived from the concept of obtuse meaning. It certainly departs from a standard way of reading images and films politically. Rather, the move Barthes makes seems to be one of withdrawal and retreat from any of the possible political consequences of an interpretation of images and texts.

To conclude, what about your own Bildungsroman with respect to Roland Barthes? How did you read him? When did you meet him, admire him, adhere to or ignore his ideas?

I first read Barthes' *Mythologies* in the late 1950s and early 1960s, and he was very important for me at the time because he was the person who could establish links between the grand outlines of Marxist theory and an analysis of the common objects of our everyday lives. That was something I could embrace thoroughly: it was well attuned to the vision of the world of a young, Marxist student in 1960 who saw Barthes as the best interpreter of everyday life and of the production of messages and images in the world in which he lived.

In the 1970s, I didn't read Barthes and I wasn't concerned with how he was changing. I read "The Reality Effect" twenty or thirty years after it came out. In fact, I read authors and see films at moments in my life that are completely out of sync with their publication or release. In the 1970s, I hardly read anything considered "theory." I stayed away from theoretical debate and wasn't following Barthes' work at all during that period. Much later, when I was trying to develop my own thinking about images and literature, toward the early 2000s and not when Barthes died, I picked up Barthes again and read the books that I hadn't read. I knew there was something in his key texts about interpreting the politics of literature and of images. From that point on, I referred quite often to Barthes in my work, in *The Future of the Image, The Emancipated Spectator,* and *Le Fil perdu,* because he somehow incarnated a particular theoretical paradigm and its reversal.

Looking back, I can see that for me, Barthes embodied what it meant to be a Marxist critic of literature and of images in the 1960s—and to reverse that position later on. He exemplified the reversal that made the image into a kind of reality emanating from the body itself and coming toward the spectator. At a time when I needed to think about how images affect us, Barthes was an absolute must-read, he was the keenest observer because he always had the integrity to consider all the possible consequences of the interpretive principles that he adopted. In the early 2000s, I could have read fifty or a hundred different authors on images or on narrative, but Barthes was enough. I caught up with his text on "The Reality Effect" in the late 1990s, thanks to Paul Ricoeur who, talking about historical revisionism, told me that it was the reality effect that had twisted people's minds. I hadn't read it, but I knew that I had to. And when I did, I completely understood a particular political vision of literature.

For me, Barthes is someone who incarnates the "modernist" misunderstanding about modernity—but in such a rigorous way that I find him to be an absolutely ideal partner. And he also consistently put his views to the test of examples that were in charge of illustrating and confirming them, but also, by the same token, that were made available potentially to contradict these views. From the little that he says about Flaubert and about the famous barometer in "The Reality Effect," I was able to define my own thinking about what this barometer could mean as a revolution, and develop the idea that literature was exactly the opposite of what Barthes thought it was. He saved me from wasting my time reading all the *Tel Quelian* texts—and for that I'm extremely grateful.

In the same way, *Camera Lucida* was also, at a certain point in time, a summary of the iconophilic reversal that Godard and Lyotard also witnessed. So when I wanted to think about photography, I put myself in front of the images on which Barthes had commented and I could point out exactly where he took us for a ride. When he says that he was attracted to this young man not because he was handsome but because he was dying, I had to point out that nothing in this photo suggests that the young man is going to die. Similarly, when Barthes talks about the little boy's Danton collar, I understood how he managed to see death in photos where there is no death. From this perspective, he is absolutely exemplary, and no one can take his place.

---

[1] This interview was translated by Deborah Glassman. It took place in Paris on December 5, 2014.

[2] Barthes, "Mother Courage Blind," in *Critical Essays*, trans. Richard Howard (Evanston: Northwestern University Press, 1972), 33–36.

[3] Barthes, "Power and 'Cool,'" in *Mythologies: The Complete Edition*, trans. Richard Howard and Annette Lavers (New York: Hill and Wang, 2013), 76–78.

[4] Barthes, "To the Seminar," in *The Rustle of Language*, trans. Richard Howard (Berkeley: University of California Press 1989), 340.

Nine Texts on the Cinema by Roland Barthes

Translated from the French by

DEBORAH GLASSMAN

ANGELS OF SIN (LES ANGES DU PÉCHÉ, 1943)

Directed by Robert Bresson, script by Father
Bruckberger, dialogue by Jean Giraudoux

Those Angels are no fools; they are the nuns who take in bad girls when they get out of prison, dress them in Dominican garb, listen to and support them, teach them to behave, and occasionally see their tender efforts rewarded when one of them converts or another discovers her vocation. Renée Faure, a silly little chatterbox who has just left her comfortable bourgeois nest, is one of "God's seamstresses." She has the calling but is also proud; fervent but reckless; very gay but somewhat arrogant; beloved by some of the sisters and envied by others. With her electric personality, she is attempting to save a lost soul: Jany Holt, who has hateful black eyes, stubborn mien, and bitter mouth. Released from prison, Jany has just killed the man who had double-crossed her in an earlier affair. Her calculated decision is to seek refuge in the convent. The wolf meets the lambs, and for the imperfect angel Renée Faure, Jany is Beelzebub. Renée Faure wants to save Jany Holt at any cost, but only manages to incense her, to stalk, suffocate, wound, and threaten her with her good intentions. Jany takes her revenge and using a little black cat, Beelzebub in animal form in the service of this female Beelzebub, she incites the good but timorous Renée Faure to rebel against the compassionate convent. The Angel quits her paradise but leaves her heart behind; returning at night to sneak around, tortured by love and pride, the poor little bird has lost her gay white wings and is struck down by a storm in the convent's dark garden one cold rainy night. The sisters find her in the morning—she has pneumonia—and bring her to the convent infirmary where a happy end leads her to heaven. This is the price of Jany Holt's soul; in the end she is vanquished by a charitable act so incautious that it led to death.

Many aspects of this effective film could have made it unbearable: the title, the set, the script. The décor was treacherous; we know what filmmakers make of a convent and nuns, since despite their considerable talent, set designers can never manage to create a chapel in a studio; too many pillars here, too many flowers there, too many bells and organs. And movie actresses, despite the malleability of their characters, never play nuns well; here are eyebrows that are too arched and lips over-rouged, there the effort to appear saintly taints the faces with hypocrisy, the makeup fails to cover the stigmata of a very secular life (see the end of the film *Ramuntcho* [1938]). Bresson's film suffers from none of these problems; the convent is modest, subtle, and clean; the chapel isn't over-done; occasionally we see a the lines of a cloister gallery but most often a small, sunny garden, a sewing room, a kitchen, a corridor; no organ, a bell rings once or twice; a couple of pure songs, the dialogue is simple, steady, virile. Bresson's nuns are credible: not too made up, they know how to wear the garb, how to walk, pray, and speak; they aren't forever raising their eyes heavenward or looking down at the ground; they are fresh without being touched up, gracious without being provocative. In Sylvie, the Prioress, with her umbrella, delicate mouth, and honest lovely eyes, we finally have someone who resembles a nun rather than a pimp in disguise. The images are of good quality. The dark, simple material of the sackcloth, the brilliant, vibrant, torrid lime wash on the walls, the subtle, bright gauze of the light—the cameraman moved among these three dimensions while the dialogue moves us into the universe above, where the intimacy of the convent is as warm and calming as the sackcloth; where pride and penitence burn bright like the lime washed walls; and where compassion and spirituality resemble the aerial movements of the light.

The script was also risky. Films with messages rarely work, and religious films are always hard to take, as they bring together the two worst enemies of art: an absence of talent and good intentions. Watching *L'Appel du silence* (*The Call of Silence*, 1936), a film about le Père de Foucauld, the viewer squirms in discomfort and embarrassment. But the script for our film was written by Father Bruckberger, a Dominican priest (who is also the author of a study entitled *Ligne de faîte*, on the Thomism of Claudel, Maritain, and Bernanos). I think that even in its author's mind, the script had no grand pretentions; what mattered above all was to create a tableau, and so simply to create a plot in which these Angels of Sin would be brought together for two hours on a few meters of movie screen. The subject was subtly conceived and has some depth, and I give credit to Father Bruckberger for having understood the intolerable personality of Sister Anne-Marie (Renée Faure) and the understandable rebellion of Therese (Jany Holt). It is surely Anne-Marie who triumphs (for a Christian, a good death means victory), and Goodness wins out, but at what price? During the whole film we felt that Goodness was not so far from Evil, that there was some solid common ground between these two forces, where they blended until they became inseparable, just as in life; had he not been a Dominican, this pessimistic vision might have linked the scriptwriter to the great tragic tradition. The fact that the Father belongs to the Church ensured that we receive the soothing ascension of the final *Salve Regina* which brought many viewers in the movie theatre to tears; but it was also surely for this reason that that ridiculous storm struck the good nuns' orchard with full force; for Father Bruckberger, Anne-Marie had to die. But to die because of a storm? Does one die from defeat? Unfortunately not, but we know how much both Dominicans and filmmakers, each for their own reasons, love the spectacle of a beautiful death.

The dialogue reminds us of Giraudoux's considerable talent, though not his style. Listening to this film is tremendously pleasurable for the mind and for the heart. Not a single sentimental sentence or pedantic remark, no catechism, no emotional outbursts; the dialogue is humane and full of grandeur and goodness; it grabs and holds the soul without any of the artifices of religious eloquence; occasionally it even gives us a glimpse of the more exquisite nourishments of mischievousness and tenderness.

Existences 30 (August 1943)

ON CINEMASCOPE

If, for lack of technical expertise, I am unable to define the Henri Chrétien process, I can at least judge its effects, which are, to my mind, surprising.[1] Enlarging the image to the size of binocular vision inevitably transforms the film lover's inner sensibility. In what sense? Stretching the frontal perspective approximates the form of a circle, which is to say, the ideal space of the great dramatic arts. Until now, the spectator's gaze has been that of a subterranean corpse ensconced in darkness and receiving cinematic nourishment in much the same way as an invalid does, passively through a catheter or a pipette. Here the position is entirely different: I am on a huge balcony and move comfortably within the limits of the visual field, freely culling what interests me; in short I begin to be immersed and to replace my larval sensibility with a euphoria born of circulating equally between the spectacle and my body.

Darkness itself is transformed; in an ordinary movie theater, darkness is tomb-like, and I am still in the cavern of myth where a small tongue of light flickers far above me, and I receive the truth of the images like some heavenly grace. But here, by contrast, what binds me to the screen is no longer filiform, thread-like; rather, a whole volume of brightness launches itself starting from me. I do not receive the image via those long filaments of light we see pierce and infuse the stigmatized; I lean into the very breadth of the spectacle and, emerging from a larval state, become a bit godlike; for I am no longer beneath the image but before it, in the midst of it, separated from it by this ideal distance essential for creation: it's no longer the distance of the gaze but of an arm's reach (God and painters always have long arms). Of course this larger space must be filled in a new way; the close-up may not survive, or at least its function will change: kisses, drops of sweat, psychology, this may all merge with the shadows and the background. A new dialectic must surface, between humans and the horizon, between humans and objects, a dialectic of solidarity and no longer one of decor. This space, properly speaking, should be the space of History; and technically speaking, the epic dimension is born. Imagine yourself watching *Battleship Potemkin*, no longer positioned behind a spyglass but pressed up against the very air, the stone, the crowd: this ideal *Potemkin*, where your hand can finally reach out to the insurgents, where you can share in the light and receive the blow of the tragic Odessa Steps right to your chest as it were—that is what now becomes possible; the balcony of History is ready. It remains to be seen what will be shown there, whether it will be *Potemkin* or *The Robe*, Odessa or Saint-Sulpice, History or Mythology.

Les Lettres Nouvelles 12 (February 1954)

---

[1] Editors' note: Barthes here displays his chauvinism and some knowledge of film history by opening his essay with reference to the Frenchman who invented the anamorphic process that could squeeze a wide image onto standard 35 mm film. Henri Chrétien could never capitalize on his invention, leaving it to Hollywood to do so more than a quarter century later.

VERSAILLES AND ITS ACCOUNTS

On Sacha Guitry's film Royal Affairs in Versailles
(Si Versailles m'était conté . . ., 1954)

I confess that Sacha Guitry's *Versailles* took me by surprise. We had gone in expecting some truculence in the nonsense, a pleasant showing-off, clichés, of course, but cynical and piquant in their excess, in a word, something to enliven the inner verve. What we got was everything but: a lethally boring film whose stupidity really corrupts; you come out of there feeling soiled.

Start by imagining the star, cinema's most degrading tool, and then multiply that by twenty or thirty. In thrall to a mindset where Money, meaning numbers, creates value, Guitry drowns his film in stars. Managing to do just the reverse of Hegel, he turns quality into quantity. Note that this value-by-numbers is also supposed to account for History: here, France is nothing more than a collection of names of grade-school fame. These poor celebrities (let's assume here the real faces of those attending this charming *five o'clock tea*, where Guitry brings together Louis XVI, Marie-Antoinette, Madame de Lamballe,

Robespierre, Lavoisier, and Chénier)—these nominal grandees must all be lined up as if on an abacus, handled, moved around, shifted and grouped together, added or subtracted; every once in a while a surprise "subtotal"; then a quick table and, in one fell swoop, because everything has to be done quickly, another batch awaits its turn: La Fontaine-Molière-Boileau-Racine-Madame de Sévigné, and voilà, the Grand Siècle has been "summed up."

Truth be told, this operation-by-star has its own cunning logic, consisting as it does in popularizing History through Cinema while glorifying Cinema through History. It's a deal deemed mutually beneficial to both bodies: Georges Marchal lends a bit of his erotic glory to Louis XIV who, in exchange, yields a bit of his monarchical luster to Georges Marchal. Louis XIV has nothing to complain about. Two birds, a single stone; one character, two values: a good investment.

Except that the deal leaves a sinister residue. Instead of being ennobled through this usage, it is the stars who drag History into generalized prostitution. Confronted with their historical archetype, they lose their masks and appear in their terminal vulgarity, deflated and ridiculous at the merest nominal contact with the illustrious dead. Right, so that's Molière over there, that cocky mug of Fernand Gravey whom we've seen so often slouching around in movies set in dives? And Voltaire is that venerable third-rate thespian who strikes "mental poses" while deploying the full arsenal of theatrical art? Louis XIV, that's that painted face gone to seed, whose labored artifice is an insult to Versailles' enduring and pure decor, here truly sullied by man? This is surely the actors' revenge on centuries of taboo: History in its entirety is swallowed up by a bunch of histrionics who humiliate her by trying to pass themselves off as her. (The only one to escape the disaster is Danièle Delorme, the sole actress and living being in this film of cadavers.)

We must, however, dive deeper yet in this morass. History and Sacha Guitry! Serious people have complained about the film's errors. It's truly comical to level the same complaints at Guitry as at Michelet. Historical error is something grown-ups do commit, but how can it possibly be of concern in this proto-history of imbecility? At most we can decry the fundamental ineptness of the imagery. Here the objects are by no means simple—on the contrary, they are stupidly and inexpressibly complicated. The costumes, for all the obscene flurry of copying, are dull and pinched. Had Sacha Guitry wanted to create a popular work, he really should have learned something from the costumes at the Folies-Bergère, where each period piece is false, of course, but superbly false, showing a gorgeous disdain for any verity, designed to give the costuming an epic dimension. Nothing is grand in these images: the platitude of those wigs! The History of France? A succession of head covers, like the hat page in the Larousse: a History of Wigs.

What's more, everything in this film is flabby, and you can't even use the excuse of excess: the cast's wigs are askew, their posture sloppy. Everything is geared toward an audience assumed to be comprised of idiots, whose capacity to perceive is of the lowest order: imagined to be more or less blind and dumb, capable of grasping only the crudest of signs, the sash of some grand medal, a cardinal's hat, a tricolor against a blue sky, one (or rather, many) "Messieurs, the King!" and other toys for overgrown children.

In a word, the film aims to humiliate: humiliate Versailles, France, History, the history of France, cinema, humanity, men, everything really. Going back to its truly obsessive fixation on the theme of adultery: tossing the cuckolded husband at the audience to get a laugh. It's pure reflex, one we know and can count on, no need to take it even a single step further. People are treated like Pavlov's dogs: the ring of a doorbell, a "set of horns," the audience drools or laughs, a pattern of pure reflex, drained of all humanity. The viewers are a priori taken to be brainless. This film is not for people; it's for animals. Not that that isn't common coin in French cinema, of course. Nonetheless, the Pavlovization of the viewer bears the State's imprimatur in this case, given the chateau, and likely its millions as well.

As for the chateau, it is barely visible in the film. We see a tiny bit of it at the beginning and a big chunk of the staircase at the end (both shots ruined by the actors who are dragged into them), and that's it. For Sacha Guitry, Versailles is, more than anything, an antechamber. Here is Eternal France: the room where one waits, chats, polishes platitudes, learns to be a servant. Regimes come and go, the antechamber stays—as does Talleyrand-Guitry in fact, because of the infallible logic that only the boring endure.

Versailles has thus endured—what with its antechambers, boudoirs, and nooks—and must go on enduring (says Mr. Cornu). Why? Because Versailles is a moneymaker. Under careful scrutiny, Sacha Guitry's pompous syllogism is clear: grandeur comes from money; as Versailles cost a lot of money, Versailles is grand. A second syllogism folds in the first: whatever costs money has to make money; Versailles cost a lot, so it must make a lot. Sacha Guitry prefers to argue from economics rather than from genius. He takes it for granted that his viewers will be sensitive to glory, but then placates the more cold-hearted by explaining how the investment will turn a profit. Louis XIV gave lots and lots of money so that in some future time Anglo-Saxon tourists, armed with dollars and guided by that three-headed human buffoon (Larquey, Tissier, and Bourvil), would give back to the French Republic what the King so conscientiously deposited in its savings booklet. (Was he a spendthrift? Oh no, for had that been the case, he wouldn't be worthy of respect). So History is a community of accounts, and how childish to change political regimes—right, Mr. Guitry?—since France basically equals a continuity of big bucks at good returns. What a marvel, this History of France that makes it possible for a little Louis XIV buck, hatched by Mr. Cornu, to keep on bearing offspring.

Naturally, the public is terrorized by this financial syllogism. I suspect (and for its sake, hope) that it is bored, but it's impossible to own up to that when the logic of Money coincides so well with the logic of the State. Preceded by every imaginable form of intimidation (a budget in the millions, the national interest, the charitable work, artistic restoration, ministerial support, the bevy of stars, the extra length, specially priced tickets), the film has eluded that premier act of collective censure, and the one it most deserves, namely boredom.

It isn't the least among the devious tactics of this undertaking that the viewer has been prematurely trapped in wily, half-patriotic, half-financial moralizing devised to sublimate or else to redeem this turkey through a blend of panache and *interest*, one of the old secrets of bourgeois terror. How could we not laugh at the cuckold when it's for France, and when one has paid 400 francs for the ticket?

Les Lettres Nouvelles 15 (May 1954)

CINEMA RIGHT AND LEFT

(on Claude Chabrol's Le Beau Serge, 1958)

As I recall the opening images of *Le Beau Serge*, I say to myself yet again that here in France talent is with the right and truth with the left, that it is this fatal disjunction between form and meaning that stifles us, and that the reason we aren't able to free ourselves from the aesthetic is that our aesthetic is always a pretext for conservation. The paradox here is that in our society, art is the outside limit of a culture as well as the beginning of a nature, and that the only thing artistic freedom has managed to achieve is to thrust upon us an inert image of mankind.

I would have given a lot to strip *Le Beau Serge* of its plot. I'm not even sure its author thinks it makes any sense. It might be that its anecdote becomes a melodrama because it really is of so little consequence; it might be that truth resides in the style, while concession is in the content; it might be a paradox of structure that the existence of a narrative is merely an attribute of its form. Hence the generalized divorce between a truth of signs—the whole modern way of seeing the world strictly as surface—and the pretense of plots and roles sloppily borrowed from the crudest bourgeois folklore of a Paul Bourget or a Graham Greene. A casual gaze may yield sarcasm, or affection, that is, a truth; but casualness when it comes to the subject matter yields a lie. No other art can endure for long under this contradiction; a story's naiveté quickly spoils the form's modernity. The terrible thing about cinema is that it makes this monstrosity viable. We might even say that our current avant-garde lives off this contradiction: true signs, false meaning.

Everything on the surface of *Le Beau Serge* is accurate (except when it translates the story directly: the snow is fake, for example): the fields, the village, the hotel, the town square, the clothes, objects, faces and gestures, everything that bears up under the gaze, everything that is literal, that only signifies an insignificant existence or an existence whose significance is well beyond the consciousness of the characters. A fundamental elegance infuses the beginning of the film where, thankfully, nothing happens apart from a subtle contradiction of rural life, *cut short*—a must, so that there's something to look at—by the appearance of a young bourgeois in a duffel coat and wafting scarf, reading *Cahiers du Cinéma* and drinking bad coffee in the local bar. So long as it doesn't give birth to the monstrous Anecdote, this kind of light touch works well, meaning, that it's sensuous. I for one could have done entirely without Sentiment; I would have gladly spent hours watching the unfolding of that double existence hidden entirely in its most intelligent signs, would have relished the appropriateness of a description taking on not the village itself (nothing is more annoying than a realism of the sticks or of a bunch of old drunks), but rather this patient dialectic, where the urbanity of the young dandy is brought together with the deformity of "Nature." In a word, the best part of this film is what we might call its microrealism, the adroitness of its choices. Chabrol has a capacity for *exactitude*: he knew for instance how to find the essential gestures of the children playing soccer in the street, those that convince through a "*discharge of evidence*," to use a phrase of Claudel's. Formally, in its descriptive surface, there is something flaubertian about *Le Beau Serge*.

The difference—and it is substantial—is that Flaubert never wrote a *story*. Through a profound understanding of his own ambitions, he knew that the value of his realism lay in its insignificance, that the world signifies only that it signifies nothing. Flaubert's genius lies in this awareness of—and this courage for—the tragic deflation of signs and their signifieds. By contrast, Chabrol imbues his realism with a pathos and a moral, that is to say, with an ideology—whether or not it is intended. No story is innocent: for the last century Literature has been wrestling with this inevitability. In a move at once too offhand and too heavy-handed, Chabrol refuses the anecdote all asceticism; he narrates massively, producing moral tales: *love can save a human being*. But save him from what? Wherein lies the ugliness of handsome Serge? In having had his first child be deformed? In being a social failure? Is his ugliness also that of his village, dying because it possesses, *is*, nothing? The confusion of these questions, and an indifference to the answers, is what defines right-wing art, an art always interested in bits and pieces of human misery but never in the connections between them. The farmers drink. Why do they drink? Because they are very poor, because they have nothing to do. Why this misery, this neglect? Here the investigation stops or dissipates: surely these farmers are just animals; it's in their nature. We aren't asking here for a lesson in political economy on the causes of rural misery. But an artist must know that he is fully responsible for the *implications* [*terms*] of his explanation: at a certain point art inevitably renders the world static, and the later this happens the better. I call right-wing art this fascination with inertia, which then leads to describing results without ever asking, not so much about their causes (art cannot be determinist) but about their functions.

The despair of handsome Serge *applies*, one way or another, to all of France: here is the basis of true art. And as a work of art is neither a chart, nor a balance sheet, nor a political analysis, it is through their ties with one another that we grasp the totality of the world that has shaped them. In Visconti's *La Terra Trema*, the relationship of the two brothers involves, in its intimacy, all of Sicilian capitalism; the impossible love of the sister and the young bricklayer is crushed by the full weight of the earth. Because Chabrol wanted his creatures to relate to each other intensely, his village remains folkloric: he offers a "human" drama in a "specific" framework—a formula that exactly describes the inversion of reality that Marx attributes to bourgeois ideology, for here in fact, it is the drama that is "specific," and the frame "human."

In sum, what the anecdote lets Chabrol dodge is, precisely, the real. Whether it is because of his rebelliousness or because of his inability to give his world some depth, the social geology of Balzac, for example (our young cinema has nothing but contempt for the "outdated" heavy-handedness of committed art), Chabrol has in any case refused flaubertian asceticism, the wasteland of a realism without signification. Too refined to accept politics, he is too complacent to at least give his refusal some ethical meaning. Melodrama (the insipid story of the snow, the childbirth) is the huge vessel into which he voids his irresponsibility. *Be good*? Does Chabrol think it's enough to want to be good? The real problem starts when a Chabrol film ends. The existence of goodness doesn't absolve it of its specific modes, and its modes are joined to the entire world, so a person can never simply be good by himself. Too bad these talented youths don't read Brecht. There they would have found the picture of an art that knows to start a problem precisely at the point where they think they have finished with it.

Les Lettres Nouvelles 2 (second series) March 11, 1959

ON LEFT-WING CRITICISM

Left-wing criticism: it is quite difficult to sort out this question, which touches on the very structure of our society, its illusions, and its contradictions. Especially since we immediately get caught in a vicious circle: if we are talking about what leftist criticism *is*, we must acknowledge that what is said about a film in leftist newspapers (and what other criterion is there?) isn't very different from what is said about them elsewhere. Whereas if we are talking about what leftist criticism *should be*, we can't assign its tasks without first having an idea about what the Left is. In order to make myself as clear as possible, let me replace your main line of inquiry with four specific questions.[1]

1. Must a Political Choice Inevitably Entail an Ideological Choice?

Who can answer this question beyond what the choice itself dictates? To say that man is a totality, that his choices are his full commitment, is already to take a position. But to rally in favor of "freedom" of choices (that is to say, of their independence) is to take a position too. There is no innocent answer to this question.

What, then, is the situation? How does the criticism penned today respond to this solidarity of the political and the ideological? With more and more glibness. It is well known that Marxism practices an unbridled eclecticism in France (cf. *Les Lettres Françaises*). As for the rest, with the exception of a few reviews with tiny readership, leftist criticism is "liberal." Meaning that it in no way requires that there be a connection between how it votes or what its political reading is and what it thinks about the works it sees (or for that matter produces). It takes the immixing of the political into the cultural to be the beginning of terror, seeing it as a form of Zhdanovism.

Perhaps we need to go further: the culture of the leftist reader is, by and large, petit bourgeois, and with the exception of a few sensitive issues (such as racism, for example), essentially *depoliticized*. It is quite telling that *France Observateur* has never been able to politicize its cultural pages, especially when it comes to theater and cinema: its "left-wing" public apparently in no way demands the elaboration of a socialist culture, even given the risk of errors or excess. They would probably find the very idea unbearable.

2. What Can Be the Left's Ideological Criteria?

Since the banner of the Left gathers both revolutionaries and liberals, the call for freedom remains always an ambiguous theme, and it isn't here that we should hope to find a unified left, unless we propose to cheat. No question that such unity can only be grasped in the deepest zones of consciousness, within a theme that is very general. I believe that for whatever Left we are talking about, this theme is that man is not a fixed fact: man is mobile, never a prisoner of himself, there is no essence, there is only human history. Thus any work that immobilizes man, enclosing him in an essence of love or of unhappiness, which leads us to say "man is made this way or that way," leads implicitly to tragedy, be it of the cheerful or the glib variety—all such works should (albeit with all imaginable nuance) be the target of leftist criticism. The theme of an unchanging human nature is always concealed, especially in cinema (with its thirteen billion annual viewers), where a position can't ever be intellectualized. But it is precisely because deciphering this is so necessary that criticism is legitimate. There is so much explaining to do that leftist criticism needn't be concerned about being normative: let it simply tell us what a film offers as reasons for living, for taking action, for suffering, for fighting (or for doing nothing), and the alibis the film serves up—and further, whether its model of humanity has man owing his unhappiness to himself, or to others, or to human *nature*. We'll ask it for no other instruction.

3. Is There a Leftist Aesthetic?

How could form, too, not be "committed," or, to put it more precisely, responsible? Here again we run into the misdeeds of Zhdanovism: because one given political regime imposed one particular kind of realism, and because that realism was generally recognized as devoid of all aesthetic value, the conclusion is drawn that all managed art is doomed to be poor art, which leads to a swing toward the opposite extreme, with doors open wide to unrealism, as if the artist enjoyed some special privilege and "form" soared in the sublime heavens of the universal.

There is, however, someone who has taught us to think about political engagement in artistic form, and that is Brecht. The point is not to apply Brecht to cinema wholesale, for everything is always yet to be invented. But at least we now know that audacity, and even theoretical audacity, can pay off: let's dare to demand *everything* of a work of art—not just its ideas and its morality, but also its language: man can be signified by the positioning of a spotlight [*réflecteur*]. And inversely, admirable works of deeply political language can produce an argument that is unclear and insufficiently worked through: I'm thinking about what a perfect leftist film *Come back, Africa* (1959) might have been.

4. Isn't the Politicization of Criticism Dangerous?

Once again Zhdanovism casts its long shadow. Because the politicization of art took place under a regime that imposed it through the most cruel coercion, we reject it out of hand, to the point of sometimes turning the rejection of terror into a counterterror. Is it really so difficult to tell them apart? It is one thing, and a detestable thing, to limit the creator's liberty, but it is a different thing to ask the artist to take responsibility for his work.

What's more, in a paradox that is nothing but a ruse of history, it is exactly because we (still) live in a liberal democracy where the artist is (relatively) free that his political responsibility ought to be fully developed. It is in a bourgeois regime that one must demand politicized criticism, and saying so is no sophism. Material freedom, political responsibility—this should be, to my mind, the first watchword of a socialist culture.[2]

Positif 36 (November 1960)

Response to a survey on leftist criticism. Other respondents include Raymond Borde, Bernard Dort, Marcel Martin, and Louis Marcorelles.

---

[1] I am not concerned with the ways in which film criticism differs from other forms of art criticism. The reflections offered here apply to cinema and theater but less to Literature, and even less to painting and music. Why? Because the *relay points* multiply.

[2] I admire, for instance, that Ionesco is being produced in Yugoslavia and equally deplore that there is no political critique of Ionesco to be had.

"TRAUMATIC UNITS" IN CINEMA: RESEARCH PRINCIPLES

At the moment when, several decades after its birth, cinema is recognized as the model for *mass media*, the humanities [*sciences humaines*], for their part, are undergoing an extraordinary period of development with an increasingly coherent exploration of psychic mechanisms, increasingly refined observations of the processes of perception and their consequences, and an extension of the theory of information into complex sign systems, particularly of language. All of this drives the need for a synthesis, whose privileged object is the filmic image, thanks to its dynamic and "total" nature.

We already have some indication of how this synthesis goes: advancing the very notion of *signification*, which tends to include both perceptual phenomena and the procedures of communication. The processes of signification were studied initially in a specialized area of linguistics—semantics—yet in fact, as we see increasingly, they touch upon many other human activities. Whether men are exchanging goods,[1] ideas, images, or values,[2] every social act, from the moment that it is broad-based, presents itself in a certain way as a communication of signs, which is why the study of the signifying function continues to expand and to attach itself legitimately to new disciplines.

The task remains enormous, however. To date, the communication systems that have been sketched out deal with purely intellectual content. Yet the example of film commits us to reinvesting as well in all the affective density of perception via a general theory of signification, and to seeking the cognitive or emotive elements of the filmic sign underpinning the signaling system, whether these elements constitute or contest it—in a word, to define a complete signifying *unit* as it mobilizes all levels of complex cerebral activity simultaneously. It goes without saying that this research addresses every aspect of cinematographic reality, content notwithstanding, including heroic, political, erotic, or more ordinary themes that appear together in films accidentally or intentionally.

The difficulty of this kind of research has to do both with the contradiction in nature between, on the one hand, the diachronic character of the film image—active only in a perpetual movement of being established and of disappearing—and, on the other, with the constraints of any systematic analysis, which can only use immobile elements. We could say that the filmic image is purely diachronic or temporal, while structural research implies, at least in the way it represents itself, a stabilization and something like an atemporality of identified functions. But it's exactly because the gap between genesis and structure, and between process and tableau, continues to profoundly confuse modern epistemology that we ought to address this head on, insofar as film is a privileged object of study from this perspective because the spectator experiences it as a *given*, whereas in fact it's a product, something that can be submitted to intentional variations; afterward, the image can be repeated, although it never stops being lived: thus it's possible to carry out *in vivo* experimentation, so to speak, since lived experience here is both a situation taken from daily life and a laboratory situation; finally, in films made for experiments (especially in Thematic Film Tests, which we discuss below), the subject, when asked what he has seen, aware that it's possible to rerun the bit of the film being discussed, recognizes that an event can be reversed, which changes the nature of his judgments.

We'd like to use this set of experimental advantages to address the problem of signification in film as exactly as possible.

What are the sites, forms, and effects of signification in film? And more exactly, does everything in a film signify, or, to the contrary, are the signifying elements discontinuous? What is the nature of the relationship that unites filmic signifiers and their signifieds?

For the moment, the issue is to distinguish within filmic continuity the signifying units that, *all things being equal*, are analogous to those of any semantic chain, or even more abstractly, of any coded message. Once these units have been identified and classified, we will be able to study the mental ramifications of signification by linking what we already know about how film is conceptualized to the results of a structural analysis.[3]

As to the nature of signifying units in filmic continuity, we have a working hypothesis that has proven to be a good way to make a refined analysis of the process of signification: we can use the operational concepts worked out by structural semantics based on Saussure's observations on language.[4] But we must make one thing absolutely clear: by using linguistic instruments we are in no way claiming to recognize that cinema is a language in the exact sense of the term, as the popular metaphor all too frequently implies.[5] One of the contributions of Saussurian thinking was to extend the frameworks of signification far beyond articulated language, by postulating a general science of signs—semiology—of which linguistics would be only one part. As an example of extralinguistic semantics Saussure used pantomime, a relatively simple semiological system where the relationship linking the gesture to its signified is codified, drawn from traditional rhetoric.[6] Cinema obviously raises more complex semantic problems. Like all western art, it claims to link a signifier with a signified through an exhaustively analogous relationship (which involves the myth of *natural* art). But as soon as an equivalence is established between two terms, one of which actualizes, or as is incorrectly said, *reproduces* the other (meaning an image

and whatever content it refers to), the semiological analysis is legitimate; this is how we can talk about logomorphism in cinema. Let's say
that cinema is a *logos*, it is not a language. These are the epistemological
boundaries of our analysis.

The working hypothesis here would be useless if we did not have
access to a few simple examples. Fortunately, while we await the oppor-
tunity to refine a complete set of tests concerning signification, we do
have some filmic material from which to take our first examples: the
Thematic Filmic Tests (TFTs) done at the Filmological Institute.[7] This
material offers two advantages for our discussion. First, some of these
films exist in different versions that modify particular points in the film
and change how it is understood; this is an excellent way of getting as
close as possible to the thresholds of meaning, and therefore to the signifying units. Next, although we're trying to establish purely qualitative
models in our search for systemic functions, a statistical measurement
of types of comprehension will prove essential initially for analyzing the
usual signifieds of the sequence (every structural analysis ought to infer
the signifiers from the signifieds), in other words, the normal *range* of
possible interpretations. It takes the message at its point of reception,
which is an important precaution if we hope to avoid, as any good sociologist should, speculating about the "intentions" of the filmmaker. Our
study addresses the message as it is perceived, and not as it is launched.[8]

Let's take TFT number 8.[9] The film shows a young man (YM)
and an older woman (OW). The first question that comes up after seeing the film is about the identities of the two characters: who are they?
Depending on whether the viewer believes that they are a mother and
son, or two characters in love, or even, and above all, that it shows is a
filial relationship colored by ambiguity ("mother and son with a problem"), the various peripeties appear as so many *signs* that support, complicate, or disturb the clarity of the relationship. This sort of strategic
position on human relations justifies our seeing it as the overall signified
of the TFT. We should point out that if further experimentation were
to make it possible to generalize this remark and determine the exact
degree to which filmic signifieds are defined by the relationships among
the film's characters, we might be able to discern a very consequential
structural law that is both symmetrical to, and the converse of, the one

that Propp defined for folk tales.[10] Unlike the folk tale that is organized around actions (*what?*[11]), a film's structure would be organized around the dramatis personae (*who?*),[12] which is a significant change that would call into question the universal status of the human imagination by suggesting the existence of two contrasting imaginary structures, one for rural societies and one for modern, technical societies.

We are thus are in the presence of the signified: the status of the relationship between the YM and the OW. What is its content? We've seen that when asked, viewers defined the characters in three ways: a mother and son, lovers, or a mother and son with a problem. As the last interpretation lies somewhere between the first two, we'll choose it as the signified of reference. But before inferring the signifiers from the signified, which is our basic task here, we have to remember that the analyst has drawn the signified from the oral and written answers of the film's viewers, which is to say that it was relayed by articulated language, which has its consequences: to be expressed, the filmic signifier requires another semantic system, which is language itself, and it's from this fragile, sensible contact between the two systems—the one verbal and the other visual—that the trauma is born, in that either the filmic signified immediately encounters a verbal stereotype that fully conveys it (*a mother and her son*), or, to the contrary, the signified has to struggle with the necessity of an original or impotent verb to clarify the signification (*a mother and her son, but with something disturbing between them and I can't or don't want to say what it is*, etc.). In general, we can say that the entire content is traumatic, but that it is divided into units by language.

We see that any piece of an overall signified can be localized in language. For example, from the relational signified that concerns us here we can extract an extremely subtle signified, verbalized by the single word *but* . . . in a phrase like *a mother and her son, but* . . . We can already surmise that the entire traumatic thrust lies in this tiny signified, which merely verbalizes the incest taboo, but what we will later consider above all (since we're not analyzing the content here) is that language not only provides the largest units (nouns and adjectives) for the filmic signified, but its finest, most fluid, most abstract units as well, as in our example where it's a matter of the purely paratactic expression of a relationship of adversity (the conjunction *but*).[13] So, as much as possible, our research on the visual signifiers whose inventory we'd like to establish should be guided by the smallest signified, however it is expressed verbally.[14]

Once such a signified has been defined (by studying the answers to the questionnaire), we can imagine two methods for identifying with some precision the signifier (or signifiers) that constitute the signified as a sign.[15]

The first method is to deepen the investigation by asking the subject to clarify point by point the visual elements that led to a particular interpretation: a signified, for example the choice of the YW (young girl or woman) between two young men (TFT no. 7) would lend itself to being read through the body language, gestures, and behavior that the subject recalls during this thorough questioning, by isolating these factors in the diachrony as complex, discontinuous signifiers.[16] The second, stricter, more experimental method, which however produces fewer results, is to have several versions of each film. In each version we modify some single detail, one that experience had proven was not pinpointed, or even noticed by the spectator. We then observe how these participants (who are not informed about the modification) register any changes in meaning across the different versions. There are several versions of TFT no. 8 (A, B, C, etc.). If in version B the YM's eyes linger on the OW (shot 8) slightly longer than in version A, the signified changes and the relationship between the two people is clearly deemed to be a love relationship. This second method corresponds rather exactly to what structural linguistics (Hjelmslev) calls *the commutation test,* in which the place and oppositional structure of a signifying unit are established by experimentally determining the smallest formal change that alters their meaning (for example, *pole/mole* makes it possible to distinguish the phonological opposition between p and m[17]).

We can hope that the initial results of a combination of these two methods will enable us to discern some operational concepts with which to subsequently establish a commented inventory of filmic signifiers. For the moment, we've seen that we need not study the signified in itself; it merely helps us identify the signifiers. Once the signifiers are located, they must be structured; in other words, we must discern the smallest formal element whose variation, however tiny, creates meaning, since the thresholds and amplitude of variation create the structure.

Shot 8 in TFT no. 8 (YM looking toward the OW) is an excellent example of the subtlety of the film's semantic process, defined as signifying by the test of commutation. Since the YM's gaze appears in two versions with different meanings, it can't be the trigger for meaning, strictly speaking, though we might be tempted to claim this, were we postulating (as is commonly done) that it's the *expressivity* of that look that signifies love. The gaze is, of course, no stranger to signification, which wouldn't exist without it, but in a certain way it's merely the *support* or base for meaning. For it to attain the status of a signifier, it needs another element: *duration*.[18] We initially identified two elements in the complex signifier (shot no. 8)—but neither the gaze nor its duration, taken independently, can produce the meaning that one would try to impose on it. Though each is necessary, it is their association that defines the threshold of signification. We've already called the first of these elements the *support* of signification. Of the two elements this is the most material one, corresponding as it does to a fragment of filmic space; it has a *syntagmatic* reality. The second element plays something like the role of a *morpheme* in language. It holds the signifying charge without being able to signify by itself: for the moment, let's call it "morpheme" (or variant). Its function is topmost, as it "coordinates," so to speak, the terms of opposition that make signification possible (gaze: long/short); its reality-status is *systematic* insofar as the variant it develops is virtual, which is to say that it cannot be realized *at the same time* with the same support: a gaze cannot be *simultaneously* long and short.[19] Our example now provides us with a provisional structure for a signifying unit, which we sketch out as follows, even though it should be clear that the spatial representation of these structures can be no more than metaphoric:

SIGNIFYING UNIT		
Support	*Morpheme*	
	Duration	
GAZE	*Terms of Opposition*	
	Short	Long

We are beginning to see the direction in which our inventory should proceed, namely, we should attempt to distinguish between support-elements and morpheme-elements in the signifying units we have collected. This will obviously raise several problems, including quite subtle ones, since the rule is to discern the smallest "pertinent" variation, meaning one that produces meaning. The inventory may perhaps need to be complicated by other notions, or at least by other schemata. A whole series of relay-supports may for instance exist between the initial "raw" support and the final morpheme; it is also possible that simple units $(SM)^{20}$ organize themselves into more complex, structurally open-ended units, with such units in turn becoming the simple support for another morpheme, in a pattern of amplification):

$$\underline{\quad S \quad \cdot \quad M \quad}$$
$$\underline{\quad S \quad \cdot \quad M \quad}$$
$$S \qquad \cdot \qquad M \quad \text{etc.}$$

In other words, as with any semiological system, the research task is twofold: first, to establish an inventory of the signifying units; this is essentially a matter of establishing limits; filmic continuity is cut up into as many slices as there are distinct signifieds. Then the signifying units must be compared to one other (with no reference to the chain of images) and grouped into pathways of oppositions, whose interplay engenders meaning.

This method is, *for the time being*, identical to the one used in linguistics. Nevertheless, a warning to guard against excessive fidelity to the models of linguistic analysis would be nothing more than a rhetorical precaution, for it goes without saying that cinema is not a language, and that fundamental differences will continue to emerge as research progresses (we have already seen, for instance, that language has no *supports* for signification, since everything in language signifies: the word doesn't support meaning, it *is* the meaning). All the same, oral and filmic discourse do share a basic schema; both entail signifieds and signifiers joined in the form of a sign,[21] and the sign is our point of departure.

It remains to be seen, of course, what happens to the sign when it is "read," since, fatally, the visual sign encounters the (internal) verbal sign, and language has a "right to reclaim" the filmic sign. And as this "reclaiming" can be done in different ways and be differently paced (saturation, waiting, deception, revolt), we could say that there is something the filmic sign "ventures" that the linguistic sign does not (or only barely), and it is on this level of "venturing" that trauma is probably constituted. It is, to take an example, in the instant when the duration of the gaze as a visual sign confronts the various stereotypes of passionate or else filial love that the traumatic unit arises (if the two signs are in conflict), or is avoided (if they coincide). At issue here is the problem of *conceptualization*, as discussed by Gilbert Cohen-Séat.[22] And the special interest of the filmic discourse is precisely that it consists of two articulated levels—a level of signalization, and an "open-ended" level of conceptualization. *How does the verbal code assimilate the visual code?* This is the fundamental question, to be one day answered by research we've just outlined here.

Revue internationale de filmologie (July–September 1960)

---

[1] See Claude Lévi-Strauss, *Les Structures élémentaires de la parenté* (Paris: Presses Universitaires de France, 1949); G.-G. Granger, *Méthodologie économique* (Paris: Presses Universitaires de France, 1955).

[2] Roland Barthes, *Mythologies* (Paris: Le Seuil, 1957).

[3] We have to immediately clarify that the ramifications don't add to signification, but rather constitute it, which is probably what defines the originality of film. We dissociate the two only for the purposes of the analysis.

[4] Ferdinand de Saussure, *Cours de linguistique générale* (Paris: Éditions Payot, 1955).

[5] On cinema and language, see G. Cohen-Séat, *Essai sur les principes d'une philosophie du cinéma* (Paris: Presses Universitaires de France, 1946), 117–152.

[6] The gestural code is most rigorous in oriental theater, where symbols are determined by an ancestral "grammar."

[7] G. Cohen-Séat, C. Bremond, J.-F., Richard, "Étude d'un matériel filmique thématique," in *Revue international de filmologie*, VIII: 30–31 (1958).

[8] See Cohen-Séat's distinction between efficiency and effectiveness adopted by the 2nd International Filmology Conference (1955): "As effectiveness refers to the quality of a method that makes it possible to get certain specifically intended effects, we propose here to understand efficiency, for any given phenomenon, as the fact of doing any action inherent in its own nature."

[9] See "Étude d'un matériel filmique thématique," 91, for the shot by shot action of this TFT.

[10] Vladimir Propp, *Morphology of the Folktale* (Indianapolis: University of Indiana Press, 1958).

[11] Translator's note: In the original this and other related interrogative pronouns are given in English, in italics, and in parentheses.

[12] Recall journalism's rule for defining an event, also known as the five Ws: Who? What? Where? When? Why?

[13] It goes without saying that silence can become a verbal unit in the affective "grammar" required here.

[14] Remember that the TFTs we are studying are silent and soundless.

[15] We can obviously imagine simultaneous signifiers (sets and gestures).

[16] A signified can have several signifiers.

[17] Translator's note: The binary Barthes provides in French is *pot/mot*.

[18] The duration is perfectly quantifiable in number of seconds and images. But signification is the production of an opposition (long/short), and not of an accumulation.

[19] The problem of knowing whether the oppositions in a paradigm are binary (long/short) or complex is serious, and continues to be debated in linguistics, which makes the question all the more premature for film.

[20] S = Support; M = Morpheme. The dot is a sign for combination, as in formal logic.

[21] In the Saussurean sense of sign, meaning the union of signifier and signified.

[22] G. Cohen-Séat, "Étude d'un matériel filmique thématique."

PREFACE TO *LES INCONNUS DE LA TERRE* (*STRANGERS OF THE EARTH*, MARIO RUSPOLI, 1961)

It's not easy to talk about poor farmers. Too sincere to be romantic, and deprived of the political prestige of the proletariat because they are, after all, landowners: they are a mythically disinherited class.

But Mario Ruspoli, assisted by Michel Brault and Jean Ravel, has managed to make a film on this thankless yet burning subject that hits the mark, a film that edifies and seduces at one and the same time. The film is a genuine investigation; Ruspoli lets his farmers speak and they immediately convey, through their direct, concrete language, the problems of the French peasantry today: their pitiful revenues, the antiquated technology, the generational antagonism between young and old, the conflict between the individual and the group, the demand for better living conditions and more freedom. Before our very eyes, class-consciousness awakens and speaks of its own accord.

This film is true, yet it manages to avoid the temptation of being gloomy, as its images, objects, and dialogue are infused with a certain flavor, warmth, and clarity; mutual trust triggers vibrant exchanges between the people, the landscapes, and the camera, between those asking the questions and those being questioned. This is surely why we have no impression of spectacle here and look on these images of truth with trust, pleasure, and benefit.

Artsept 2 (April–June 1963)

ANSWER TO A QUESTION ABOUT JAMES BOND

Once upon a time, our modern hero was a complete man: always the strongest, he also thought and he knew; he was the one to see things clearly. That was what we could read in the roles and even the eyes of a Gary Cooper or a Humphrey Bogart. As for Bond, he never appears to be thinking, yet has always decided. He understands obstacles but knows neither resistance nor fatigue. Not only is he invulnerable, he is also never worn out or blemished: a good-looking object that manipulates other objects, he fits in perfectly with the world of gadgets in which he lives. All of that is just fine as long as Bondism lets itself be a spectacle and always includes a small dose of parody: in his way, James Bond is a distanced hero.

Nouvel Observateur (December 15, 1965)

Answer to a survey about James Bond. Other respondents include Georges Balandier, Roger Caillois, and Jean Duvignaud.

SADE—PASOLINI

(On Pier Paolo Pasolini's Salò, or the 120 Days of Sodom, 1976)

Fascists do not like Salò. Yet, since for some among us Sade has become a kind of precious legacy, there were cries of protest: "Sade has nothing to do with fascism!" Meanwhile the rest, who are neither fascists nor Sadeans, stick to the unwavering and handy position of finding Sade "boring." Thus, Pasolini's film can't count on anyone's support. And yet, judging from evidence, it does touch us somewhere. But where?

What touches us in Salò, and has an impact, is the letter [rather than the spirit—trans.] Pasolini filmed his scenes literally, as they had been described (I am not saying written) by Sade; the scenes thus have a melancholy, cold, precise beauty resembling those grand illustrations in encyclopedias. Forcing someone to eat excrement? Excising an eye? Lacing food with needles? You see everything: the plate, the turds, the smearing, the package of needles (purchased in Salò from the neighborhood Upim store), the texture of the polenta; you are, as the saying goes, spared nothing (the very premise of the letter). Given such rigor, what is ultimately laid bare is not the world painted by Pasolini but our own gaze: our gaze laid bare, that is, the effect of the letter. In Pasolini's film (something specific to him, I think) there is no symbolism. On the one hand, there is the crude analogy (fascism, sadism); on the other, the letter—detailed, insistent, elaborated, burnished like a naïve painting; allegory and letter, but never symbol, metaphor, or interpretation (the same language, but gracious, is in *Teorema*).

That said, the letter has a curious, unexpected effect. We might think that the letter would be on the side of the truth, and of reality. Not so: the letter deforms the objects of consciousness on which we are to take a position. In remaining faithful to the letter of the Sadean scenes, Pasolini ends up deforming the Sade-object and the fascism-object: the Sadeans and the political types are thus right to be outraged, or to disapprove.

The Sadeans (the readers infatuated with Sade's text) won't ever recognize Sade in Pasolini's film, for one general reason: Sade simply is not figurable. Just as there is no portrait of Sade (other than a fictional one), so no picture of Sade's universe is possible: that universe, by the imperious decision of Sade-the-writer, is granted entirely to the power of writing. And if that is so, it's doubtless because there is a privileged relationship between writing and fantasy. Both have *gaps*: fantasy isn't the same as dream; it does not follow the lines, however forked, of a story; and writing isn't painting, it doesn't follow the contours of the object; fantasy can only be written, it can't be described. That's why Sade will never be filmed, and from a Sadean perspective (from the vantage point of the Sadean text) Pasolini could be nothing but wrong—which he was, stubbornly (following the letter is being stubborn).

Pasolini was also wrong from a political perspective.[1] Fascism is too serious a danger, and too insidious, to be dealt with by simple analogy, as if the fascist masters were "simply" replacing the libertines. Fascism is a constrictive object: it *demands* that we think about it in terms that are precise, analytical, and political. The only thing art can do with it, if it's going to take it on at all, is to make it credible, to *demonstrate* how it arises, not to *depict* what it looks like: I can really only see it being dealt with *à la Brecht*. Put otherwise, there is a responsibility to present this fascism as a perversion: who, facing *Salò*'s libertines, wouldn't be relieved to say "*I'm not like them, I'm not a fascist since I don't like shit!*"

In a word, Pasolini did what shouldn't have been done, and twice over. From the perspective of *value*, his film loses out on both accounts—because anything that makes fascism *less real* is bad, and everything that makes Sade *look real* is bad.

And yet, what if . . . ? What if, on the level of emotions, there were indeed some Sade in fascism (a banality), and more to the point, there were some fascism in Sade? *Some fascism* doesn't mean *fascism*. For there is "fascism-as-system" and there is "fascism-as-substance." Where the system requires a precise analysis and reasoned discernment to ascertain that not just any random form of oppression is called fascism, the substance can meanwhile circulate everywhere: after all, it is just one among the modes in which political "reason" colors the death drive— which, according to Freud, remains invisible unless it is imbued with some phantasmagoria. It is this substance that *Salò* stirs up, from the base of a political analogy, which here only has the effect of a signature.

Failed as figuration (both of Sade and of the fascist system), Pasolini's film is valuable as an obscure recognition within each of us, poorly mastered but certain to embarrass: it embarrasses everyone, because, given Pasolini's particular *naiveté*, it makes it impossible for anyone to *claim innocence*. That is why I wonder if, at the end of a long chain of errors, Pasolini's *Salò* mightn't *ultimately* be a properly Sadean object, one that is beyond recuperation: indeed, it seems no one can recuperate it.

Le Monde (June 16, 1976)

---

[1] Editors' note: the French text gives Sade's name here rather then Pasolini's. It is likely that this was either a copyediting error or an oversight.

NOTES

Preface

1. A bibliography of works dedicated to Roland Barthes and cinema can be found at the end of this volume.

2. For instance, chapter 6, "The Melodramatic Imagination," mentions Barthes' participation in André Téchiné's film *The Brontë Sisters*, but does not refer to Barthes' own review of the movie, "Il n'y a pas d'homme." It is safe to say that, had he had time, Phil Watts would have considered this 1979 piece whose final lines confirm the analyses of chapter 4: Barthes's interest in cinema and his personal connection to the work of certain directors are to be inscribed in a "politics of friendship." Another text Phil Watts would have certainly addressed had he had the time is the fragment from *Camera Lucida* in which Barthes comments on the automaton in *Fellini's Casanova*.

3. On this topic, though, one can read Phil Watts' 2011 article "Camus and Film," originally written for a French online journal, and republished in a special issue of the *Romanic Review* devoted to his work, 105.1–2 (2014), 133–142.

4. See the comments about *Wrestling* that Michel Brault delivers in the 2005 film by Gilles Noël, *Le Cheval de Troie de l'esthétique* (Nanouk Films).

5. See Scott MacKenzie, "The Missing Mythology: Barthes in Québec," *Canadian Journal of Film Studies* 6.2 (1997): 65–74.

6. Although consensus holds that Barthes does not appear in the film, Godard confirmed Barthes' cameo in a 2004 discussion with art historian Jean-Claude Conesa. He further explained that while Barthes agreed to take part in one well-chosen scene, he also asked that his presence remain undetectable.

Accordingly, the cameo takes place in the dark; when seen today, only the camera movement suggests where he might have been sitting during super-computer Alpha 60's lecture at the "Institut de Sémantique Générale." See Alain Fleischer, *Morceaux de Conversations avec Jean-Luc Godard*, Disc 3: "Jean-Luc Godard avec Jean-Claude Conesa" (Paris: Éditions Montparnasse, 2010). Alain Bergala's meticulously researched account of the film's production gives further information about this sequence, which initially cast Barthes as the lecturer. See Bergala, *Godard au Travail: Les Années 60* (Paris, Cahiers du Cinéma, 2006), 244–245.

7. Charlotte Garson, "Roland Barthes, voix-off du cinéma: *Inclusum labor illus-trat*," *Revue des sciences humaines*, Special Issue *Sur Barthes*, ed. Claude Coste, 268 (Oct.–Dec. 2002), 73–74.

8. Ibid., 80–81.

9. Ibid., 81.

10. Ibid., 81. Barthes constantly stressed the importance of letting ones' eyes wander off the page while reading a book. For the contrast with the cinematic experience, see Dominique Païni, "D'une théorie douce à une lecture poé-tique: Barthes et le cinéma," *Cinémaction* 20 (July 1982), 132–142, and James S. Williams, "At the Reader's Discretion: On Barthes and Cinema," *Paragraph* 21.1 (March 1998), 45–56.

11. While commenting in class on Barthes' article "The Third Meaning," Gilles Deleuze presents him as a cinephobe: "he doesn't give a damn about cinema . . . what interests him are the individual frames" (*Cours du 29 janvier 1985*, www2.univ-paris8.fr/deleuze/article.php3?id_article=299).

12. Charlotte Garson opens her article with a quote in which Barthes explains that even if the *Cahiers du Cinéma* wanted him to write a book opening a series devoted to movies, "they let [him] free to choose [his] topic, and [he] chose photography"! (ibid., 73.) See also on this topic Steven Ungar, "Persistence of the Image: Barthes, Photography and the Resistance to Film," in *Critical Essays on Roland Barthes*, ed. Diana Knight (New York: Hamm and Co., 2000), 236–249.

13. Garson, "Roland Barthes, voix-off du cinéma," 89. See also Jean-Louis Calvet, "Barthes et le cinéma: la disparition du signifiant," *Cinémaction* 60 (July 1991), 140–145.

14. Roland Barthes, "From Science to Literature," in *The Rustle of Language*, trans. Richard Howard (Berkeley: University of California Press 1989), 9.

15. Barthes, *Sade, Fourier, Loyola*, trans. Richard Miller (Berkeley: University of California Press, 1976), 9.

16. Barthes, "La Chronique: Tempo II," in *Œuvres complètes*, vol. V (Paris, Seuil, 2002), 651. Our translation. Further references to this five-volume edition will be cited as *OC*.

17. See Robert Bresson, *Notes on Cinematography* (New York: Urizen Books, 1977).

NOTES

18. Barthes, "Dear Antonioni," trans. G. Nowell-Smith in his *L'avventura* (London: British Film Institute, 1997), 63–69. For an alternative translation by Nora Hoppe, including Antonioni's response, "Dear Friend," see *L'avventura*, Michelangelo Antonioni director; Seymour Chatman and Guido Fink eds. (New Brunswick, NJ: Rutgers University Press, 1989), 209–213.

19. On the relation between Barthes and Deleuze, see Yves Citton and Philip Watts, "GillesDeleuzeRolandBarthes. Cours croisés, pensées parallèles," *Revue Internationale des Livres et des Idées* 5 (May 2008), 6–10.

20. Barthes, "Dear Antonioni," 67–68.

21. Vilém Flusser, *Towards a Philosophy of Photography* [1983], ed. Derek Bennett, (Göttingen: European Photography, 1984) and *Into the Universe of Technical Images* [1985], trans. Nancy Ann Roth (Minneapolis: University of Minnesota Press, 2011).

22. The ethical-political stakes of such counterrhythmic gestures have been developed by Barthes in his 1976 Collège de France lectures. See *How to Live Together: Novelistic Simulations of Some Everyday Spaces*, trans. Kate Briggs (New York: Columbia University Press, 2012). For "slow cinema," see Ira Jaffe, *Slow Movies: Countering the Cinema of Action* (London: Wallflower Press, 2014) and Justin Remes, *The Cinema of Stasis* (New York: Columbia University Press, 2015).

23. On the role this theory of excess may have played in later film studies, see Kristin Thompson, "The Concept of Cinematic Excess," *Ciné-Tracts* I:2 (Summer 1977), 54–63.

24. Barthes, "Dear Antonioni," 65.

25. For more on this, see Yves Citton, "Literary Attention: The Hairy Politics of Details" and Vincent Debaene, "Reading (with) Phil Watts," *Romanic Review*, 105.1–2 (2014), 111–121, and 97–101.

26. See for instance Jussi Parikka, *What Is Media Archaeology?* (Cambridge: Polity, 2012); Erkki Huhtamo and Jussi Parikka, *Media Archaeology: Approaches, Applications, Implications* (Berkeley: University of California Press, 2011); Jeffrey Sconce, *Haunted Media: Electronic Presence from Telegraphy to Television* (Durham, NC: Duke University Press, 2000); Friedrich Kittler, *Gramophone, Film, Typewriter* (Redwood City, CA: Stanford University Press, 1999).

27. Claude Coste, *Bêtise de Barthes* (Paris: Klincksieck, 2011).

28. "Interview with Jacques Rancière," in this volume.

29. Barthes, "Of What Use Is an Intellectual?" in *The Grain of the Voice* (Berkeley: University of California Press, 1985), 272–273.

30. Tiphaine Samoyault, *Roland Barthes* (Paris: Seuil, 2015).

31. Barthes, "Dear Antonioni," 63–64.

32. Ibid., 68.

33. Michelangelo Antonioni, "Dear Friend," in *L'avventura*, eds. Chatman and Fink, 213–214.

Introduction

1. Michel Foucault's speech "Voici, en bien peu de temps . . ." was delivered to the Collège de France in honor of Roland Barthes at his death and published in *Roland Barthes au Collège de France*, ed. Nathalie Léger (Éditions de l'IMEC, 2002), 103–104. The translation of this sentence is that of the editors; this holds true for all instances when a published translation is not cited.
2. Marie Gil, *Roland Barthes. Au lieu de la vie* (Paris: Flammarion, 2012), 316.
3. Roland Barthes, *Roland Barthes by Roland Barthes*, trans. Richard Howard (Berkeley: University of California Press, 1977), 54.
4. Editors' note: the idea that Barthes was not the "cinephobe" he is so often described as lies at the heart of a pioneering article by Jonathan Rosenbaum which Phil Watts apparently did not know. See "Barthes & Film: 12 Suggestions," *Sight and Sound* 52:1 (Winter 1982–1983), 50–53.
5. *Roland Barthes by Roland Barthes*, 54.
6. Barthes, "To the Seminar," in *The Rustle of Language*, trans. Richard Howard (Berkeley: University of California Press 1989), 340.
7. Commenting on the Marx Brothers' film *A Night at the Opera*—"a work I regard as an allegory of many textual problems"—Barthes explained how being a professor, professing in front of a class, is similar to the Marx Brothers, disguised as Russian aviators, whose beards fall off little by little. Barthes, "Writers, Intellectuals, Teachers," in *The Rustle of Language*, 313.
8. D. N. Rodowick, *The Crisis of Political Modernism: Criticism and Ideology in Contemporary Film Criticism* (Berkeley: University of California Press, 1995).
9. Dudley Andrew, *Concepts in Film Theory* (New York: Oxford University Press, 1984), 6.
10. Barthes, *The Pleasure of the text*, trans. Richard Miller (New York: Hill and Wang, 1975), 66–67.
11. David Bordwell, *Making Meaning: Inference and Rhetoric in the Interpretation of Cinema* (Cambridge: Harvard University Press, 1991), 1.
12. See for instance the "comité de parrainage" of *L'Écran Français*, which included Jacques Becker, Henri Langlois, and Georges Sadoul, but also Sartre and Camus.
13. Martin Jay, *Downcast Eyes: The Denigration of Vision in Twentieth-Century French Thought* (Berkeley: University of California Press, 1993).
14. See Philip Watts, "Camus and Film," *Romanic Review* 105.1-2 (2014), 133–142.
15. Stanley Cavell, "More of *The World Viewed*," in *The World Viewed: Reflections on the Ontology of Film* (Cambridge, MA: Harvard University Press, 1979), 162–230.
16. Barthes calls himself a "hedonist" in *Roland Barthes by Roland Barthes*, trans. Richard Howard (Berkeley: University of California Press, 1977), 43.

17. Michael Fried, *Absorption and Theatricality: Painting and Beholder in the Age of Diderot* (Chicago: University of Chicago Press, 1989).

18. Barthes also exercised a significant influence on Anglophone film studies, where his views were promulgated consistently in the British journal *Screen* in the early 1970s.

19. The problem of interdisciplinarity is central to the French academic field after 1968. It is the intellectual buzzword of the 1970s and lies at the heart of the project labeled "sciences humaines." See François Dosse, *Gilles Deleuze & Félix Guattari: Intersecting Lives*, trans. Deborah Glassman (New York: Columbia University Press, 2010). Barthes practiced this kind of systematic interdisciplinarity with skepticism and growing disdain. His writings on cinema also reflect this increasing disciplinary uneasiness.

Chapter 1

1. Roland Barthes, "On CinemaScope," trans. Deborah Glassman, in this volume.

2. Barthes, "Towards a Semiotics of Cinema: Interview with Michel Delahaye and Jacques Rivette," in Jim Hillier, ed., *Cahiers du Cinéma 1960–1968* (Cambridge, MA: Harvard University Press, 1986), 276.

3. Barthes, *Mythologies: The Complete Edition*, trans. Richard Howard and Annette Lavers (New York: Hill and Wang, 2013), ix. Subsequent quotations, given in parentheses, are from this English edition.

4. See Barthes, *S/Z*, trans. Richard Miller (New York: Hill and Wang, 1975). Barthes speaks about modes of reading in capitalist society and explains how the act of reading has become tied to mass consumption: books are meant to be read once and then discarded. In his 1968 seminar on the Balzac story, he applied this idea to the movies: "The ideology of consumption that reaches its peak in cinema, technologically born at the height of capitalist civilization (an alienation which we ignore a bit too often when we talk about this art form): a film, *in concrete terms*, cannot be seen more than once. This is why, perhaps, the *cultural* (revolutionary) future of cinema depends on the possibility of repeated viewing-readings: the task is to replace the *irreversibility* of vision with a new temporality, that of perpetual rewriting. Is the Cinémathèque the answer?" See Barthes, *'Sarrasine' de Balzac: Séminaires à l'École Pratique des hautes études (1967–1968 et 1968–1969)*, ed. Claude Coste and Andy Stafford (Paris: Seuil, 2011), 81.

5. Miriam Hansen, *Cinema and Experience* (Berkeley: University of California Press, 2012), 4.

6. See Kristin Ross, *Fast Cars, Clean Bodies: Decolonization and the Reordering of French Culture* (Cambridge, MA: MIT Press, 1995).

NOTES

7. See Michael Sheringham, *Everyday Life: Theories and Practices from Surrealism to the Present* (New York: Oxford University Press, 2006).

8. Barthes, *Mythologies*, 62.

9. See Kristin Ross, "Yesterday's Critique, Today's Mythologies," in *Sites: Contemporary French and Francophone Studies* 12:2 (2008), 231–242. Ross distinguishes Barthes and Lefebvre from the Frankfurt School's "disdain for the tainted and shared realities of popular culture" (234). In Lefebvre, according to Ross, "alienation in daily life must be situated in dialectical tension with forces of critique and emancipation" (234). The critiques of everyday life that one finds in the 1950s were thus often double sided. Along with the demystification, Ross continues, one finds hints that thinking about and writing about everyday life might also bring "the possibility of the realization of human needs and desires" (234), and that in order to be thought, "the everyday, it seems, must first be fictionalized" (236).

10. Éric Marty, *Roland Barthes, le métier d'écrire* (Paris, Seuil, 2006), 77: "The only reality that belonged to him was writing. Nothing, whether in his gestures, in his remarks, in his look, in his phone calls, in his laugh, nothing drifted outside a page of writing, nothing seemed able to fall into the ordinary triviality of life, into the incoherent, profane, and gray sphere of everydayness."

11. Editors' note: Between January 1953 and January 1959, the journal that was, and later became again, *La Nouvelle Revue Française* was published as *La Nouvelle Nouvelle Revue Française*. It had been obliged to alter its title to meet French press laws regarding publications that had fallen into the hands of the Nazis during the Occupation.

12. Louis-Jean Calvet, *Roland Barthes: A Biography* (Cambridge: Polity Press, 1994), 125–126.

13. Did Barthes have Sartre's *La Nausée* in mind? The novel, after all, is about looking at everyday objects—"the table, the street, the people, my pack of tobacco"—in a new, unfamiliar way. The one object that doesn't inspire Roquentin's disgust, the one thing he really likes to look at, is his hair—"Still, there is one thing which is pleasing to see, above the flabby cheeks, above the forehead; it is the beautiful red flame which crowns my head, it is my hair." (Jean-Paul Sartre, *Nausea*, trans. Lloyd Alexander (New York: New Directions Publishing Company, 1964), 16.)

14. Barthes uses the English/French term "folklore" in "Cinema Right and Left," trans. Deborah Glassman, in this volume. Originally published in 1959, several years after Seuil's *Mythologies* collection.

15. Barthes is thinking more of theater as practiced by Stanislavsky in Russia and the Soviet Union than of the students of the Stanislavsky method in the United States. Otherwise, he might have mentioned that Marlon Brando, one of the stars of *Julius Caesar*, had trained at the Actors Studio and was, precisely, an adept of an acting style that Barthes describes as "deeply rooted,

NOTES

somehow invented on each occasion, presenting an inward, and secret face, the signal of a moment and no longer of a concept." Barthes, "Romans in the movies," in *Mythologies*, 21.

16. Barthes, "A Sympathetic Worker," in *Mythologies*, 70–72. Barthes' reference to movie critics may have had in mind André Bazin, whose review of Kazan's feature notes that the union in the film seemed "peu sympathique" (uncongenial), but that one would have needed to know the exact conditions of New York dock workers to judge this representation. André Bazin, "Sur les Quais," *France Observateur* 245 (January 20, 1955), 28–29.

17. In his autobiography, Kazan writes: "When Brando at the end yells at Lee Cobb, the mob boss, 'I'm glad what I done—you hear me?—glad what I done!' that was me saying, with identical heat, that I was glad I'd testified as I had . . . So when critics say that I put my story and my feelings on the screen, to justify my informing, they are right." Elia Kazan, *A Life* (New York: Knopf, 1988), 500.

18. Victor Navasky, *Naming Names* (New York: Viking Press, 1980), 199, 206–207.

19. The film critic Ado Kyrou compares *On the Waterfront* to the 1933 Nazi propaganda film *Hitler Youth Quex*. "Atmosphère d'un mois cinématographique," *Les Lettres Nouvelles* 3:27 (May 1955), 783. See also Lindsay Anderson, "The Last Sequence of *On the Waterfront*," *Sight and Sound* 24:3 (January–March 1955), 127–130.

20. Barthes, "Suis-je marxiste?" *Les Lettres Nouvelles* 29 (July–August, 1955).

21. Philippe Roger, "Barthes with Marx," in *Writing the Image After Roland Barthes*, ed. Jean-Michel Rabaté, (Philadelphia: University of Pennsylvania Press, 1997), 177.

22. See Philip Watts, *Allegories of the Purge. How Literature Responded to the Postwar Trials of Writers and Intellectuals in France* (Redwood City, CA: Stanford University Press, 1998), 47–51, 108–109.

23. Barthes, "Billy Graham at the Vel' d'Hiv," in *Mythologies*, 109–112.

24. While Kristin Ross underscores the distance between the Frankfurt school and French cultural critics on the left, she has also shown how the work of German writers prepared this intellectual current in France. In "Yesterday's Critique, Today's Mythologies," 233, she asserts that "Thinking about the moment of Barthes and Lefebvre makes it clear that it was the Germans— Simmel, Kracauer, Walter Benjamin and later Wolfgang Schivelbusch—who in fact *invented* French cultural studies at an earlier moment, beginning in the 1930s. They invented it with their intricate analysis of 19th century Paris . . . But it was the French themselves who set out after World War II to debate the discontents and anxieties surrounding modernization ideology and the adoption of American-style consumption practices in an array of interdisciplinary experiments."

NOTES

25. Bazin's article appeared in *L'Écran Français*, December 17, 1946. It has been translated by Hugh Gray in Bazin, *What is Cinema?* Volume II (Berkeley: University of California Press, 1971), 158–162.
26. Barthes, "Romans in the Movies," in *Mythologies*, 20.
27. Henri-François Rey, "Hollywood fabrique des mythes comme Ford des voitures," *L'Écran Français* 150 (May 11, 1948), 6.
28. Jean Thévenot, "Le cinéma garde-mythes: le médecin (façon Hollywood)," *L'Écran Français* 317 (August 1–7, 1951), 12–13.
29. Edgar Morin, *Les Stars* [1957] (Paris: Seuil, 1972), 7. The preface to the 1972 edition does not appear in the English translation.
30. Morin, *The Stars*, trans. Richard Howard (Minneapolis: University of Minnesota Press, 2005), 145. Chapter 3 is titled "The Stellar Liturgy."
31. Barthes, *Mythologies*, 274.
32. Editors' note: The term *doxa* recurs throughout *Roland Barthes by Roland Barthes*, trans. Richard Howard (Berkeley: University of California Press, 1977); see especially Barthes' text "Doxa/Paradoxa" on page 71. See also Anne Herschberg-Pierrot, "Barthes and Doxa," *Poetics Today* 23.3 (2002), 427–442.
33. Barthes, "Angels of Sin," trans. Deborah Glassman, in this volume.
34. See, for example, "Dominici, or the Triumph of Literature" in *Mythologies* about the trial of the shepherd Gaston Dominici. Condemning the prosecution's abuse of power during the trial, Barthes writes that Dominici was judged by a system that transformed an event, the murder of British tourists, into a rhetorical display: "Antitheses, metaphors, flights of oratory, it is the whole of classical rhetoric which accuses the old shepherd here" (51).
35. Philippe Roger clarifies this point: "In the early 1950s, theatre had thus become for Barthes what literature could not be. In *Writing Degree Zero*, Barthes had condemned modern literature to exposing only the impasse of a divided society and to bearing testimony, through a degraded and compromised language, of its own impotency. Not so with theater. While no new language could be pure enough to quench the writer's thirst, the wind now blowing on the stage would relieve and revive those 'Frenchmen like me [R. B.] stifling under the bourgeois evil.' When literature could be no more than an 'empty sign,' theatre emerged in Barthes' provisional *Weltanschauung* as the greatest of expectations for mind and body and the collective body of society: for 'theatre is in advance emasculated if one does not crave it with one's entire body, and if that craving is not shared by an entire community.' . . . A global experience by nature, a civic medium by tradition, theater and only theater, in Barthes' view, can bring together what bourgeois society has divided: art and politics, classes and languages." Roger, "Barthes with Marx," 183–184.
36. Barthes, *Mythologies*, 274.

NOTES

37. The term is from Harold Beaver's 1981 essay "Homosexual Signs (*In Memory of Roland Barthes*)," published in *Critical Inquiry* 8:1 (Autumn 1981) and reprinted in *Camp: Queer Aesthetics and the Performing Subject* ed. Fabio Cleto (Ann Arbor: University of Michigan Press, 1999).
38. Susan Sontag, "Notes On 'Camp,'" in *Camp*, 61. See also Gerald Mast and Marshall Cohen eds., *Film Theory and Criticism: Introductory Readings* (New York: Oxford University Press, 1974), Parker Tyler, "The Garbo Image," in *The Films of Greta Garbo*, ed. Michael Conway et al. (New York: The Citadel Press, 1963) and Greg Taylor, *Artists in the Audience: Cults, Camp, and American Film Criticism* (Princeton, NJ: Princeton University Press, 2001). It seems likely that American film students in the 1970s first encountered Barthes through this essay, which was included in the 1974 edition of the Mast anthology. Surprisingly, it appeared in a section of articles debating "auteur theory" as support for the argument that an actor could be as important as a director.
39. See Morin, *The Stars*, 99–109, esp. 102. But a crucial section about the new star as "neurotic hero" is lost in the abridged English version. "James Dean introduces a new kind of hero . . . the hero as washout, the tormented hero, the hero with problems, even with neuroses . . . the evil is inside him, he's caught up in a living contradiction, in impotence, in hope, in errant quests. As such, James Dean inaugurated the era of heroes from modern adolescence." *Les Stars* (Seuil, 1972), 146. This passage, translated here by the editors, was added by Morin for the later edition and does not appear in the 1957 original in either English or French.
40. See Jacques Doniol-Valcroze's review of *Sabrina* in *France Observateur* (February 10, 1955).
41. André Bazin, "La Reine Christine," in *France Observateur* (February 17, 1955), 30–31.

Chapter 2

1. Roland Barthes, "Préface à Stendhal, *Quelques promenades dans Rome*" (La Guilde du Livre, 1957), collected in *OC I*, 913–914.
2. The source for Barthes' use of this term is most likely Edgar Morin's *Cinema or the Imaginary Man*, trans. Lorraine Mortimer (Minneapolis: University of Minnesota Press, 2005), published in French in 1956. Quoting earlier theorists, Morin defines *photogénie* as "'that extreme poetic aspect of beings and things' (Delluc), 'that poetic quality of beings and things' (Moussinac), 'capable of being revealed to us only by the cinematographe' (both Moussinac and Delluc)" (15). He adds, "Everything unfolds as if, before the photographic image, empirical sight were doubled by oneiric vision, analogous to what

Rimbaud called *voyance*" (16). According to Jean Epstein, the poetry of cinema, *photogénie*, resides outside of plot ("De quelques conditions de la photogénie," *Cinéa-Ciné pour tous* 19 (August 15, 1924), 6–8). See Christophe Wall-Romana, "Epstein's photogénie as Corporeal Vision: Inner Sensation, Queer Embodiment, and Ethics," in Sarah Keller and Jason Paul, eds., *Jean Epstein: Critical Essays and New Translations* (Amsterdam: Amsterdam University Press, 2012), 51–72.

3. Barthes, "On CinemaScope," trans. Deborah Glassman, in this volume.
4. Walter Benjamin, "The Work of Art in the Age of Mechanical Reproduction," in *Illuminations: Essays and Reflections* (New York: Schocken Books, 1968), 234.
5. Barthes, "The Poor and the Proletariat," in *Mythologies*, 35–37.
6. François Truffaut, "Sacha Guitry the Villain," in *The Films in My Life* (New York: Simon and Shuster, 1978), 216–218.
7. François Truffaut (writing under the pseudonym R. L.), "Si Versailles m'était conté," *Cahiers du Cinéma* 34 (April 1954), 64.
8. For many years, Guitry had been known as a comic, somewhat *mondain* personality whose films almost always reached a large audience despite the fact that his opportunism and reactionary politics had led him to support Pétain and the Vichy government during the Occupation. In the wake of his 1944 film *MCDXXIX-MCMXLII (De Jeanne d'Arc à Philippe Pétain)* as well as his public pronouncements in favor of the Vichy régime, he was jailed for sixty days at the Liberation. See Jean-Pierre Bertin-Maghit, *Le Cinéma français sous l'Occupation* (Paris: Perrin, 2002), 230–235 [Editors' note: As counterpoint to Watts' argument, we should point out that Guitry's films were equally important to filmmakers on the political left after the war, especially Alain Resnais and Nicole Vedrès. For complimentary, and sometimes contrasting analysis of Guitry's career in pictures, see *Sacha Guitry, Cinéaste*, Philippe Arnaud, ed. (Crisnée: Éditions Yellow Now, 1993). On Guitry's support for Pétain and the film *MCDXXIX-MCMXLII*, see Bernard Eisenschitz, "De Jeanne d'Arc à Philippe Pétain," http://lemagazine.jeudepaume.org/2013/03/bernard-eisenschitz-de-jeanne-darc-a-philippe-petain/, and Ivone Margulies, "Sacha Guitry, National Portraiture and the Artist's Hand," *French Cultural Studies* 16:3 (2005), 241–258.]
9. Barthes, "Versailles and its Accounts," trans. Deborah Glassman, in this volume.
10. André Bazin makes the same point. In a later review of Guitry's *Napoléon*, he writes: "Starting from *Si Versailles m'était conté*, Sacha Guitry . . . understood that highly expensive films earn even more money than those made cheaply. . . *Si Versailles* thus combined an indecently penurious technique with luxurious casting, decor (natural) and costumes," *France Observateur* 255 (March 31, 1955), 30.

11. Michel Marie, *The French New Wave: An Artistic School*, trans. Richard Neupert (Malden, MA: Blackwell Publishing, 2003), 12–13.
12. Barthes, "Cinema Right and Left," trans. Deborah Glassman, in this volume.
13. Ibid. Barthes does not develop exactly what he means by "Flaubertian asceticism," but one can think of the pages of *Writing Degree Zero* in which he analyzes Flaubert's rejection of plot in favor of a "*Gregorian codification* of literary *language*" that signifies nothing beyond itself and that "transmutes the writing handed down to him [the writer] by history into an *art*" (*Writing Degree Zero*, trans. Annette Laver and Colin Smith [New York: Hill & Wang, 1968]), 65.
14. "*L'Express* talks with Roland Barthes," in *The Grain of the Voice: Interviews 1962–1980* (New York: Hill and Wang, 1985), 95.
15. Editors' note: On the *doxa*, see especially Barthes' text "Doxa/Paradoxa" in *Roland Barthes by Roland Barthes*, trans. Richard Howard (Berkeley: University of California Press, 1977), 71.
16. Barthes was well acquainted with *Positif*. Given his prominence at the time, his previous writing on film, and his critique of Chabrol, it is not surprising that the review would ask him to respond to a survey on criticism and the left published in their November 1960 issue. See his answer, "On Left-Wing Criticism," trans. Deborah Glassman, in this volume.
17. Robert Benayoun, "The Emperor Has No Clothes," trans. Peter Graham in *The French New Wave: Critical Landmarks*, in G. Vincendeau and Graham, eds. (London: British Film Institute, 2009), esp. 163–168. The original appeared in *Positif* 46 (June 1962), 1–14. [Editors' note: Indeed Truffaut, Godard, and Rohmer all wrote copiously for *Arts*, though Chabrol did not. See the impressive dossier of essays on this fascinating journal, collected in *Film Criticism* XXXIX: 1 (Winter 2015), particularly Marc Dambre, "*Arts* and the Hussards in Their Time," which establishes the alliance of Truffaut, Rohmer, and Godard with Jacques Laurent, publisher of *Arts* and a Vichy apologist, as well as a staunch supporter of French Algeria.]
18. Bernard Dort, "Lettre à Claude Chabrol," *Les Temps Modernes* 158 (April 1959), 1673–1681.
19. Barthes also finds such materialism present in the photographic portraits that Agnès Varda and Thérèse Le Prat made of French actors. See "Visages et Figures," in *OC I*, 273. This essay was partially reprinted as "The Harcourt Actor" in *Mythologies*, 15–18.
20. Editors' note: This quote appears in publicity material Argos Films prepared for *Chronicle of a Summer*. See Anatole Dauman, *Souvenir-écran* (Paris: Éditions du Centre Pompidou, 1989), 136.
21. Barthes, "Preface to *Les Inconnus de la terre*," trans. Deborah Glassman, in this volume. This brief article originally appeared in Argos Film's pressbook *Les Inconnus de la terre. Une enquête cinématographique de Mario Ruspoli, rédigée*

par Jean Ravel, Paris, Argos Films, 1962, [n.p.]. It received its first commercial publication in *Artsept* 2 (April–June 1963), 76.

22. See Colin MacCabe, *Godard: A Portrait of the Artist at 70* (London: Bloomsbury, 2003), 103, where he refers to Truffaut's article excoriating the journal *Positif*. François Truffaut, "*Positif*: Copie zéro," *Cahiers du Cinéma* 79 (Jan. 1958), 60–62.

23. On the importance of these interviews as the journal moves from classicism to modernity, see Antoine de Baecque, *Les Cahiers du Cinéma, Histoire d'une revue Tome II: Cinéma, tours détours 1959–1981* (Paris: Cahiers du Cinéma, 1991).

24. Barthes, "Towards a Semiotics of Cinema: Interview with Michel Delahaye and Jacques Rivette," in Jim Hillier, ed., *Cahiers du Cinéma 1960–1968* (Cambridge, MA: Harvard University Press, 1986), 276. Further citations to this translated interview are provided as page numbers in parentheses.

Chapter 3

1. Paul Willemen, "Reflections on Eikhenbaum's Concept of Internal Speech in the Cinema," *Screen* 15.4 (Winter 1974/75), 59–70.

2. Roland Barthes, *Camera Lucida: Reflections on Photography*, trans. Richard Howard (New York: Hill and Wang, 1981), 115.

3. See Colin MacCabe, "Barthes and Bazin," in *Writing the Image After Roland Barthes*, ed. Jean-Michel Rabaté (Philadelphia: University of Pennsylvania Press, 1997); Dudley Andrew, "The Ontology of a Fetish," *Film Quarterly* 61:4 (Summer 2008), 62–66; Adam Lowenstein, "The Surrealism of the Photographic Image: Bazin, Barthes, and the Digital *Sweet Hereafter*," *Cinema Journal* 46:3 (Spring, 2007), 54–82.

4. André Bazin, "Nous autres chevaliers de l'avant-garde," *Combat* 1565 (July 16, 1949).

5. Bazin, "Will CinemaScope Save the Cinema?" in *André Bazin's New Media*, trans. Dudley Andrew (Berkeley: University of California Press, 2014), 267–287. "Le cinémascope sauvera-t-il le cinéma?" originally appeared in *Esprit* 21:207–208 (October–November 1953), 672–683. Bazin's article is a summary of the state of Hollywood in 1953 and ends with an enthusiastic endorsement of CinemaScope, as a way of renewing the potential of cinema. Still, Bazin has some doubts about the new technology and, in his conclusion, he asks these two questions: "What the cinema gains for its spectacular genres, doesn't it give up in psychological resources and, more generally, in its capacity for intellectual expression, which is to say precisely in its more evolved genres? Spread out across this bay window that now may replace the older rectangle, what will become of the sacrosanct close-up, the cornerstone

of montage?" (284). Barthes, for his part, rejoices in this technological revolution: "The close-up may not survive, or at least its function will change: kisses,
drops of sweat, psychology, this may all merge with the shadows and the
background." See "On CinemaScope," in this volume.

6. Bazin, "Sur les Quais," France Observateur 245 (January 20, 1955), 28–29.
7. Barthes, "Comment Démystifier," Les Lettres Nouvelles 25 (March 1955)
478–480. When he republished the essay in Mythologies Barthes changed
the title to "A Sympathetic Worker" ["Un ouvrier sympathique"]. Barthes,
Mythologies: The Complete Edition, trans. Richard Howard and Annette
Lavers (New York: Hill and Wang, 2013), 70–72.
8. Bazin, "La Reine Christine," France Observateur 249 (February 17, 1955),
30–31.
9. Bazin, "Continent Perdu," France Observateur 296 (January 12, 1956), 18.
10. Barthes, "Continent Perdu," in Mythologies: The Complete Edition, 184–186.
11. In his response to a Positif questionnaire on left-wing criticism in 1960,
Barthes asserted that cultural criticism from the left was nearly inexistent in
France. He cites as an example France Observateur, which he claims, in a line
that downplays the work he and Bazin were doing for the weekly, "has never
been able to politicize its cultural pages, especially when it comes to theater
and cinema" ("On Left-Wing Criticism," in this volume).
12. Vincent Debaene, Far Afield: French Anthropology between Science and
Literature, trans. Justin Izzo (Chicago: University of Chicago Press, 2014).
13. On Bazin's relation to academic criticism see Dudley Andrew's "The Core
and The Flow of Film Studies," Critical Inquiry 35:4 (Summer 2009). Andrew
uncovers an article in which Bazin "cattily reports" on the success of Cohen-
Séat, one of the very few university professors of film in the 1950s. As Andrew
makes clear, Bazin's article gives voice to a struggle taking place between
cinephiles and the academics at the Institut de Filmologie, who showed a "calculated disinterest" in films but who had managed to wrangle institutional
support from the Sorbonne. Barthes, it seems to me, is somewhere between
the cinephile and the scientist.
14. Hervé Joubert-Laurencin, "A Binocular Preface," in Opening Bazin: Postwar
Film Theory and its Afterlife, ed. Dudley Andrew and Hervé Joubert-Laurencin
(Oxford: Oxford University Press, 2011), xiv. See also Colin MacCabe,
"Barthes and Bazin," where he writes (in Rabaté, Writing the Image After
Roland Barthes, 75): "Bazin's Catholic humanism and realist aesthetic had
banished him from the theoretical reading lists of the 1960s and 1970s."
15. Barthes, "Rhetoric of the Image," in Image, Music, Text, trans. Stephen Heath
(New York: Hill and Wang, 1977), 32–51.
16. Barthes, "Rhetoric of the Image," 44.
17. Three years before, in the very first issue of Communications (1961, pages
220–222) while reviewing a volume titled Civilisation de l'image (recherches

et débats du Centre Catholique des Intellectuels Français), Barthes had put into question the very possibility of "an 'ontology' of the image," describing the word "ontology" as "evasive," and adding that only Sartre's book *The Imaginary* had gotten close to a convincing classification of the image. See Roland Barthes, "La Civilisation de l'image," in *OC II*, 564–566. Editors' note: This review appears right after Claude Bremond's review of Bazin's *Qu'est-ce que le cinéma?* vol. 3, "Cinéma et Sociologie."

18. Bazin, "The Ontology of the Photographic Image" in *What is Cinema?* vol. 1, trans. Hugh Grey (Berkeley: University of California Press, 2005), 13. This essay first appeared in English in *Film Quarterly* 13:4 (Summer, 1960), 4–9.

19. Editors' note: The original edition of Lévi-Strauss' phenomenally successful *La Pensée Sauvage* bore a botanical drawing of a *viola tricolor* on its cover. The common French term for this flower is a homonym of the book's title and translates as "wild pansy."

20. Barthes, "Towards a Semiotics of Cinema: Interview with Michel Delahaye and Jacques Rivette," in Jim Hillier, ed., *Cahiers du Cinéma 1960–1968* (Cambridge, MA: Harvard University Press, 1986), 277.

21. Ibid., 281–282.

22. Barthes, "Cinema Right and Left," trans. Deborah Glassman, in this volume.

23. Adam Lowenstein, "The Surrealism of the Photographic Image," 54, 57.

24. Barthes, "Préface à Stendhal, *Quelques promenades dans Rome*," in *OC I*, 914.

25. Bazin, "The Ontology of the Photographic Image," 15.

26. See Barthes, "Dear Antonioni," trans. G. Nowell-Smith in his *L'avventura* (London: British Film Institute, 1997), 63–69.

27. Jean-Paul Sartre, *The Imaginary: A Phenomenological Psychology of the Imagination*, (New York: Routledge, 2004), 181. Barthes uses the expression "*cela a été*" ("that has been," "that once existed") on several occasions in his writing career. In *The Pleasure of the Text*, he mentions how much he enjoys reading the details of the "daily life" of characters—schedules, habits, meals, clothes, etc. All this constitutes what Barthes calls the *cela a été* of the characters' reality. See *The Pleasure of the Text*, trans. Richard Miller (New York: Hill and Wang, 1975), 53, or the original French in *OC IV*, 252.

28. Bazin, *What is Cinema?* trans. Timothy Barnard (Montreal: Caboose, 2009), 193. For an alternate translation, see *What is Cinema?* vol. 1, trans. Hugh Gray, 105.

29. Pascal Bonitzer writes: "The visual field in cinema doubles as a blind field. The screen is a mask and vision is always partial." See his *Le Champ aveugle* (Paris: Cahiers du Cinéma, 1982), 96.

30. Adam Lowenstein, "The Surrealism of the Photographic Image," 63.

31. Barthes, "Dear Antonioni," 68.

32. Bazin, "Evolution of the Language of Cinema," in *What is Cinema?* vol. 1, 35–36.

Chapter 4

1. Editors' note: Barthes' essay uses the French spelling "Nordine." In 1970 Saïl founded *Cinéma 3*, a film journal linked with the Fédération Marocaine des Ciné-Clubs. The title of this journal, which Barthes mentions in the dedication, is a reference to Fernando Solanas and Octavio Getino's 1969 manifesto "Towards a Third Cinema." In their preface to the first issue, the editors open its pages to anyone who wishes to contribute to the "emergence and development" of an authentic Third World cinema, and Barthes is listed as one of the contributors to (or a subject of?) a forthcoming volume. Although the promised collaboration never took place, this web of connections underscores the extent to which Barthes' title "The Third Meaning" carries faint yet deliberate echoes of the Third World project, and the politicized struggle for a Third Cinema that was being waged at the time. See "Cinéma 3," *Cinéma 3* 1:1 (January 1970), 3–5.

2. Roland Barthes, "The Third Meaning," in *Image, Music, Text* trans. Stephen Heath (New York: Hill and Wang, 1977), 59. Subsequent page references to this article come from this collection and appear in parentheses.

3. See, for example, Sergei Eisenstein, *Réflexions d'un cinéaste* (Moscow: Éditions en langues étrangères, 1958); *Ma conception du cinéma* (Paris: Buchet-Chastel, 1971). *Cahiers du Cinéma* featured texts by and about Eisenstein in almost every issue from number 208 (January 1969) to number 234/235 (January/February 1972). Between 1973 and 1980, writers associated with Cahiers prepared a series of books which presented the filmmaker's major writings to a French audience: *Mettre en Scène* (Paris: Union Générale des Éditions, 1973); *Au-delà des étoiles* (Paris: UGE, 1974); *La non-indifférente nature* (2 vols, Paris: Union Générale d'Éditions, 1976/1978) and *Mémoires* (3 vols, Paris: Union Générale d'Éditions, 1978/1980). Several other books and catalogues appeared in France during this period; for a detailed list, see www.cinematheque.fr/sites-documentaires/eisenstein/index.php.

4. Editors' note: 1968 produced a complex set of relations between the PCF and such radicalized journals as *Cahiers du Cinéma, Cinéthique*, and *Tel Quel*. In some ways, this post-'68 period was the closest that the critical left came to the Party itself. Barthes' pieces on Eisenstein, however, prefer to sidestep questions of ideological allegiance and move, as Watts suggests, from politics proper to micropolitics.

5. Adam Lowenstein, "The Surrealism of the Photographic Image: Bazin, Barthes, and the Digital *Sweet Hereafter*," *Cinema Journal* 46:3 (Spring, 2007), 64.

6. Victor Burgin, "Barthes' Discretion," in *Writing the Image After Roland Barthes*, ed. Jean-Michel Rabaté (Philadelphia: University of Pennsylvania Press, 1997), 27.

7. Barthes, "Diderot, Brecht, Eisenstein," in *Image, Music, Text*, 69–78. Citations from this English edition will be given in parenthesis. Barthes mentions "découpage" immediately in this essay. His use of this term follows the etymology of "couper" (to cut), which, while it may be common in art history, is out of synchronization with how the term developed in postwar French film theory. André Bazin employed it extensively in his essays on Welles and particularly in his long essay "William Wyler, Jansenist of Mise-en-scene," where it generally refers to the filmmaker's initial plan or layout of how a scene will be organized to appear on-screen. And so, while it does involve cutting (i.e., editing), it equally involves the mise-en-scene, or distribution of actors and props within the setting, and the placement and movement of the camera to cover the situation. For a complete discussion of this fascinating term, see Timothy Barnard, *Découpage* (Montreal: Caboose Press, 2015).

8. Philippe Roger, "Barthes with Marx," in *Writing the Image After Roland Barthes*, 182.

9. Réda Bensmaïa, *The Barthes Effect: The Essay as Reflective Text*, trans. Pat Fedkiew (Minneapolis: University of Minnesota Press, 1987). See especially 42–45, from which the quotations in this paragraph are drawn.

10. Sylvia Harvey, *May '68 and Film Culture* (London: British Film Institute, 1980), 45.

11. Antoine de Baecque, *Les Cahiers du Cinéma: Histoire d'une revue Tome II: Cinéma, tours détours 1959–1981* (Paris: Cahiers du Cinéma, 1991), 221.

12. Though Barthes did make a brief but crucial reference to *Battleship Potemkin* in his 1954 essay on CinemaScope. See chapter 2 as well as the translation of this essay in this volume.

13. Cahiers had asked to interview Barthes, but he declined, offering to submit a text instead: "The Third Meaning." See Jean Narboni, *La Nuit sera noire et blanche* (Paris: Capricci, 2015), 32–34.

14. See Julien Bourg, *From Revolution to Ethics: May 1968 and Contemporary French Thought* (Montreal: McGill-Queens University Press, 2007); Jacques Rancière, *Althusser's Lesson*, trans. Emiliano Battista (London: Continuum Books, 2011); Kristin Ross, *May '68 And Its Afterlives* (Chicago: University of Chicago Press, 2002).

15. Wole Soyinka, *The Critic and Society: Barthes, Leftocracy and Other Mythologies* (Ile-Ife: University of Ife Press, 1982). Citations henceforth are to pages of this book given in parentheses.

16. Steven Ungar, *Roland Barthes, The Professor of Desire* (Lincoln: University of Nebraska Press, 1983), 153.

17. Thomas Waugh, *The Fruit Machine: Twenty Years of Writings on Queer Cinema* (Durham, NC: Duke University Press, 2000), 59.

Chapter 5

1. Two articles by Barthes exemplify this approach, both published in 1960 in *La Revue Internationale de Filmologie*: "Le problème de la signification au cinéma" (no. 32–33) and "Les 'unités traumatiques' au cinéma" (no. 34). The latter essay can be found in translation at the end of this volume. See also Vincent Debaene's *Far Afield* on Barthes' view of the relationship between literature and anthropology (Chicago: University of Chicago Press, 2014, 299–302).

2. Roland Barthes, "From Science to Literature," in *The Rustle of Language*, trans. Richard Howard (Berkeley: University of California Press 1989), 3.

3. Barthes, "'Traumatic Units' in Cinema," trans. Deborah Glassman, in this volume. "La vedette: enquêtes d'audience?" can be found in *OC II*, 202–233. Barthes here comments on three transcripts out of the dozen interviews recorded by a mass communication research group. Violette Morin, a leader of the group, composed her article "Les Olympiens" for the same issue.

4. Barthes, "Préface à l'*Encyclopédie Bordas*, tome VIII: L'aventure littéraire de l'humanité," [1970], in *OC III*, 627; 630.

5. Dudley Andrew, "The Core and the Flow of Film Studies," *Critical Inquiry* 35:4 (Summer 2009), 889.

6. Barthes, "'Traumatic Units' in Cinema."

7. Barthes, "Leaving the Movie Theater," in *The Rustle of Language* (University of California Press, 1989), 345–349.

8. See notably Martin Jay, *Downcast Eyes: The Denigration of Vision in Twentieth-Century French Thought* (Berkeley: University of California Press, 1993), 458.

9. Georges Friedmann, "Avant-propos," in *Communications* 21 (1974), 1–7.

10. Christian Metz, "Le signifiant imaginaire," *Communications* 23 (1975), 15. In English, *The Imaginary Signifier*, trans. Celia Britton et al. (Bloomington: University of Indiana Press, 1982), 20.

11. Félix Guattari, "Le divan du pauvre," *Communications* 23 (1975), 96–103.

12. Metz, *The Imaginary Signifier*, 50 ("Le signifiant imaginaire," 35); Barthes "Leaving the Movie Theater," 347.

13. Editors' note: A recent anthology takes up precisely the meaning of this term and focuses on the mid-1970s when it played a large role in film theory. François Albera and Maria Tortajada, eds., *Cine-dispositives: essays in Epistemology across Media* (Amsterdam: Amsterdam University Press, 2015).

14. Barthes, "En sortant du cinéma," in *OC IV*, 778. Editors' note: In this case Watts prefers his own translation, which is more literal than the one published in *The Rustle of Language*, 345.

15. On Barthes, the body, and theater, see the passage from Philippe Roger's essay "Barthes with Marx" reproduced in chapter 1, note 35.

16. Editors' note: Phil Watts' notes mention the importance to his views here of the work of Diane Morgan, who writes on the pertinence for Kant of architecture. See her *Kant Trouble* (New York: Routledge, 2000).
17. Barthes, "Leaving the Movie Theater," 349.
18. Marielle Macé, *Le Temps de l'essai: Histoire d'un genre en France au XXe siècle* (Paris: Belin, 2006), 215–231.
19. Cf. Gilles Deleuze's description of Jean-François Lyotard's book *Discours, Figure*: "Appréciation," in *La Quinzaine Littéraire* 141 (May 15, 1972), 19.
20. Metz, *The Imaginary Signifier*, 64.
21. Metz, *The Imaginary Signifier*, 64–65.
22. This quote also helps answer Martin Jay's claim that Metz's work was an example of a "profound suspicion of vision" among French intellectuals (*Downcast Eyes*, 14). It seems to me that Metz's suspicion lies not with vision itself, but with a specific object, cinema, which takes on the role of a degraded work of art.
23. Metz, *The Imaginary Signifier*, 66.
24. Metz, *The Imaginary Signifier*, 79.
25. Metz "Primary Figure, Secondary Figure,' in *The Imaginary Signifier*, 161–163.
26. "Film is like a mirror. But it differs from the primordial mirror in one essential point: although, as in the latter, everything may come to be projected, there is one thing only that is never reflected in it: the spectator's own body." Metz, *The Imaginary Signifier*, 42.
27. Barthes, "Leaving the Movie Theater," 349.
28. See Philip Rosen, *Narrative, Apparatus, Ideology: A Film Theory Reader* (New York: Columbia University Press, 1986). This anthology includes the canonical essays by Baudry and Mulvey from the mid-1970s. See also Miriam Hansen, *Babel and Babylon: Spectatorship in American Film* (Cambridge, MA: Harvard University Press, 1991).
29. D. A. Miller, *Bringing Out Roland Barthes* (Berkeley: University of California Press, 1992), 38–39. Editors' note: coincidentally, it was also in 1992 that Donald Richie published *Lateral View: Essays on Culture and Style in Contemporary Japan* (Berkeley: Stone Bridge Press). Richie was perhaps the most prominent gay non-Japanese writer living in Japan, the Empire of Signs.

Chapter 6

1. Éric Marty, *Roland Barthes, le métier d'écrire* (Paris: Seuil, 2006), 67.
2. Fredric Jameson, *Postmodernism, or, The Cultural Logic of Late Capitalism* (Durham, NC: Duke University Press, 1991), 286.
3. Serge Daney, *La Maison Cinéma et le Monde*, vol. I (Paris: POL, 2001), 219.

4. Editors' note: Daney's sepulchral vision of the New Wave is equally informed by the *politique des auteurs'* preference for older directors and the backward gaze of the postwar cinephile. See also his comments on nostalgia and melancholy in "Ce drôle de temps," *La Maison Cinéma et le Monde,* vol. 3 (Paris: POL 2012), 295–297.

5. See Robert Stam, *François Truffaut and Friends: Modernism, Sexuality, and Film Adaptation* (New Brunswick, NJ: Rutgers University Press, 2006), esp. 57–62.

6. Sam Di Iorio, "Bad Objects: Truffaut's Radicalism," in *A Companion to François Truffaut,* Dudley Andrew, Anne Gillain, eds. (Malden, MA: Wiley-Blackwell Publishing, 2013), 356.

7. Cf. Michel Marie, *The French New Wave: An Artistic School* (Malden, MA: Blackwell Publishing, 2003); Richard Neupert, *A History of The French New Wave Cinema* (Madison: University of Wisconsin Press, 2002).

8. Editors' note: In his fine monograph *André Téchiné* (Manchester: Manchester University Press, 2007), Bill Marshall lists the very same films as Philip Watts does in this paragraph before going on to comment on Barthes' view of *The Brontë Sisters.* See pp. 23 and 25. Marshall also alludes to Téchiné's "imaginative use of melodrama" in relation to his earlier film, *Souvenirs d'en France,* and tallies up numerous filiations between Barthes and Téchiné (16, 11).

9. François Cusset, *La décennie: le grand cauchemar des années 1980* (Paris: La Découverte, 2006).

10. *Moi, Pierre Rivière, ayant égorgé ma mère, ma sœur et mon frère . . .* (Paris : Gallimard, 1973), 269.

11. Michel Foucault, *Abnormal: Lectures at the Collège de France, 1974–1975,* ed. V. Manchetti and A. Salomoni, trans. Graham Burchell (New York: Picador, 2004), 61.

12. E. P. Thompson, *The Making of the English Working Class* (New York: Vintage Books, 1963), 12.

13. Peter Brooks, *The Melodramatic Imagination: Balzac, Henry James, Melodrama, and the Mode of Excess* (New Haven, CT: Yale University Press, 1976), 56–62.

14. Anne Gillain and Dudley Andrew, "Interview with Arnaud Desplechin, Part I: Truffaut and his Position," in *A Companion to François Truffaut,* 14.

15. Vincent Canby, "*The Last Metro*: Melodrama by Truffaut" *The New York Times,* February 11, 1981.

16. Di Iorio, "Bad Objects," 356.

17. T. Jefferson Kline, "Anxious Affinities: Text as Screen in Truffaut's *Jules et Jim,*" chapter 1 of *Screening the Text: Intertextuality in New Wave French Cinema* (Baltimore: Johns Hopkins University Press, 2002).

18. Thomas Elsaesser, "Tales of Sound and Fury: Observations on the Family Melodrama," *Monogram* 3 (1972), 2–15. Reprinted in Barry Keith Grant, ed., *Film Genre Reader* (Austin: University of Texas Press, 1986), 278–308.

19. Patrice Maniglier and Dork Zabunyan, *Foucault va au cinéma* (Montrouge: Bayard, 2011), 36.

20. Ibid., 102.

21. Michel Foucault, *Discipline and Punish: The Birth of The Prison*, trans. Alan Sheridan (New York: Pantheon Books, 1977), 17.

22. Brooks, *The Melodramatic Imagination*, 43.

23. Foucault, *Abnormal*, 95–96.

24. Ibid., 94–95. See also 337, where Foucault's words are quoted in the appendix, "Course Context," drawn up by the editors V. Manchetti and A. Salomoni.

25. Foucault cites an apocryphal text attributed to Radcliffe, *Les Visions du château des Pyrénées*. As Manchetti and Salomoni suggest in their notes to Foucault's lecture, her novel *The Romance of the Forest* provides a better example. See Foucault, *Abnormal*, 107, notes 36–37. On the relationship between the gothic novel and melodrama, see Brooks, *The Melodramatic Imagination*, especially 17–20.

26. Foucault, *Discipline and Punish*, 15, 17, 29.

27. Christine Gledhill, ed., *Home is Where the Heart is: Studies in Melodrama and the Woman's Film* (London: British Film Institute, 1987).

28. Editors' note: See Emmanuelle André, *Le Choc du sujet: de l'hystérie au cinéma* (Rennes: Presses Universitaires de Rennes, 2011).

29. Pascal Kané, "Entretien avec Michel Foucault," *Cahiers du Cinéma* 271 (November 1976), 53.

30. Foucault "Le Retour de Pierre Rivière" quoted in Maniglier and Zabunyan, *Foucault va au cinéma*, 154. Watts' translation.

31. René Allio, *Carnets* (Paris: Lieu commun, 1991), 44.

32. Editors' note: Though Charlotte does finally marry after losing her siblings to sickness and addiction, the film insists on her autonomy from her husband.

33. Editors' note: Barthes was among those who noticed this. See his comments about participating in the film in "Il n'y a pas d'homme," in *OC V*, 659–661.

34. Ludovic Cortade rightly makes the link between the still image at the end of Truffaut's *Les Quatre Cents Coups* and Barthes' reflections on photographs in *La Chambre claire*. See Cortade, *Le Cinéma de l'immobilité* (Paris: Presses de la Sorbonne, 2008), 46. The tie between Barthes and Truffaut's 1978 film seems even more compelling.

35. Barthes, *Camera Lucida*, trans. Richard Howard (New York: Hill and Wang, 1981), 115.

36. In fact, we know that Barthes did not see Truffaut's film but that he was aware of, and drawn to, *La Chambre verte*. In an account of their friendship, Éric Marty mentions that one night, shortly after his mother's death, Barthes wanted to see Truffaut's film but that Marty, worried that Barthes was too depressed, convinced him to see the comedy *One, Two, Two: 122 rue de*

NOTES

Provence instead. That night, Marty concludes, "I discredited myself." Marty, *Roland Barthes*, 97.

37. The collection was published after Truffaut's death, but according to its editors Jean Narboni and Serge Toubiana, Truffaut had chosen the title before he died. See Truffaut, *Le Plaisir des yeux* (Paris: Cahiers du Cinéma/Seuil, 1987), 7.

38. Editors' Note: This line appears in the Dziga Vertov Group film *Vent d'Est* (1969). In *Camera Lucida*, Barthes renders it as "Not a just image, just an image" and attributes the phrase to Godard (70). More recently, however, David Faroult has suggested that it was put into circulation by his partner Jean-Pierre Gorin. See Faroult, "Du *Vertovisme* du Groupe Dziga Vertov," in *Jean-Luc Godard: Documents* (Paris: Éditions du Centre Pompidou, 2006), 134.

39. Pierre Bourdieu, *Photography: A Middlebrow Art* (Redwood City, CA: Stanford University Press, 1990).

40. Ibid., 5.

Conclusion

1. See "L'image fraternelle (Entretien avec Jacques Rancière)," *Cahiers du Cinéma* 268–269 (July–August 1976), 7–19; Jacques Rancière, "Fleurs intempestives (*La communion solennelle*)," *Cahiers du Cinéma* 278 (July 1977), 17–20.

2. Kristin Ross, "Yesterday's Critique, Today's Mythologies," *Contemporary French and Francophone Studies* 12:2 (2008), 239–240. Jacques Rancière, *Chronicles of Consensual Times* (London: Continuum, 2010).

3. Roland Barthes, "To the Seminar," in *The Rustle of Language*, trans. Richard Howard (Berkeley: University of California Press 1989), 332–342. Barthes, *The Neutral: Lecture Course at the Collège de France (1977–1978)*, trans. Rosalind E. Krauss and Denis Hollier (New York: Columbia University Press, 2005).

4. Edgar Morin, *Les Stars* (Paris: Seuil, 1972), 7. Watts' translations, as this preface does not appear in the English version.

5. Barthes, "Change the Object Itself: Mythology Today," trans. Stephen Heath in *Image, Music, Text* (New York: Hill and Wang, 1977), 166.

6. Barthes, *Mythologies: The Complete Edition*, trans. Richard Howard and Annette Lavers (New York: Hill and Wang, 2013), 272.

7. Barthes, "Change the Object Itself," 169.

8. Barthes, "La Chronique: Démystifier," in *OC V*, 649–650. The translation here is that of the editors.

9. Barthes, "Sur la théorie," in *OC III*, 692.

10. Barthes, "La Chronique: Démystifier," 649.

BIBLIOGRAPHY

The bibliography that follows is divided into three sections: the first includes the articles Roland Barthes devoted to cinema as well as a selection of Barthes' texts that mention films and filmmakers. Whenever possible, we have given three sources for these references: the English translation (if one exists), the original French publication, and the relevant pages in the five-volume reference edition of Barthes' complete works which Les Éditions du Seuil published in 2002.

The following section provides an overview of secondary material devoted to the relationship between Barthes and cinema. It relies on Philip Watts' research as well as earlier bibliographies compiled by Charlotte Garson (2002) and Vincent Joly (2004). It does not include studies devoted to Barthes' writing on photography. The third section lists all other works cited in Watts' text.

I. Roland Barthes Cinema

ARTICLES AND INTERVIEWS

"Angels of Sin" translated by Deborah Glassman in this volume. Originally published as "Les Anges du péché," *Existences* 30 (August 1943) and available in *Œuvres complètes*, vol. I (Paris: Les Éditions du Seuil, 2002), 50–51. Further references to this five-volume edition will be cited here as *OC*.

"Visages et figures," *Esprit* 204 (July 1953) and available in *OC I*, 268–279.

"The Romans in Films" in *Mythologies*, translated by Richard Howard and Annette Lavers (New York: Hill and Wang, 2012), 19–21. Originally published as "Jules César au Cinéma" in *Les Lettres Nouvelles* 11 (January

1954) and reprinted as "Les Romains au Cinéma" in *Mythologies* (Paris: Les Éditions du Seuil, 1957). Available in *OC I*, 691–693.

"On CinemaScope" translated by Deborah Glassman in this volume. Originally published as "Au Cinémascope" in *Les Lettres Nouvelles* 12 (February 1954) and available in *OC I*, 456–457.

"Versailles and Its Accounts" translated by Deborah Glassman in this volume. Originally published as "Versailles et ses comptes" in *Les Lettres Nouvelles* 15 (May 1954) and available in *OC I*, 482–485.

"The Poor and the Proletariat" in *Mythologies*, translated by Richard Howard and Annette Lavers (New York: Hill and Wang, 2012), 35–37. Originally published as "Le Pauvre et le prolétaire" in *Les Lettres Nouvelles* 21 (November 1954), collected in *Mythologies* (Paris: Les Éditions du Seuil, 1957), and available in *OC I*, 701–702.

"A Sympathetic Worker" in *Mythologies*, translated by Richard Howard and Annette Lavers (New York: Hill and Wang, 2012), 70–72. Originally published as "Comment Démystifier" in *Les Lettres Nouvelles* 25 (March 1955) and reprinted as "Un Ouvrier sympathique" in *Mythologies* (Paris: Les Éditions du Seuil, 1957). Available in *OC I*, 722–724.

"The Face of Garbo" in *Mythologies*, translated by Richard Howard and Annette Lavers (New York: Hill and Wang, 2012), 73–75. Originally published as "Le Visage de Garbo" in *Les Lettres Nouvelles* 26 (April 1955) and collected in *Mythologies* (Paris: Les Éditions du Seuil, 1957). Available in *OC I*, 724–725.

"Power and 'Cool'" in *Mythologies*, translated by Richard Howard and Annette Lavers (New York: Hill and Wang, 2012), 76–78. Originally published as "Puissance et désinvolture" in *Les Lettres Nouvelles* 26 (April 1955) and collected in *Mythologies* (Paris: Les Éditions du Seuil, 1957). Available in *OC I*, 725–727.

"*Continent perdu*" in *Mythologies*, translated by Richard Howard and Annette Lavers (New York: Hill and Wang, 2012), 184–186. Originally published in *Les Lettres Nouvelles* 35 (February 1956), and collected in *Mythologies* (Paris: Les Éditions du Seuil, 1957). Available in *OC I*, 798–800.

"The Harcourt Actor" in *Mythologies*, translated by Richard Howard and Annette Lavers (New York: Hill and Wang, 2012), 15–18. Originally published as "L'Acteur d'Harcourt" in *Mythologies* (Paris: Les Éditions du Seuil, 1957) and available in *OC I*, 688–690.

"Cinema Right and Left" translated by Deborah Glassman in this volume. Originally published as "Cinéma droite et gauche" in *Les Lettres Nouvelles* 2 (Second Series; March 11, 1959) and available in *OC I*, 943–945.

"Le problème de la signification au cinéma," *Revue Internationale de Filmologie* 10:32–33 (January–June 1960) and available in *OC I*, 1039–1046.

"On Left-Wing Criticism" translated by Deborah Glassman in this volume. Originally published as "Sur la critique de gauche" in *Positif* 36 (November 1960) and available in *OC I*, 1083–1086.

"Civilisation de l'image," *Communications* 1 (1961) and available in *OC I*, 1137–1139.

"'Traumatic Units' in Cinema" translated by Deborah Glassman in this volume. Originally published as "Les 'Unités traumatiques' au cinéma: Principes de recherche" in *Revue Internationale de Filmologie* 10:34 (July–September 1960) and available in *OC I*, 1047–1056.

What is Sport? [1961] translated by Richard Howard (New Haven, CT: Yale University Press, 2004). Originally published as *Le Sport et les hommes: Texte du film* Le Sport et les hommes *d'Hubert Aquin* (Montreal: Presses de l'Université de Montréal, 2004).

"Preface to *Les Inconnus de la terre*" translated by Deborah Glassman in this volume. Originally published as "Préface aux *Inconnus de la terre*" in *Artsept* 2 (April–June 1963), 76.

"La Vedette: Enquêtes d'audience?" *Communications* 2 (1963), 197–216, and available in *OC II*, 202–233.

"Towards a Semiotics of Cinema: Interview with Michel Delahaye and Jacques Rivette" translated by Jim Hillier in *Cahiers du Cinéma 1960–1968* (Cambridge, MA: Harvard University Press, 1986), 276–285. Originally published as "Entretien avec Roland Barthes" in *Cahiers du Cinéma* 147 (September 1963) and available in *OC II*, 255–266.

"Semiology and Cinema" translated by Linda Coverdale in *The Grain of the Voice* (New York: Hill and Wang, 1985), 30–37. Originally published as "Sémiologie et cinéma (entretien avec P. Pilard et M. Tardy)" in *Image et Son* 175 (July 1964) and available in *OC II*, 622–628.

"Answer to a Question about James Bond" translated by Deborah Glassman in this volume. Originally published as "Réponse à une question sur James Bond" in *Le Nouvel Observateur* (December 15, 1965) and available in *OC V*, 1026.

"The Third Meaning" in *Image, Music, Text*, translated by Stephen Heath (New York: Hill and Wang, 1977), 52–68. Originally published as "Le troisième sens. Notes de recherche sur quelques photogrammes de S. M. Eisenstein" in *Cahiers du Cinéma* 222 (July 1970) and available in *OC III*, 485–506.

"Diderot, Brecht, Eisenstein" in *Image, Music, Text*, translated by Stephen Heath (New York: Hill and Wang, 1977), 69–78. Originally published in *Cinéma, Théorie, Lectures*, a special issue of *Revue d'esthétique* (1973) and available in *OC IV*, 338–344.

"*Le Pélican* de Gérard Blain," *Le Nouvel Observateur* (February 14, 1974) and available in *OC IV*, 512.

"Leaving the Movie Theater" in *The Rustle of Language*, translated by Richard Howard (Berkeley: University of California Press, 1989), 345–349. Originally published as "En sortant du cinéma" in *Communications* 23 (1975) and available in *OC IV*, 778–782.

"To Learn and to Teach" in *The Rustle of Language*, 176–178. Originally published as "Apprendre, enseigner" in *Ça cinéma* 7–8 (May 1975) and available as "Apprendre et Enseigner" in *OC IV*, 793–795.

"Ce qui est bon," *Le Monde* (September 18, 1975) and available in *OC IV*, 797–799.

"Sade-Pasolini" translated by Deborah Glassman in this volume. Originally published in *Le Monde* (June 16, 1976) and available in *OC IV*, 944–946.

"Day by Day with Roland Barthes," especially the following short entries: "Leni," "Very French," "Limelight," "Perceval," "Roberte ce soir," translated by Marshall Blonsky in *On Signs* (Baltimore: Johns Hopkins University Press, 1985), 98–117. These texts are part of a series which appeared weekly in *Le Nouvel Observateur* between December 18, 1978 and March 26, 1979. Available as "La Chronique" in *OC V*, 625–653.

"Il n'y a pas d'homme," *Le Nouvel Observateur* (May 14, 1979) and available in *OC V*, 659–661.

"Dear Antonioni" in *L'avventura*, translated by G. Nowell-Smith (London: British Film Institute, 1997), 63–69. Originally published as "Cher Antonioni" in *Cahiers du Cinéma* 311 (May 1980) and available in *OC V*, 900–905.

SELECTED TEXTS RELATED TO CINEMA

"Témoignage sur Robbe-Grillet," *Clarté* 39 (December 1961) and available in *OC I*, 1117 [Resnais' *Last Year at Marienbad*].

"The Last Word on Robbe-Grillet?" translated by Richard Howard in *Critical Essays* (Evanston: Northwestern University Press, 1972), 197–204. Originally published as "Le point sur Robbe-Grillet?" a preface to Bruce Morrissette, *Les Romans de Robbe-Grillet* (Paris: Les Éditions de minuit, 1963) and collected in *Essais critiques* (Paris: Les Éditons du Seuil, 1964). Available in *OC II*, 452–459. [Robbe-Grillet as novelist and filmmaker]

"Baudelaire's Theater" in *Critical Essays*, 25–31. Originally published as "Le théâtre de Baudelaire" in *Théâtre populaire* 8 (July–August 1954), collected in *Essais critiques*, and available in *OC II*, 304–310. [Theatricality, cinema, and the novel.]

"The Diseases of Costume" in *Critical Essays*, 41–50. Originally published as "Les maladies du costume de théâtre" in *Théâtre populaire* 12 (March–April 1955), collected in *Essais critiques*, and available in *OC II*, 316–324. [Guitry's *Royal Affairs in Versailles*, Dreyer's *The Passion of Joan of Arc*.]

"Cayrol and Erasure" translated by Richard Howard in *The Rustle of Language* (New York: Hill and Wang, 1986), 181–190. Originally published as "La

Rature" a preface to Jean Cayrol, *Les corps étrangers* (Paris: Union Générale d'Éditions-10/18, 1964) and available in *OC II*, 595–599. [Resnais' *Muriel*.]

"Japon: l'art de vivre, l'art des signes," *Image et Son* 222 (December 1968) and available in *OC III*, 84–85. [Vadim's *Nutty, Naughty Chateau*.]

"Une problématique du sens," *Cahiers Média* 1 (1970) and available in *OC III*, 507–526. [Godard's *Alphaville*.]

"Writers, Intellectuals, Teachers" in *The Rustle of Language*, 309–331. Originally published as "Écrivains, intellectuels, professeurs" in *Tel Quel* 47 (Autumn, 1971) and available in *OC III*, 887–907. [Wood's *A Night at the Opera* and the Marx Brothers.]

"Une leçon de sincérité" [1972] *Poétique* 47 (September 1981) and available in *OC IV*, 133–143. [On a "filmic reading" of Lucan's *Pharsalia*.]

The Pleasure of the Text translated by Richard Miller (New York: Hill and Wang, 1975). Originally published as *Le Plaisir du texte* (Paris: Les Éditions du Seuil, 1973) and available in *OC IV*, 217–264. [Murnau's *City Girl*.]

"L'essai en fête," [1975], presented by Nicole Brenez, *Trafic* 78 (Summer 2011), 86–94. [Eisenstein, the concept of the Third Meaning.]

Roland Barthes by Roland Barthes translated by Richard Howard (New York: Hill and Wang, 1977). Originally published as *Roland Barthes par Roland Barthes* (Paris: Les Éditions du Seuil, 1975) and available in *OC IV*, 575–771. [Fragments: "Charlot," "Le plein du cinéma," "L'emblème, le gag" (on Wood's *A Night at the Opera*), and "Pause: anamnèses" (on Buñuel's *Un Chien Andalou*).]

All Except You. Saul Steinberg [1976] Originally published as Roland Barthes, Saul Steinberg *All Except You* (Paris: Repères, 1983) and available in *OC IV*, 949–975. [Fragment: "Charlot".]

How To Live Together: Novelistic Simulations of Some Everyday Spaces. Notes for a Lecture Course and Seminar at the Collège de France (1976–1977), translated by Kate Briggs (New York: Columbia University Press, 2013). Originally published as *Comment vivre ensemble. Cours et séminaires au Collège de France (1976–1977)* (Paris: Seuil / IMEC, 2002). [Chaplin's *Modern Times*, Fellini's *Satyricon*, Becker's *It Happened at the Inn*.]

A Lover's Discourse: Fragments, translated by Richard Howard (New York: Hill and Wang, 1978). Originally published as *Fragments d'un discours amoureux* (Paris: Les Éditions du Seuil, 1977) and available in *OC V*, 25–296. [Pasolini's *Teorema*, Buñuel's *The Discreet Charm of the Bourgeoisie*.]

"Sur La Plage," *Le Monde* (March 24, 1977) and available in *OC V*, 309–310. [Straub and Huillet's *Othon*, Resnais' *Providence*.]

The Neutral: Lecture Course at the Collège de France (1977–1978), translated by Rosalind E. Krauss and Denis Hollier (New York: Columbia University Press, 2005). Originally published as *Le Neutre. Cours au Collège de France (1977–1978)* (Paris: Seuil/IMEC, 2002). [Jacquot's *Closet Children*.]

"Inaugural Lecture, Collège de France" translated by Richard Howard in *A Barthes Reader* (New York: Hill and Wang, 1982), 457–478. Originally published as *Leçon* (Paris: Les Éditions du Seuil, 1978) and available in *OC V*, 429–446. [Pasolini's *Trilogy of Life*.]

The Preparation of the Novel: Lecture Courses and Seminars at the Collège de France (1978–1979 and 1979–1980), translated by Kate Briggs (New York: Columbia University Press, 2011). Originally published as *La Préparation du roman I et II. Cours et séminaires au Collège de France (1978–1979 et 1979–1980)* (Paris: Seuil / IMEC, 2003). [Mizoguchi's *Ugetsu Monogatari*; photography and cinema; Fellini's *Casanova* and *Fellini Satyricon*.]

Camera Lucida: Reflections on Photography, translated by Richard Howard (New York: Hill and Wang, 1981). Originally published as *La Chambre claire* (Paris, Les Éditions du Seuil, 1980) and available in *OC V*, 785–892. [Fragments 36 and 47, on Antonioni's *Blow-Up* and *Fellini's Casanova*.]

II. Selected Writings on Roland Barthes and Cinema

Attridge, Derek, "Roland Barthes' Obtuse, Sharp Meaning and the Responsibilities of Commentary" in Jean-Michel Rabaté, ed., *Writing the Image After Roland Barthes*, (Philadelphia: University of Pennsylvania Press, 1997), 77–89.

Bérubé, Renald, "Roland Barthes et Hubert Aquin, lecteurs sportifs," *Lettres québécoises: la revue de l'actualité littéraire* 115 (2004), 45–46.

Brenez, Nicole, "Invention du corps subtil. Barthes et Eisenstein" in Catherine Coquio and Régis Salado, ed., *Barthes après Barthes. Une actualité en question* (Pau: Publications de l'université de Pau, 1993), 167–172.

Brown, William, "Roland Barthes: What Films Show Us and What They Mean" in Murray Pomerance and R. B. Palmer, *Thinking in the Dark: Cinema, Theory, Practice* (New York: Rutgers University Press, 2015), 113–124.

Burgin, Victor, "Barthes's Discretion" in Jean-Michel Rabaté, ed., *Writing the Image After Roland Barthes* (Philadelphia: University of Pennsylvania Press, 1997), 19–31.

Calvet, Jean-Louis, "Barthes et le cinéma: la disparition du signifiant," *Cinémaction* 60 (July 1991), 140–145.

Carasco, Raymonde, "L'image-cinéma qu'aimait Roland Barthes (le goût du filmique)," *Revue d'esthétique* 6 (1984), 71–78.

Garson, Charlotte, "Résistance au cinéma, insistance du cinéma. Un parcours de Barthes," *Variations* 4 (2000), 43–53.

Garson, Charlotte, "Roland Barthes, voix-off du cinéma: *Inclusum labor illustrat*," *Revue des sciences humaines* 268 (Oct.–Dec. 2002), 73–74.

Gil, Marie, *Roland Barthes: Au lieu de la vie* (Paris: Flammarion, 2012).

Le Forestier, Laurent, "Comment peut-on encore être 'cinémato-barthésien'?" *1895* 50 (December 2006), 137–146.

Lesage, Julia, "*S/Z* and *The Rules of the Game*," *Jump Cut* 12/13 (1976), 45–51.

Lowenstein, Adam, "The Surrealism of the Photographic Image: Bazin, Barthes, and the Digital *Sweet Hereafter*," *Cinema Journal* 46:3 (Spring 2007), 54–82.

MacCabe, Colin, "Barthes and Bazin. The Ontology of the Image" in Jean-Michel Rabaté, ed., *Writing the Image After Roland Barthes* (Philadelphia: University of Pennsylvania Press, 1997), 71–76.

MacKenzie, Scott, "The Missing Mythology: Barthes in Québec," *Canadian Journal of Film Studies* 6:2 (1997), 65–74.

Mayne, Judith, "*S/Z* and Film Criticism," *Jump Cut* 12/13 (1976), 41–45.

Miller, D. A., "Second Time Around: Chabarthes," *Film Quarterly* 65 (Winter 2011), 16–17.

Mouren, Yannick, "Les intellectuels français dissertent du cinéma (Barthes, Foucault et quelques autres)," *Cahiers de la cinémathèque* 70 (1999), 75–84.

Païni, Dominique, "D'une théorie douce à une lecture poétique. Barthes et le cinéma," *Cinémaction* 20 (August 1982), 132–142.

Petric, Vlada, "Barthes versus Cinema," *Sight & Sound* (Summer 1983), 205–207.

Polan, Dana B., "Roland Barthes and the Moving Image," *October* 18 (Fall 1981), 41–46.

Rosenbaum, Jonathan, "Barthes & Film: 12 Suggestions," *Sight and Sound* 52:1 (Winter 1982–1983), 50–53. Reprinted in *Placing Movies: The Practice of Film Criticism* (Berkeley: University of California Press, 1995), 45–53.

Thompson, Kristin, "The Concept of Cinematic Excess," *Ciné-Tracts* 1:2, 54–63.

Ulmer, Gregory L., "'A Night at the Text: Roland Barthes's Marx Brothers," *Yale French Studies* 73 (1987), 38–57.

Ungar, Steven, "Persistence of the Image: Barthes, Photography and the Resistance to Film" (1989) in Diana Knight, ed., *Critical Essays on Roland Barthes* (New York: Hamm and Co., 2000), 236–249.

Williams, James S., "At the Reader's Discretion: On Barthes and Cinema," *Paragraph* 21:1 (March 1998), 45–56.

III. Works Cited

Albera, François and Tortajada, Maria, eds., *Cine-dispositives: Essays in Epistemology across Media* (Amsterdam: Amsterdam University Press, 2015).

Allio, René, *Carnets* (Paris: Lieu commun, 1991).

André, Emmanuelle, *Le Choc du sujet: de l'hystérie au cinéma* (Rennes: Presses Universitaires de Rennes, 2011).

Anderson, Lindsay, "The Last Sequence of *On the Waterfront*," *Sight and Sound* 24:3 (January–March 1955), 127–130.

Andrew, Dudley, *Concepts in Film Theory* (New York: Oxford University Press, 1984).

Andrew, Dudley, "The Ontology of a Fetish," *Film Quarterly* 61:4 (Summer, 2008), 62–66.

Andrew, Dudley, "The Core and The Flow of Film Studies," *Critical Inquiry* 35:4 (Summer 2009), 879–915.

Andrew, Dudley and Gillain, Anne, eds., *A Companion to François Truffaut* (Hoboken: John Wiley & Sons, 2013).

Antonioni, Michelangelo, "Dear Friend," trans. Nora Hoppe, in *L'avventura*, Michelangelo Antonioni director; Seymour Chatman and Guido Fink, eds. (New Brunswick, NJ: Rutgers University Press, 1989), 213–214. Originally published as "Cher ami," *Cahiers du Cinéma* 311 (May 1980), 11.

Arnaud, Philippe, ed. *Sacha Guitry, Cinéaste* (Crisnée: Éditions Yellow Now, 1993).

Barnard, Timothy, *Découpage* (Montreal: Caboose Press, 2014).

Barthes, Roland, *Writing Degree Zero*, trans. Annette Laver and Colin Smith (New York: Hill & Wang, 1968). Originally published as *Le degré zéro de l'écriture* (Paris: Les Éditions du Seuil, 1953); available in *OC I*, 169–225.

Barthes, Roland, "Suis-je marxiste?" in *Les Lettres Nouvelles* 29 (July–August, 1955). Available in *OC I*, 596.

Barthes, Roland, "Billy Graham at the Vel' d'Hiv" in *Mythologies*, trans. Richard Howard and Annette Lavers (New York: Hill and Wang, 2012), 109–112. Originally published as "Billy Graham au Vel d'Hiv" in *Les Lettres Nouvelles* 29 (July–August 1955), 180–183. Collected in *Mythologies* (Paris: Les Éditions du Seuil, 1957) and available in *OC I*, 746–749.

Barthes, Roland, "Préface à Stendhal, *Quelques promenades dans Rome*" (La Guilde du Livre, 1957). Available in *OC I*, 912–918.

Barthes, Roland, "Rhetoric of the Image," in *Image, Music, Text*, trans. Stephen Heath (New York: Hill and Wang, 1977), 32–51. Originally published as "Rhétorique de l'image" in *Communications* 4 (November 1964), 40–51. Available in *OC II*, 573–588.

Barthes, Roland, "From Science to Literature," in *The Rustle of Language*, trans. Richard Howard (Berkeley: University of California Press, 1989), 3–10. Originally published in English as "Science versus Literature" in the *Times Literary Supplement*, September 28, 1967. The French text, "De la science à la littérature," is available in *OC II*, 1263–1270.

Barthes, Roland, *'Sarrasine' de Balzac: Séminaires à l'École Pratique des hautes études (1967–1968 et 1968–1969)*, ed. Claude Coste and Andy Stafford (Paris: Les Éditions du Seuil, 2011).

Barthes, Roland, *S/Z*, trans. Richard Miller (New York: Hill and Wang, 1975). Originally published by Les Éditions du Seuil in 1970 and available in *OC III*, 119–345.

Barthes, Roland, "Préface à l'*Encyclopédie Bordas*, tome VIII: L'aventure littéraire de l'humanité" [1970]. Available in *OC III*, 627–631.

Barthes, Roland, "Sur la théorie," Originally published in *VH 101* (Summer 1970) and available in *OC III*, 689–696.

Barthes, Roland, "*L'Express* talks with Roland Barthes" in *The Grain of the Voice: Interviews 1962–1980* (New York: Hill and Wang, 1985), 95. Originally published as "L'Express va plus loin avec . . . Roland Barthes" in *L'Express*, May 31, 1970. Available in *OC III*, 671–688.

Barthes, Roland, "Change the Object Itself: Mythology Today," trans. Stephen Heath in *Image, Music, Text* (New York: Hill and Wang, 1977), 166. The original French essay was titled "Changer l'objet lui-même" and appeared in the April 1971 issue of *Esprit*. It is available as "La mythologie aujourd'hui" in *OC III*, 873–876.

Barthes, Roland, *Sade, Fourier, Loyola*, trans. Richard Miller (Berkeley: University of California Press, 1976), 9. Originally published by Les Éditions du Seuil in 1971, and available in *OC III*, 699–868.

Barthes, Roland, "To the Seminar" in *The Rustle of Language*, trans. Richard Howard (Berkeley: University of California Press, 1989), 340. Originally published as "Au séminaire" in *L'Arc 56* (1974); available in *OC IV*, 502–511.

Barthes, Roland, "Of What Use Is an Intellectual?" in *The Grain of the Voice* (Berkeley: University of California Press, 1985), 272–273. Originally published in *Le Nouvel Observateur* (January 10, 1977) and available in *OC IV*, 364–382.

Barthes, Roland, La Chronique: Démystifier," in *OC V*, 649–650; "La Chronique: Tempo II," in *OC V*, 651. Part of a series of articles published in *Le Nouvel Observateur* between December 18, 1978 and March 26, 1979. While the translations used in this book are those of the editors, the reader may locate an English version of these articles in the anthology *On Signs*, ed. Marshall Blonsky (Baltimore: The Johns Hopkins University Press, 1985), 114; 115–116.

Bazin, André, "Le cinémascope sauvera-t-il le cinéma?" *Esprit* 207–208 (October–November 1953), 672–683.

Bazin, André, "Sur les Quais," *France Observateur* 245 (January 20, 1955), 28–29.

Bazin, André, "La Reine Christine," *France Observateur* 249 (February 17, 1955), 30–31.

Bazin, André, "*Napoléon* de Sacha Guitry," *France Observateur* 255 (March 31, 1955), 28–29.

Bazin, André, "Continent Perdu," *France Observateur* 296 (January 12, 1956), 14.

Bazin, André, *What is Cinema?* vol. 1, trans. Hugh Grey (Berkeley: University of California Press, 1968).

Bazin, André, *What is Cinema?* vol. 2, trans. Hugh Grey (Berkeley: University of California Press, 1971).

Bazin, André, *What is Cinema?* trans. Timothy Barnard (Montreal: Caboose, 2009).

Beaver, Harold, "Homosexual Signs (*In Memory of Roland Barthes*)" in Fabio Cleto, ed. *Camp: Queer Aesthetics and the Performing Subject* (Ann Arbor: University of Michigan Press, 1999).

Benjamin, Walter, "The Work of Art in the Age of Mechanical Reproduction" in *Illuminations: Essays and Reflections* (New York: Schocken Books, 1968), 217–251.

Bensmaïa, Réda, *The Barthes Effect: The Essay as Reflective Text*, trans. Pat Fedkiew (Minneapolis: University of Minnesota Press, 1987).

Bergala, Alain, *Godard au Travail: Les Années 60* (Paris: Cahiers du Cinéma, 2006).

Bertin-Maghit, Jean-Pierre, *Le Cinéma français sous l'Occupation* (Paris: Perrin, 2002).

Bordwell, David, *Making Meaning: Inference and Rhetoric in the Interpretation of Cinema* (Cambridge, MA: Harvard University Press, 1991).

Bontemps, Jacques, "Roland Barthes: bref lexique du spectateur," *Trafic* 95 (Autumn 2015), 112–122.

Bourdieu, Pierre, *Photography: A Middle-brow Art*, trans. Shaun Whiteside (Redwood City, CA: Stanford University Press, 1990).

Bourg, Julien, *From Revolution to Ethics: May 1968 and Contemporary French Thought* (Montreal: McGill-Queens University Press, 2007).

Bresson, Robert, *Notes on Cinematography* (New York: Urizen Books, 1977).

Brooks, Peter, *The Melodramatic Imagination: Balzac, Henry James, Melodrama, and the Mode of Excess* (New Haven, CT: Yale University Press, 1976).

Calvet, Louis-Jean, *Roland Barthes: a Biography* (Cambridge: Polity Press, 1994).

Canby, Vincent, "*The Last Metro*: Melodrama by Truffaut," *The New York Times*, February 11, 1981.

Cavell, Stanley, *The World Viewed: Reflections on the Ontology of Film* (Cambridge, MA: Harvard University Press, 1979).

Citton, Yves, "Literary Attention: The Hairy Politics of Details," *Romanic Review* 105:1–2 (2014), 111–121.

Cortade, Ludovic, *Le Cinéma de l'immobilité* (Paris: Presses de la Sorbonne, 2008).

Coste, Claude, *Roland Barthes moraliste* (Caen: Presses Universitaires du Septentrion, 1998).

Coste, Claude, *Bêtise de Barthes* (Paris: Klincksieck, 2011).

Cusset, François, *La décennie. Le grand cauchemar des années 1980* (Paris: La Découverte, 2006).

Daney, Serge, *La Maison Cinéma et le Monde*, vol. 1 and vol. 3 (Paris: POL, 2001; 2012).

Dauman, Anatole, *Souvenir-écran* (Paris: Éditions du Centre Pompidou, 1989).

de Baecque, Antoine, *Les Cahiers du Cinéma, Histoire d'une Revue T. II: Cinéma, tours détours 1959–1981* (Paris: Cahiers du Cinéma, 1991).

Debaene, Vincent, *Far Afield: French Anthropology between Science and Literature*, trans. Justin Izzo (Chicago: University of Chicago Press, 2014).

Debaene, Vincent, "Reading (with) Phil Watts," *Romanic Review* 105.1–2 (2014), 97–101.

Deleuze, Gilles, "Appréciation," *La Quinzaine Littéraire* 141 (May 15, 1972), 19.

Deleuze, Gilles, *Cours du 29 janvier 1985*, www2.univ-paris8.fr/deleuze/article. php3?id_article=299.

Di Iorio, Sam, "Bad Objects: Truffaut's Radicalism" in Dudley Andrew and Anne Gillain, eds., *A Companion to François Truffaut* (Hoboken: John Wiley & Sons, 2013), 356–374.

Doniol-Valcroze, Jacques, "*Sabrina*," *France Observateur* (February 10, 1955), 28–29.

Dort, Bernard, "Lettre à Claude Chabrol," *Les Temps Modernes* 158 (April 1959), 1673–1681.

Dosse, François, *Gilles Deleuze & Félix Guattari: Intersecting Lives*, trans. Deborah Glassman (New York: Columbia University Press, 2010).

Eisenschitz, Bernard, "De Jeanne d'Arc à Philippe Pétain," http://lemagazine. jeudepaume.org/2013/03/bernard-eisenschitz-de-jeanne-darc-a-philippe-petain/.

Eisenstein, Sergei, *Réflexions d'un cinéaste* (Moscow: Éditions en langues étrangères, 1958).

Eisenstein, Sergei, *Mettre en Scène* (Paris: Union Générale d'Éditions, 1973).

Eisenstein, Sergei, *Au-delà des étoiles* (Paris: Union Générale d'Éditions, 1974).

Eisenstein, Sergei, *La non-indifférente nature*, 2 vols. (Paris: Union Générale d'Éditions, 1976; 1978).

Eisenstein, Sergei, *Mémoires*, 3 vols. (Paris: Union Générale d'Éditions, 1978/ 1980).

Epstein, Jean, "De quelques conditions de la photogénie," *Cinéa-Ciné pour tous* 19 (August 15, 1924), 6–8.

Faroult, David, "Du *Vertovisme* du Groupe Dziga Vertov" in *Jean-Luc Godard: Documents* (Paris: Éditions du Centre Pompidou, 2006), 134–138.

Fleischer, Alain, *Morceaux de Conversations avec Jean-Luc Godard* DVD, Disc 3: "Jean–Luc Godard avec Jean-Claude Conesa" (Paris: Éditions Montparnasse, 2010).

Flusser, Vilém, *Towards a Philosophy of Photography*, ed. Derek Bennett (Göttingen: European Photography, 1984).

Flusser, Vilém, *Into the Universe of Technical Images*, trans. Nancy Ann Roth (Minneapolis: University of Minnesota Press, 2011).

Foucault, Michel, ed., *Moi, Pierre Rivière, ayant égorgé ma mère, ma sœur et mon frère . . .* (Paris: Gallimard, 1973).

Foucault, Michel et al., eds., *Discipline and Punish: The Birth of The Prison*, trans. Alan Sheridan (New York: Pantheon Books, 1977).

Foucault, Michel, *Abnormal: Lectures at the Collège de France, 1974–1975*, ed. V. Manchetti and A. Salomoni, trans. Graham Burchell (New York: Picador, 2004).

Foucault, Michel, "Voici, en bien peu de temps . . .," in *Roland Barthes au Collège de France*, Nathalie Léger, ed. (Paris: Éditions de l'IMEC, 2002), 103–104.

Fried, Michael, *Absorption and Theatricality: Painting and Beholder in the Age of Diderot* (Chicago: University of Chicago Press, 1989).

Friedmann, Georges, "Avant-propos," *Communications* 21 (1974), 1–7.

Gledhill, Christine, ed., *Home Is Where the Heart Is: Studies in Melodrama and the Woman's Film* (London: British Film Institute, 1987).

Guattari, Félix, "The Poor Man's Couch" in *Chaosophy: Texts and Interviews 1972–1977* (Cambridge, MA: MIT Press, 2009), 257–267.

Hansen, Miriam, *Babel and Babylon: Spectatorship in American Film* (Cambridge, MA: Harvard University Press, 1991).

Hansen, Miriam, *Cinema and Experience: Siegfried Kracauer, Walter Benjamin, and Theodor W. Adorno* (Berkeley: University of California Press, 2012).

Harvey, Sylvia, *May 68 and Film Culture* (London: British Film Institute, 1980).

Huhtamo, Erkki and Parikka, Jussi, *Media Archaeology: Approaches, Applications, Implications* (Berkeley: University of California Press, 2011).

Jaffe, Ira, *Slow Movies: Countering the Cinema of Action* (London: Wallflower Press, 2014).

Jameson, Fredric, *Postmodernism, or, The Cultural Logic of Late Capitalism* (Durham, NC: Duke University Press, 1991).

Jay, Martin *Downcast Eyes: The Denigration of Vision in Twentieth-Century French Thought* (Berkeley: University of California Press, 1993).

Kané, Pascal, "Entretien avec Michel Foucault," *Cahiers du Cinéma* 271 (November 1976), 52–53.

Kline, T. Jefferson, *Screening the Text: Intertextuality in New Wave French Cinema* (Baltimore: Johns Hopkins University Press, 2002).

Joubert-Laurencin, Hervé, "A Binocular Preface" in *Opening Bazin: Postwar Film Theory and its Afterlife*, Dudley Andrew and Hervé Joubert-Laurencin, eds. (Oxford: Oxford University Press, 2011), ix–xvi.

Kazan, Elia, *A Life* (New York: Knopf, 1988).

Kittler, Friedrich, *Gramophone, Film, Typewriter* (Redwood City, CA: Stanford University Press, 1999).

Kyrou, Ado, "Atmosphère d'un mois cinématographique," *Les Lettres Nouvelles* 3:27 (May 1955), 783.

MacCabe, Colin, *Godard: A Portrait of the Artist at 70* (London: Bloomsbury, 2003).

Macé, Marielle, *Le Temps de l'essai: Histoire d'un genre en France au XXe siècle* (Paris: Belin, 2006).

Maniglier, Patrice and Zabunyan, Dork, *Foucault va au cinéma* (Montrouge: Bayard, 2011).

Margulies, Ivone, "Sacha Guitry, National Portraiture and the Artist's Hand," *French Cultural Studies* 16:3 (2005), 241–258.

Marie, Michel, *The French New Wave: An Artistic School*, trans. Richard Neupert (Malden, MA: Blackwell Publishing, 2003).

Marshall, Bill, *André Téchiné* (Manchester: Manchester University Press, 2007).

Marty, Éric, *Roland Barthes, le métier d'écrire* (Paris: Les Éditions du Seuil, 2006).

Mast, Gerald and Cohen, Marshall, eds., *Film Theory and Criticism: Introductory Readings* (Oxford: Oxford University Press, 1974).

Metz, Christian, "Le signifiant imaginaire," *Communications* 23 (1975), 3–55.

Metz, Christian, "The Imaginary Signifier" in *The Imaginary Signifier: Psychoanalysis and the Cinema*, trans. Celia Britton et al. (Bloomington: University of Indiana Press, 1982), 1–87.

Metz, Christian, "Primary Figure, Secondary Figure," in *The Imaginary Signifier*, 154–167.

Miller, D. A., *Bringing Out Roland Barthes* (Berkeley: University of California Press, 1992).

Morgan, Diane, *Kant Trouble* (London: Routledge, 2000).

Morin, Edgar, *Cinema or the Imaginary Man* [1956], trans. Lorraine Mortimer (Minneapolis: University of Minnesota Press, 2005).

Morin, Edgar, *Les Stars* (Paris: Seuil, 1972).

Morin, Edgar, *The Stars*, trans. Richard Howard (Minneapolis: University of Minnesota Press, 2005).

Narboni, Jean, *La Nuit Sera Noire et Blanche: Barthes*, La Chambre claire, Le Cinéma (Paris: Capricci, 2015).

Navasky, Victor, *Naming Names* (New York: Viking Press, 1980).

Neupert, Richard, *A History of The French New Wave Cinema* (Madison: University of Wisconsin Press, 2002).

Parikka, Jussi, *What Is Media Archaeology?* (Cambridge: Polity Press, 2012).

Rancière, Jacques, *Althusser's Lesson*, trans. Emiliano Battista (London: Continuum Books, 2011).

Rancière, Jacques, "L'image fraternelle (Entretien avec Jacques Rancière)," *Cahiers du Cinéma* 268–269 (July–August 1976), 7–19.

Rancière, Jacques, "Fleurs intempestives (*La communion solennelle*)," *Cahiers du Cinéma* 278 (July 1977), 17–20.

Rancière, Jacques, *Le fil perdu* (Paris: La Fabrique, 2014).

Remes, Justin, *The Cinema of Stasis* (New York: Columbia University Press, 2015).

Rey, Henri-François, "Hollywood fabrique des mythes comme Ford des voitures," *L'Écran Français* 150 (May 11, 1948), 6.

Richie, Donald, *Lateral View: Essays on Culture and Style in Contemporary Japan* (Berkeley: Stone Bridge Press, 1992).

Rodowick, D. N., *The Crisis of Political Modernism: Criticism and Ideology in Contemporary Film Criticism* (Berkeley: University of California Press, 1995).

Roger, Philippe, "Barthes with Marx," *Writing the Image After Roland Barthes*, ed. Jean-Michel Rabaté (Philadelphia: University of Pennsylvania Press, 1997), 174–186.

Rosen, Philip, ed., *Narrative, Apparatus, Ideology: A Film Theory Reader* (New York: Columbia University Press, 1986).

Ross, Kristin, *May '68 And Its Afterlives* (Chicago: University of Chicago Press, 2002).

Ross, Kristin, *Fast Cars, Clean Bodies: Decolonization and the Reordering of French Culture* (Cambridge, MA: MIT Press, 1995).

Ross, Kristin, "Yesterday's Critique, Today's Mythologies," *Contemporary French and Francophone Studies* 12:2 (2008), 231–242.

Samoyault, Tiphaine, *Roland Barthes* (Paris: Les Éditions du Seuil, 2015).

Sartre, Jean-Paul, *The Imaginary: A Phenomenological Psychology of the Imagination*, (New York: Routledge, 2004).

Sartre, Jean-Paul, *Nausea*, trans. Lloyd Alexander (New York: New Directions Publishing Company, 1964).

Seton, Marie, *Eisenstein* (Paris: Les Éditions du Seuil, 1957).

Sconce, Jeffrey, *Haunted Media: Electronic Presence from Telegraphy to Television* (Durham, NC: Duke University Press, 2000).

Sheringham, Michael, *Everyday Life: Theories and Practices from Surrealism to the Present* (Oxford: Oxford University Press, 2006).

Soyinka, Wole, *The Critic and Society: Barthes, Leftocracy and Other Mythologies* (Ile-Ife: University of Ife Press, 1982).

Sontag, Susan, "Notes On 'Camp'" in *Camp: Queer Aesthetics and the Performing Subject*, ed. Fabio Cleto (Ann Arbor: University of Michigan Press, 1999), 53–65.

Stam, Robert, *François Truffaut and Friends: Modernism, Sexuality, and Film Adaptation* (New Brunswick, NJ: Rutgers University Press, 2006).

Steimatsky, Noa, "Roland Barthes looks at the Stars," and "Pass/Fail: Screen, Apparatus, Subject," Chapters 2 and 4 of *The Face on Film* (New York: Oxford University Press, 2016).

Taylor, Greg, *Artists in the Audience: Cults, Camp, and American Film Criticism* (Princeton, NJ: Princeton University Press, 2001).

Thévenot, Jean, "Le cinéma garde-mythes: le médecin (façon Hollywood)," *L'Écran Français* 317 (August 1–7, 1951), 12–13.

Thompson, E. P., *The Making of the English Working Class* (New York: Vintage Books, 1963).

Truffaut, François, "Sacha Guitry the Villain" in *The Films in My Life* (New York: Simon and Schuster, 1978), 216–219.

Truffaut, François (writing under the pseudonym R. L.), "Si Versailles m'était conté...," *Cahiers du Cinéma* 34 (April 1954), 64.

Truffaut, François, "*Positif*: Copie zéro," *Cahiers du Cinéma* 79 (January 1958), 60–62.

Tyler, Parker, "The Garbo Image" in *The Films of Greta Garbo*, Michael Conway et al., eds. (New York: The Citadel Press, 1963), 9–31.

Ungar, Steven, *Roland Barthes, The Professor of Desire* (Lincoln: University of Nebraska Press, 1983).

Waugh, Thomas, *The Fruit Machine: Twenty Years of Writings on Queer Cinema* (Durham, NC: Duke University Press, 2000).

Willemen, Paul, "Reflections on Eikhenbaum's Concept of Internal Speech in the Cinema," *Screen* 15:4 (Winter 1974/75), 59–70.

INDEX